What Your Colleagues

This is a fascinating, compelling read from some of our most influential educationalists. The central purpose is to provide an evaluative framework for educators to use in determining areas of professional workload that take up considerable time without directly improving student outcomes. The process of de-implementing is explored in detail, advice about areas that might be contributing to workload are suggested, but ultimately we are offered a powerful manual for change.

The idea that more is better is challenged. The notion that much of what goes on in schools may be led by busy-ness or even "fake work" is set against a review process that privileges effectiveness and impact on learning. These arguments need to be rehearsed both within and beyond schools, optimizing teachers' time and core skills to achieve the greatest benefit for our students. Persuasively, global data shows that some systems appear to be doing less while achieving more— a lesson for us all.

—**Professor Dame Alison Peacock**, chief executive,
the Chartered College of Teaching, UK

One of the secrets of the highest-performing education systems is that they pursue fewer things at greater depth and avoid the mile-wide-inch deep implementation culture that often prevails elsewhere. But taking things away tends to be much harder in education than adding new things. *Making Room for Impact* shows it can be done and provides the research, tools, and guides to make it happen.

—**Andreas Schleicher**, director for education and skills,
Organisation for Economic Co-operation and Development (OECD), France

I don't think I have ever read an educational book quite like this, simply because the focus is not on the latest new thing you should be trying but rather a compelling argument on how to become more effective through doing less. By suggesting a range of powerful, practical processes through which you can remove, reduce, re-engineer or replace what you do, this book really empowers the reader to be bold. But this is not about taking risks; it is a powerful, evidence-informed guide on how to stop doing what you have always done (much of which we think is mandated from on high when it's not) if there are better alternatives. As Michael Bungay-Stanier reminds us in his excellent book *The Coaching Habit*, one of the key questions we need to ask ourselves is "If you are saying yes to this, what are you saying no to?" I cannot think of a better companion to have at your side than this unique and well-argued book, which has the potential to transform workload, enhance staff well-being, and improve student outcomes. I absolutely loved it!

—**Andy Buck**, founder of Leadership Matters and BASIC Coaching,
and former director of the National College for School Leadership, UK

Brilliant. Every educator recognizes that we sometimes try something new, and it doesn't work out . . . and every educator recognizes that *stopping* is not always easy! This book takes you, step by step, through the process of identifying a target for de-implementation, choosing a strategy, and implementing it. This book will be invaluable for administrators!

—**Dr. Daniel T. Willingham**, professor of psychology, University of Virginia, US; author of *Outsmart Your Brain* and *Why Don't Students Like School*

Educational improvement efforts are plagued by remnants of previous efforts that were also designed to change outcomes. These fragments, or perhaps even entire initiatives, prevent the knowledge we have now from taking hold. Implementation fails because there are too many other things that are not working but haven't been abandoned. It's as if we're at a buffet with a full plate. Instead of removing some items, we ask for another plate and pile it on. We need to learn how to stop doing things that no longer work and this guide provides a tool kit for accomplishing just that. Before trying to implement a new program or initiative, take stock and figure out what needs to go. Then follow the process outlined in this book to successfully de-implement and remove the clutter so that the good ideas take hold.

—**Dr. Douglas Fisher,** professor of educational leadership, San Diego State University, US

In this profoundly important book, Hamilton, Hattie, and Wiliam reveal why so many well-intentioned educational reforms fail and, more importantly, what we can do about it. Before you start your next initiative, take the authors' words to heart and de-implement first. With practical step-by-step advice, the *Making Room for Impact* process guides educators and leaders through the essential steps to declutter their agendas and focus on the essentials. The impressive evidence in these pages makes clear that the fragmentation associated with an abundance of initiatives is the enemy of learning. Yet it is astonishingly difficult to avoid the sunk cost fallacy—fearing that we cannot de-implement projects in which we have invested time, money, and political capital. No matter how promising the new initiative, it will fail unless you either buy a thirty-six-hour day or follow the advice in this book.

—**Dr. Douglas Reeves**, author, *Fearless Schools: Building Trust and Resilience for Learning, Teaching, and Leading*, US

Kurt Vonnegut's immortal *Cat's Cradle* featured the Bokononist mantra "busy, busy, busy." I've often thought the phrase works all too well as a description of schooling, where the mandatory and routine squeeze out the good. In *Making Room for Impact*, instead of giving school leaders yet another to-do list, the authors instead offer much-needed but far-too-rare guidance on how to focus in on what matters most and carefully de-implement the rest.

—**Dr. Frederick M. Hess**, director of Education Policy Studies at the American Enterprise Institute, Washington, DC, US

There's no end to the list of tasks teachers and schools could take on. So where can teachers find the space and time needed to make improvements, adopt better programs—or simply go home earlier? This admirable book offers the clearest answer I've yet seen. The authors offer valuable guidance in why making room for impact matters, how we can pursue it, and precisely what steps we might choose to take. Even more importantly, they offer schools license to work toward doing less and doing differently—not just more and more. The examples of how this can be done—practical and provocative alike—are also helpful. If you've ever wished you had more time, or didn't have to do something, read this book.

—**Harry Fletcher-Wood**, author,
Habits of Success and *Responsive Teaching*, UK

Hamilton, Hattie, and Wiliam provide a comprehensive guide that will assist busy educators in determining what to stop, start, and continue in their efforts to improve schools. Their model is grounded in research and provides a practical and efficient methodology for de-implementation that is long overdue and needed in education.

—**Dr. Jenni Donohoo**, author of *Collective Efficacy: How Educators'*
Beliefs Impact Student Learning and Quality Implementation, US

I cannot praise *Making Room for Impact* too highly. It took me eighteen years as a head teacher to realize that the fewer things I asked colleagues to do, the better our school became. If you read this book—the follow-up to *Building to Impact*—you won't have to spend eighteen years learning how and why to de-implement. The thing is, we can only use each hour of our lives once—that is why opportunity cost is the most important concept in the wider lives of people working in schools.

In *Making Room for Impact*, you'll find a step-by-step guide to creating the time and space for developing high quality teaching and learning by stopping doing things that don't have enough impact on our pupils' academic progress. This book will show you how to stop head teachers writing school improvement plans with fifteen priorities; how to stop deputy head teachers discussing meaningless progress data that everyone knows is meaningless; and how to stop teachers doing marking that has no impact upon learning. We need to focus more intently upon improving the quality of teaching and learning if we are going to improve the quality of provision for our pupils; this book shows you how.

What's more, if we could persuade our CEOs, governing bodies, trust boards, local authorities, and policy makers to heed the advice so clearly articulated by Hamilton, Hattie, and Wiliam, we may just reestablish teaching as a joyous profession where colleagues are able to meet the challenges of the job and avoid burnout, and by doing so solve the teacher-recruitment crisis. *Making Room for Impact* is *the* book for our times—everyone interested in the future of our schools should read it!

—**John Tomsett**, educational consultant, UK;
and coauthor of the *"Huh"* series

Unbearable workloads are a chief reason given for the teacher shortage experienced in many countries. Often teachers are exhorted to "work smarter, not harder," but they rarely receive advice about how to do this. This new book, from a team of highly regarded educators and researchers, is unique in that it provides guidance on both the "what" and the "how." It offers a process, based on principles, for removing, reducing, re-engineering, or replacing existing practices in order to concentrate on those practices likely to have the most positive impact in terms of learning outcomes.

The authors draw on extensive research from the fields of education, medicine, business, and across the English-speaking world. However, the book wears its learning lightly: It is very readable, has a strong sense of an audience of educators, and is structured in such a way that the key themes are reprised for practitioners who are likely to dip into different chapters as the need arises. It should be read not only by teachers, school leaders, and teacher educators but also by policy makers who often promote innovations with insufficient attention to value or consequences.

—**Dr. Mary James**, professor emerita,
University of Cambridge Faculty of Education, UK

An unbeatable team of authors on how to improve outcomes by decluttering—surely of interest to school leaders and teachers everywhere.

—**Sir Michael Barber**, author of *Accomplishment:
How Ambitious and Challenging Things Get Done*, UK

Two ideas came to me as I was reading this book. The first was that these are such good ideas that I wonder why it has taken so long for them to reach print. The second one is that any book that promises me a means of "getting off the hamster wheel" has to be taken seriously. So much so that I wish this movement to de-implementation had been more fully developed when I was working full time directing a large-scale education reform project in fifty secondary schools—a recipe for needing de-implementation if ever there was one. I would have benefited from the processes identified in this book immensely.

—**Dr. Russell Bishop ONZM**, emeritus professor,
University of Waikato, New Zealand

Skilled mountaineers know that to reach the summit you carry only what you need. Carrying more diminishes your chances of success and threatens your survival. In this book, Hamilton, Hattie, and Wiliam provide the practical guidance that school leaders so desperately need to lighten their packs, improve their efficiency of impact, and succeed in reaching the summit of helping all students learn.

—**Dr. Thomas R. Guskey**, professor emeritus,
University of Kentucky, US

Making Room for Impact is a refreshingly original, timely, and beautifully crafted book. I'm certain the brilliantly conceived tool kit will energize educators around the world, empowering them to make the changes they need in order to take their schools forward by breaking the cycle of forever doing more and more and more.

The de-implementation model combines a rigorous and systematic conceptual framework, intellectually satisfying in its clarity and logic, with a grounded pragmatism rooted in the wisdom you only gain by spending a lot of time around busy teachers and leaders in the manic world of education.

Having personally experienced the struggles of running a complex school with an overloaded agenda, the ideas set out here resonate completely. It goes far beyond a simplistic "less is more" mantra, providing an extremely thorough, practical guide that will help countless educators to regain balance, and get back on track, focusing their energies on the things that make the most difference.

—**Tom Sherrington**, education consultant and
author of *Teaching WalkThrus*, UK

Schools are crowded with many unnecessary and fruitless policies and practices. School leaders, teachers, and students are all overworked with futile reforms and innovations, mandatory requirements, and unproductive tasks. Schools must do less! In *Making Room for Impact*, Arran Hamilton, John Hattie, and Dylan Wiliam make compelling arguments for doing less and provide excellent guidance for schools to do less. A great read for educators!

—**Dr. Yong Zhao**, foundation distinguished professor,
University of Kansas and professor in educational leadership,
Melbourne Graduate School of Education

De-implementation, or the science and art of removing, reducing, re-engineering or replacing existing practices, is a novel concept in education, but a very important one in a world in which the limits in constantly adding more to the workload of teachers and leaders are ever more apparent. In *Making Room for Impact*, an international dream team of education researchers, Hamilton, Hattie and Wiliam, have written a practical and user-friendly guide to exactly how we can go about de-implementing in our schools, so we can make room not just for a better work-life balance but also for better results for our students.

—**Dr. Daniel Muijs**, professor of education and head of the
School of Social Sciences, Education and Social
Work, Queen's University, Belfast

Making Room for Impact (MRI) is a magnificent and unique book. It addresses a crucial, almost completely neglected topic—how to get rid of or reconstitute things that no longer work!

I am sure the reader has heard the lament that the old "grammar of school" continues to plague all efforts of reform. What reformers have traditionally done is to criticize the old way, try to implement the new only to find that they have failed time and again. How about systematically getting rid of the old as you pave the way for the new? MRI furnishes a roadmap to do just that. With fantastic graphics—a transformer's dream tool box—MRI systematically guides us through nine ways to identify, unravel, and rid the organization of distractors as you mobilize the forces for new action. The reader learns to Discover, Decide, De-Implement, and Re-decide, ending up with less work in total and a more powerful impact. MRI is a gem of a book for the action-oriented who want to affect both the small and the big picture for the better.

—**Dr. Michael Fullan**, professor emeritus,
OISE/University of Toronto

Making Room
for Impact

For educators everywhere who want to
make some room for what matters most

Making Room for Impact

A De-Implementation Guide for Educators

Arran Hamilton

John Hattie

Dylan Wiliam

FOR INFORMATION:

Corwin

A SAGE Company

2455 Teller Road

Thousand Oaks, California 91320

(800) 233-9936

www.corwin.com

SAGE Publications Ltd.

1 Oliver's Yard

55 City Road

London EC1Y 1SP

United Kingdom

SAGE Publications India Pvt. Ltd.

Unit No 323-333, Third Floor, F-Block

International Trade Tower Nehru Place

New Delhi 110 019

SAGE Publications Asia-Pacific Pte. Ltd.

18 Cross Street #10-10/11/12

China Square Central

Singapore 048423

Vice President and
  Editorial Director: Monica Eckman

Publisher: Jessica Allan

Content Development
  Manager: Lucas Schleicher

Content Development
  Editor: Mia Rodriguez

Senior Editorial Assistant: Natalie Delpino

Project Editor: Amy Schroller

Copy Editor: Lynne Curry

Typesetter: C&M Digitals (P) Ltd.

Proofreader: Larry Baker

Indexer: Sheila Hill

Cover Designer: Scott Van Atta

Marketing Manager: Olivia Bartlett

Printed in the United Kingdom

ISBN 978-1-0719-1707-7

This book is printed on acid-free paper

23 24 25 26 27 10 9 8 7 6 5 4 3 2 1

Contents

List of Figures

Foreword

Sometimes a book comes along that stops you short and causes deep contemplation. This is such a book. *Making Room for Impact* validates much of my thinking and my work. It is a key tenet of my approach that "there is no more time"—so choose wisely and get it right within the resources available.

Educators are challenged by the never-ending selection of choices that march before them like glittering answers to unsolved educational mysteries. Who is the next best guru who has landed in town? Some don't choose; they flit: "Ok, let's go there, and then there, or there." So many choices with no boundaries, no evidence of improvement, vast implementation gaps. So much to add to our systems and schools.

In contrast to the "add" syndrome, Hamilton, Hattie, and Wiliam have co-constructed a process to support educators to "subtract"—to give back precious time—whether that be for better work-life balance or alternative initiatives that generate more impact. They convincingly present their four-part de-implementation methodology, grounded in evidence, to guide de-implementation with rigor, reflection, and resilience. And they give us four different de-implementation strategies to consider (the 4Rs):

> **1. Remove** the practice completely; **2. Reduce** how frequently you do it; **3. Re-Engineer** the practice to take less time; and/or **4. Replace** it with something else that's more efficient or effective.

What makes this all the more powerful is that this is a step-by-step "How To" book with a carefully articulated four-stage process that carefully supports you to:

> **1: Discover** amenable de-implementation areas;
>
> **2: Decide** the best fit strategy (from the four "R's" above);
>
> **3: De-Implement**, including having a "Plan B" or even "C";

4: Re-Decide, which is where you confirm that you did what you set out to do and where you then iteratively decide what to do next!

In my own experience, systematic implementation and de-implementation processes are our nemesis with so many possibilities that when we experience "implementation fatigue," we buy a program, change our minds, get nervous, and alter our course further. For me, no purchasing of a program, updating policy, increasing funding, or getting the latest technology (etc.) will increase students' growth and achievement, nor will they build teachers' capacity to know how to teach all students. Nothing replaces the evidence-proven precision-in-practice of teachers and leaders that we need in every classroom. We must learn, unlearn, and relearn (Hedburg, 1981).

But almost everything we learn and "add" to our work comes with time and resourcing costs of some kind. My colleague, superintendent W. McKillican, always said, "So if we agree to add this to our work, what will we remove?" Wise but irritating words (at the time!) because we didn't know how to de-implement in a thoughtful way. This book could have helped us immensely. The authors take us through carefully crafted "baby steps" to reach wise de-implementation decisions on what is working (implementation), what is not ("fake work": Nielson & Burks, 2022; or inefficient work), and next steps, like "monitoring forever." Pure gold!

Hamilton, Hattie, and Wiliam bring this perspective to bear excellently as they give examples and practical ideas to reinforce their message. For example, they cite homework as a potential area for de-implementation. For me, another example would be "data schedules" that look at when we collect data and not "the why" and "the use" of the assessment tools—a data source that does not inform instruction needs to be de-implemented, using the four R's above. Teachers and leaders will not begrudge the time it takes to collect data when data uses are purposeful and informative. Data must inform instruction every minute of every day to be useful and warrant the administration time (Sharratt, 2019). Although, even purposeful data collection can be made more efficient (i.e., re-engineered) and this book can help with that.

Making Room for Impact is provocative. For example, wall displays that are "pretty" and not "pretty useful" need to be taken down and replaced with "The Third Teacher" Learning Walls that bring meaning to success criteria or bump-it-up walls through co-construction (Sharratt, 2019). Visible Learning at its finest.

The authors provide persuasive detail, the theory, and the practical application, asking us to consider moving from first-order change—technical changes—to second-order change, cultural change focusing on learning and improvement (Planche et al., 2008). Their approach is about giving us the tools to think through; be efficient; eliminate "waste"; and thus have more time to focus on what matters most: time to ensure students' growth and achievement. I concur with our authors: "We think de-implementation that saves time and reduces teacher workload (and increases teacher well-being)—even if student learning outcomes remain static—is a goal worth progressing." This book is about "doing the right things right" (Sharratt & Fullan, 2006).

In short, the emphasis on "subtract before you add" in this book is timely and prescient. Its conversational style, supported by statistical facts, highlights two important points that are reinforced throughout:

✓ We need robust processes and ways of working to overcome our natural tendency toward addition and not letting go. We can't just leave it to chance: the whole point of *Making Room for Impact*!

✓ Because the appropriate de-implementation actions are likely to vary by context (along with the reactions to them), it's more valuable to provide schools and systems with a framework to help them discover and implement their own strategies than simply to provide a list of recommendations or top tips.

Making Room for Impact is not just a practical guide: this book is an uplifting account of how to rigorously increase time available to focus on increasing all student outcomes. And I'm a big fan of that laudable goal!

In many ways this book is a clarion call to action asking us to do what is conceptually simple and practically difficult—what we call "simplexity" (Sharratt & Fullan, 2012, 2022). Thinking that de-implementation processes are easy would be wrong, so Hamilton, Hattie, and Wiliam support our thinking by outlining the iterative four-stage approach that is indeed simple and complex but inherently helpful and precise. And with a focus on efficiency without harming students' learning.

There are few schools and systems that are excellent without an excellent leader . . . a first among equals. Throughout *Making Room for Impact*, leadership skills are outlined directly and nuanced indirectly. Either way, leadership is discussed as the very backbone of implementation and de-implementation, completely focused on not harming outcomes for students—so laudable! I appreciate the leadership roles and responsibilities outlined in the carefully selected "Guiding Coalition," or as the authors' delineate, the "Impact Backbone Team," with members, such as:

✓ **The Sponsor(s)** – completely committed, approachable, insightful

✓ **Team Leader(s)** – tactical coaching squad

✓ **Investigator(s)** – "worker bees" on the ground

✓ **(optional) External Facilitator** – head coach and unconditional supporter

These roles lead to voluntary accountability: "we are in this together—to make a difference for students in our care." The Impact Backbone

Team members are key in hearing the voices from the field, developing action-focused inquiry questions, and aligning the strategies selected to the wider vision of this book: "every student, teacher, and leader succeeding."

Making Room for Impact is a gold mine of a book. It is clear, succinct, theoretical, and practical with thought-provoking questions throughout and written with clearly delineated "how to" steps, protocols, processes, and examples, transforming research into practical approaches.

I wholeheartedly recommend this book to all educators, wherever they are in the world, who want to master *efficiency of impact* and celebrate *work-life balance.*

Dr. Lyn Sharratt

University of Toronto, Canada

Honorary Fellow, University of Melbourne,
Graduate School of Education, Australia.

International Consultant, Practitioner, Author

Preface

You'll take the high road and I'll take the low road,
And I'll be in Scotland afore you.

The Bonnie Banks o' Loch Lomond
Roud No. 9598

Often in life there's a hard way and an *easier* way. That easier way gets you to the same destination in less time and with considerably less commotion.

But if you are already on the hard path, it's often challenging to switch. For a start, you might not (yet) know that there is an easier way. And even if you do know, you might feel guilty about making the transition. Or your "muscle memory" might push you, subconsciously, to stay firmly on the hard path—the high road—when reason suggests you would be much better off taking the low road, instead.

This begs the question: in our world of education, are we collectively on the hard path or the easier one?

We don't need to look far to find the answer. Across the predominantly English-speaking countries, teachers report exceedingly high workloads—often clocking up more than fifty hours per week (OECD TALIS, 2020). Yet, despite all the expended energy, student achievement in comparative international assessments has barely budged since 1970 (Altinok et al., 2018). And the educators working these long hours report high levels of stress: every year, large numbers of new colleagues need to be recruited and trained to replace the ones who have exited stage left.

But maybe that's just the way it is? Perhaps like the Red Queen in Alice *Through the Looking Glass*, educators simply have to run really fast just to stand still? Maybe it's the hard path or bust?

Thankfully, no. As we will go on to show, there are lots of international data showing schools and systems with shorter school days and years, less teacher preparation time, less student homework, less data collection, less form-filling, and less everything. And now for the sucker punch: many of these systems achieve just as good (and sometimes better) outcomes as the schools and systems with long hours, complicated processes, and high stress. Less really can be more.

The trouble is, though, once you have implemented all these (seemingly) shiny but additive things, they take on a life of their own. It can be very difficult to row them back—to de-implement. Understandably, you might worry that student outcomes will plummet, that parent complaints will rise, and that your colleagues in other schools will brand you lazy (or crazy).

You might also be wracked with guilt and concerned that your paymasters will haul you over the coals—for working outside "the rules." And even if you do get going, you might find yourself thwarted by that (aforementioned) muscle memory. Your mind says "take the low road," but your body, nonetheless, sleepwalks you back up the high road. All these things (and more) can make it tricky to de-implement. To pivot from the "more path" to the "less path."

We three authors were astounded at how little there was in the way of tool kits, guides, and research to support educators to overcome these pitfalls and de-implement with rigor. Hence the book you have in your hands, which (we believe) is currently the most comprehensive de-implementation guide ever written. Although it certainly won't be the last word on the subject!

The whole point of the book is to help you to focus on your *efficiency of impact*. To support you review every activity in the school day from that efficiency perspective and to ask:

What's the worst that could happen if we just stopped doing X—if we de-implemented it?

And, before you balk, there are several ways that you can de-implement. Yes, you can **Remove** the target area altogether; you can also **Reduce** how frequently you do it; or you can **Re-Engineer** the practice so that it takes less time—six 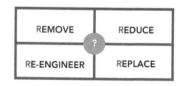 steps not sixteen; or even **Replace** it with something else. Lots of ways to go about it and lots of areas you could consider de-implementing (we even give you more than eighty suggestions to get you started!).

The process that we unpack in the following pages is called *Room for Impact*, a shorthand term derived for the book's longer title *Making Room for Impact*. It's a four-stage approach that supports you to:

1. **Discover** amenable areas for de-implementation in your local context

2. **Decide** the best-fit strategy (i.e., will you Remove, Reduce, Replace, or Re-Engineer?)

3. **De-Implement**, which is where you bring the plans to life. This also includes deploying suitable countermeasures to avoid backsliding into muscle memory or stepping on locally identified beartraps.

4. **Re-Decide**, which is where you confirm that you did what you set out to; where you triple-check that you did no harm to the learners; and where you decide what to do next!

And it's all about "making room," whether that be for positive impact in your lives outside school, the lives of your learners, or (ideally) both.

You can use this *Room for Impact* process on your own, in your professional learning community, at whole school level, or even system-level.

Many people helped and inspired us as we three collaborated on this book. Discussions with Russell Bishop, Lyn Sharratt, Douglas Reeves, Peter DeWitt, Michael Barber, Yong Zhao, Steve Saville, Christophe Mullins, Jacque Allen, Mary Sinclair, and Tina Lucas gave us many "aha!" moments. Lots of warm leads also came from pioneering de-implementation research being undertaken in the medical field, particularly the work of Susan Michie, Karina Davidson, Siqin Ye, George Mensah, Virginia Wang, Eva Verkerk, Wynne Norton, and David Chambers. We thank them for all the rich nectar!

But most of all, *Room for Impact* is about *you* and for *you*. So that you and your colleagues can identify efficiencies that you can either reinvest in greater work-life balance *or* in replacement activities that have more impact on student outcomes. It's totally about what you decide locally in your inquiry teams. We just give you the tools to systematically think it through.

Of course, you might still have a nagging doubt that the local rules and regulations don't give you the flexibility to get off the hamster wheel. But we think you might find that the (imagined) rules in your head are more complex and prohibitive than the (real) rules on paper. That you have much more leeway than you think. And as you embark on your inquiry, you are going to find out!

No one knows for sure who penned "The Bonnie Banks o' Loch Lomond." The Scottish folk song is thought to have originated in the 1700s and to tell the story of a warrior that died for his king and who (in death) simultaneously took both the "high road" (in body) and the "low road" (in spirit) back to Scotland.

But that short half-verse ("You'll take the high road and I'll take the low road, And I'll be in Scotland afore you") is arguably the most remembered part of the song. And it's also arguably taken on a life of its own, with a different and more literal meaning: That some roads just get you places faster.

And *Room for Impact* is all about helping you to do just that. So that you can reinvest the savings in the things that matter most.

Arran Hamilton
Kuala Lumpur, Malaysia

John Hattie
Melbourne, Australia

Dylan Wiliam
Florida, United States

Publisher's Acknowledgments

Corwin gratefully acknowledges the contributions of the following reviewers:

Chris Bryan
Executive/Leadership Coach
Denver Public Schools
Denver, CO

Jayne Ellspermann
CEO and Founder, Former School Principal
Jayne Ellspermann, LLC School Leadership Development
Ocala, FL

Charlotte R. LaHaye, EdD
Curriculum Coordinator
Schools of the Sacred Heard
Grand Coteau, LA

About the Authors

Arran Hamilton is group director of education at Cognition Learning Group. Previously, Dr. Hamilton has held senior positions at Cambridge University Press & Assessment, Education Development Trust, the British Council, and a research fellowship at Warwick University. His core focus is on translating evidence into impact at scale. He has overseen the design, delivery, and evaluation of large-scale education improvement programs across the United Kingdom, Australia, New Zealand, Pacific Islands, East Asia, and the Middle East. Arran's recent publications include *The Lean Education Manifesto* and *Building to Impact: The 5D Implementation Playbook for Educators.*

John Hattie is emeritus laureate professor at the Melbourne Graduate School of Education at the University of Melbourne, co-director of the Hattie Family Foundation, and chair of the Board of the Australian Institute for Teaching and School Leadership. Dr. Hattie is one of the world's best known and most widely read education experts and his Visible Learning series of books have been translated into twenty-nine different languages and have sold over two million copies. His most recent book is *Visible Learning: The Sequel: A Synthesis of Over 2,100 Meta-Analyses Relating to Achievement.*

Dylan Wiliam is emeritus professor of educational assessment at UCL Institute of Education. Dr. Wiliam started his career teaching in inner-city London schools before transitioning to educational research. He was dean of the School of Education at King's College London, senior research director at the Educational Testing Service in Princeton, US, and deputy director of the Institute of Education, University of London. His research has focused on the use of assessment to support learning (sometimes called formative assessment), and he now works with groups of teachers all over the world on developing formative assessment practices. Dylan's recent books include *Creating the Schools Our Children Need* and *Embedded Formative Assessment.*

Introduction

Work expands . . . to fill the time available for its completion

Cyril Northcote Parkinson (1955)

We have had the immense pleasure of reading and learning from thousands of books and articles on education. They all say something different. Saying the same is rarely a recipe for publication!

Some of these accounts are rearview-oriented, seeking to explain how by doing X or Y a school or system unleashed greatness. Others are forward-looking, giving suggested actions, steps, and protocols for you to implement in your own local contexts to grow your impact. And yet others double down on values: asking what it is we should care about most and prioritize for impact. But no matter their specific topic area and perspective, these publications still generally have one thing in common: a focus on improvement, on making things profoundly better for *all* students.

While the prescriptions for improvement may vary, there usually is also a second thing that unites these accounts:

The tendency to privilege addition!!!

The implicit assumption is that improvement is best unlocked by inserting *new* policies, *new* programs, *new* activities, or *new* widgets. Improvement by moving forwards and not backwards. Improvement by adding and not subtracting. More-in leading to more-out.

In many ways we should not be surprised by this. Recent psychological research suggests that we humans may be hardwired to solve problems and to innovate by attaching and inserting new ingredients rather than deleting or simplifying (Klotz, 2021). Whether this be adding more Lego bricks to a wonky bridge in a cognitive psychology lab study when removing bricks works just as well (Adams et al., 2021); or implementing *more* improvement programs, *more* technology, and *more* teaching hours in school. It seems we love to add but not subtract.

Our sister publication *Building to Impact* (2022) went with (rather than against) this psychological grain. It was specifically designed to help you with that task of implementing more, new, and better. It was also predicated on the assumption that we have good evidence about *best bets* for learning but that schools and systems still struggle to:

- select appropriate initiatives to add to their context;

- localize or adapt that new addition in a way that doesn't dilute the impact to nothing, or that actually even makes it counterproductive;

- implement the shiny new insertion with (local) fidelity;[1] and

- rigorously monitor and evaluate—to double-up the impact.

Building to Impact drew on a range of research findings on successful implementation across education, healthcare, business, and international development to present logical and sequenced steps to replicate the success of others. And it suggested that we need a new role—the implementation specialist—to keep initiatives on track and to evaluate systematically when they need to change track.

Of course, we often need to make space alongside by finding other things to stop to, then, add the new things. We need to do this because there are only twenty-four hours in a day, and there are only so many things we can do well—simultaneously—in those hours, including sleep. This is why *Building to Impact* also contained a subprocess focused on finding things to stop and then on the action of simultaneously stopping those old and less effective things while starting the new, shiny, improved things. However, the explicit assumption was that we were stopping to make space, to make room for substitution. Stopping was never about just stopping.

This book, by contrast, is *entirely* about stopping, reducing, and reversing. And we expand the three-page discussion in *Building to Impact* into a more comprehensive de-implementation process that we call *Room for Impact*.

There are at least five reasons that you might seek to get serious, rigorous, explicit, and *focused* about de-implementing:

1. **To substitute less effective practices with those that have *more* evidence and probability of impact**; that is, to free up time to focus on those more effective things (a.k.a. to **replace**).

   Often this is about swapping out good or average things that generate reasonable impact with better things that unlock far more. Because most things in education "sorta" work—very little causes actual harm. But each hour you spend on something that's only moderately effective is an hour you can't spend on something else that's very effective.

---

[1]We say "local fidelity" because we have come to the conclusion that no educational innovation can be implemented in schools in the way imagined by its inventor. Innovations have to be adapted, and so implementing with fidelity is not slavishly following instructions but finding ways to adapt the innovation in a particular context that avoids "lethal mutations."

2. **To substitute more expensive interventions with those that have the same or better outcomes at a fraction of the cost**: to use existing budgets more cost effectively (a.k.a. to **spend more wisely**)

3. **Streamlining practices that have become overengineered**, trimming an eleven-step process down to six-steps—without any loss of impact (a.k.a. to **re-engineer**)

4. **To dial down the use of a still needed process**—for example, to do it with less frequency to get the same impact or even to be selective about who delivers and receives the treatment (a.k.a. to **reduce** or even to **restrict**)

5. **To get our lives back** (a.k.a. to **Remove**, to *stop*). Yes, sometimes it's perfectly acceptable (or better, even) to just stop doing things without any intention of finding different activities to fill the void (Churches, 2020). Sometimes having that void makes us less stressed and gives us more time for introspection. And this *might* also improve our performance and learner outcomes, too.[2]

If *Building for Impact* was principally about inching forward through design space to implement new things, then *Room for Impact* is 100 percent about inching backwards—to de-implement and de-implement again: the Yang to the Yin (see Figure 0.1).

There is, however, much more research on addition. For example, our cousins in healthcare have been busy building and testing implementation frameworks since at least the 1970s and have even founded a subfield called *Implementation Science* (Bauer et al., 2015). We in education have only cottoned onto this literature and gotten serious and systematic about implementation in the last decade or so. Therefore, in developing *Building to Impact* we drew heavily from the learnings and successes within the medical field. There was so much of it!

In contrast, the business of *systematic* de-implementation, de-adoption, discontinuing, disinvesting, withdrawal, abandoning, and decommissioning is new—even to healthcare (Augustsson et al., 2021; Burton et al.,

---

[2]One of the more commonly cited definitions of de-implementation is that of Farmer et al. (2021). This states that de-implementation is about the removal of "low value" practices that have either (A) not shown to be effective; (B) are less effective than other alternatives; (C) cause harm; or (D) that are no longer necessary. We think that there is value in this definition but with the following caveats: (1) very few things in education cause genuine harm—it's more a case of some practices being less effective than others; (2) the definition plays into the education status quo—which is about the constant hunt for identifying "shiny new things" to replace existing "rusty" things—rather than just removing things; (3) it does not emphasize efficiency; that is, de-implementation focused on making existing processes take less time or resources; (4) there is no focus on financial efficiency; that is, the cost-benefit of existing actions.

FIGURE 0.1   Yin and Yang

2019; Burton et al., 2021; Davidson et al., 2017).[3] Although, in the medical field, there has been (slowly) growing interest during the last decade linked, for example, to the global *Choose Wisely* campaign, which has focused on high-cost low-impact medicines and surgeries that are routinely prescribed; and on strategies for getting healthcare practitioners to stop administering low value interventions (Grimshaw et al., 2020).

The healthcare literature on de-implementation is the current largest of any sector—and far larger than education—but it is still extremely small, with fewer than fifty major studies and systematic reviews (summarized in **Appendix 2**). And while, too, there is a growing consensus that de-implementation is *not* the same process as implementation and that unlearning is *not* the same as learning (Grisold et al., 2017; Prusaczyk et al., 2020; Visser, 2017), there are currently no healthcare-specific "oven-ready" frameworks for de-implementation that can be transplanted to our world of education; no codified manuals that take you from A to B to C to dematerialization.

Warmer leads come from the business and manufacturing sectors, in the form of the Lean Methodology and Six Sigma, which were explicitly designed for process improvement and efficiency—that is, for stopping pointless things and reducing wasteful things (Hamilton & Hattie, 2022; Harry et al., 2011; Womack & Jones, 2003). They also come from generic "get your life back" type books (e.g., Newport, 2016, 2021); and behavioral

---

[3]One reason why de-implementation research is not strong even in healthcare is that most research is done in the United States, and medical practitioners are notoriously risk averse. The risk of litigation from patients arguably makes medics more inclined to practice "defensive medicine"—that is, ordering more tests and undertaking more investigative procedures to protect from future malpractice claims. Also, because of the medical insurance system, healthcare practitioners worry less about cost.

science research on habit change, particularly addictive behaviors like giving up smoking or gambling (Gardner & Rebar, 2019; Michie et al., 2014). And even dieting.

When we turn to education, by our count, there are currently only six published education frameworks explicitly for de-implementation:

1. In 2018, England's Department for Education launched the *Teacher Workload Reduction Toolkit*, which was very strong on case studies and potential focus areas but lighter on explicit replicable processes to bring de-implementation to life and to sustain it.

2. In 2020, the Australia Northern Territory Department of Education published a short *De-Implementation Guide*, which draws on the implementation tools developed by Jonathan Sharples and colleagues at the UK's Education Endowment Foundation. However, in using an implementation framework for de-implementation, there is a hidden implicit assumption that both processes are similar. As we will go on to show, there are significant differences between the two that require different thinking and action. Same, but very different.

3. In 2021, Dan Jackson published *Work Less Teach More*, with brilliant life hacks for teachers. He has good claims about creating a "No" and "Yes" list; suggests we need to "service" ourselves like we do to our lawnmower and car; suggests we stop doing that which does not relate to our personal mission statement; and that we allow time for shallow (emails) and deep (planning, collaborating) work, and explicitly choose not to be overworked. This book is very useful as a resource for individual educators.

4. In 2022, Peter DeWitt published a mini volume on education "de-cluttering," inspired by conversations with Arran and John. Peter's work here is starting to socialize the concept of de-implementation and attune educators to the possibilities, which can only be good!

5. In 2022, Betty Burks and Gaylan W. Nielson released an excellent volume on stopping "fake work" in education. The notion of fake work is brilliantly sticky, as are the suggested protocols for identifying the activities within school that are the most valuable. But what is missing are explicit behavioral strategies for stopping the things that are not *real work*.[4]

6. In 2022, Arran and John also published *The Lean Education Manifesto*, which synthesized over fifty-three thousand studies on impact efficiency, focusing on cash-strapped developing countries. This was heavy on the research into what areas to invest and

---

[4]And in education sometimes it's not about fake work per se; instead it's often about substituting perfectly good things with even better things.

disinvest, providing a shopping list of suggestions—some of which might make you fall off the back of your chair, but we still felt we had much more to say about explicit processes for undertaking a (systematic) de-implementation inquiry cycle.

So, while these existing veins of research cast valuable light on the need for de-implementation and on some of the ways we could potentially go about it, we felt that much more needed to be done to bring it to life and give you a kit of tools to make it happen.

Therefore, *Room for Impact* is (we believe) the first book-length de-implementation model in either education or healthcare that provides a detailed and rigorous framework for use at *all* system levels. Yes, it's a Rolls-Royce model, but we have tried to highlight different routes through the book, so that you can go straight to the parts that are most relevant to you.

An Overview of the Book

None of us can abide magical mystery tours and we're sure that you are the same. So here is what you can expect from the book:

CHAPTER	KEY MESSAGES/FOCUS
PART 1: THE BIG PICTURE	
1. Why We Need to De-Implement (and Why It's Hard)	This chapter does exactly what it says on the tin. It begins by laying out three big reasons for getting serious about de-implementation (teacher workload and stress; efficiency of impact; and resource constraints). It then unpacks nine key reasons why bringing this to life is so hard. These reasons have implications that we feed forward into the *Room for Impact* Protocols. *** Suppose you are already bought into the idea of de-implementation and are less interested in the academic research underpinning it. In that case, you can skip or at least skim this chapter—and quickly exit at Chapter 2.
2. Room for Impact: The Helicopter Overview	With the big picture clearly established, we outline and unpack our suggested de-implementation processes. We also explain how you can put them to work in various contexts. This is the chapter you probably will want to come back to several times to orient yourselves, as you bring the *Room for Impact* process to life in your local context. **N.B.** For a sneak peak of the *Room for Impact* stages and steps, see Figure 0.2 and for a worked example of de-implementation decision-making in action. see Figure 0.3. ***

CHAPTER	KEY MESSAGES/FOCUS
PART 1: THE BIG PICTURE	
	With chapters 1 and 2 setting out the big picture context and the helicopter overview of the approach, the rest of the book gets deeply into the detail. Each of the chapters in parts 2, 3, 4, and 5 focuses on an individual step of the de-implementation inquiry cycle; and each is designed to be practical and hands on, giving you tools and approaches you can immediately put to use and a range of worked examples to help unlock your "aha!" moments.
PART 2: DISCOVER STAGE	
3. Permit — *Obtaining a mandate to de-implement*	De-implementation is unlikely to be successful unless you have permission to proceed from the highest levels of your organization and a backbone team to lead the charge. The *Permit*-step covers the key systems and process to make this happen. It's about establishing the mandate and laying the organizational foundations to focus on your efficiency of impact.
4. Prospect — *Searching for amenable de-implementation opportunities*	There are many things that you *could* de-implement. But some are harder than others and some come with much more risk to student outcomes. The *Prospect*-step is about explicitly identifying, sifting, and sorting the various de-implementation opportunities to decide those that offer the greatest potential in your context. We give you a range of tools and approaches to choose from.
5. Postulate — *Explaining why (potentially) unnecessary practices might have been started and sustained in the first place*	Often, the things that we do in schools are heavily ingrained, with long histories behind them. To (successfully) de-implement something, we first need to understand why it was started up in the first place and what sustains it. With that knowledge, we can then reconfirm both that it's a suitable area to de-implement and start to glean clues about the best ways to bring our intentions to life. The *Postulate*-step gives you tools and processes to explain the current situation, so you can more successfully de-implement in the (near) future. Or, so that you can conclude that de-implementing a specific area is actually a bad idea, enabling you to cross it off your list and to focus on something else instead.
PART 3: DECIDE STAGE	
6. Propose — *Developing a high-level de-implementation strategy*	This is about choosing an explicit de-implementation strategy. For example, will you *Remove, Reduce, Re-Engineer,* or *Replace* the activities in your target area? It also involves drawing on your prior understandings from the *Postulate*-step to identify countermeasures or "antidotes" for all the barriers to de-implementation that you have uncovered. This includes grappling with beliefs, social norms, and engrained habits (a.k.a. muscle memory).
7. Prepare — *Developing a more detailed de-implementation plan*	Here you are adding more meat to the bone and working up the strategy you developed during the *Propose*-step. You are fleshing this out into a more detailed implementation plan that lays out the *what, why, where, when, who,* and *how*. You are also stress testing that plan prior to de-implementation, and we give you a range of techniques, including bodystorming, pre-mortem, and side effects analysis, to choose from.

(Continued)

(Continued)

CHAPTER	KEY MESSAGES/FOCUS
PART 3: DECIDE STAGE	
8. Picture — *Laying out your success criteria and evaluation plan*	Before you get going and de-implement, you also need to picture what success looks like and set out your monitoring and evaluation plan. You get this done during the *Picture*-step.
PART 4: DE-IMPLEMENT STAGE	
9. Proceed — *De-implementing with rigor*	This is about "putting the pedal to the metal" and making de-implementation happen. Of course, what you do here is a black box (to us), because your actions will depend on your local analysis and deliberations, but we recap the key "look-fors" and lay out the critical actions.
PART 5: RE-DECIDE STAGE	
10. aPpraise — *Monitoring, evaluating, and deciding where to next*	Once you have brought your de-implementation intentions to life, you need to check that they save the intended amount of time/resources. And that you are de-implementing without harming student outcomes. Armed with those findings, you must decide what to do next. Do you continue as is? Do you abandon ship and search for a different strategy? Or do you make some tweaks to your existing approach and *Proceed* once again? These questions are the focus of the *aPpraise*-step.
11. Propel — *Longer-term considerations about sustaining and scaling*	After successfully de-implementing for some time, you must then confront longer-term decisions about sustainability and scaling. This includes whether to keep the de-implementation backbone team in place to repeat the cycle again or whether to transition to business as usual. These, and other considerations, are explored in the *Propel*-step.
PART 6: FINITO	
12. Conclusion	All things must come to an end. So, in the conclusion, we do what all conclusions do—summarize the key messages, tie the loose ends, answer a few burning questions, release the fireworks, and then let the credits roll.
Appendices	We include a range of appendices that summarize the key research findings on de-implementation and implementation. Even if you don't get to these, we included them to signal to you that a heck of a lot of research has gone into getting this book into your hands! **Appendix 1 contains a detailed "shopping list" of 80+ practical de-implementation strategies that you *could* consider! This is one that you may want to study much more closely.**

We have explicitly designed *Making Room for Impact* to be a playbook/field-guide/operating manual/kit-of-tools for de-implementation. The quickest route is to carefully read chapters 1 and 2—and skim the chapters in Parts 2–4 to get a feel for how you can use the process to undertake your local inquiry (although stop and look at chapter 5 in depth, since it has a range of detailed case studies).

Then, once you have your de-implementation team ready for action (or what we call your backbone), we suggest you work through the rest of the book chapter by chapter. Basically, you study the chapter as a team and decide how you will implement/adapt the suggested de-implementation processes locally. Then, do what you agreed, rinse, and repeat. You can also use the book on your own, leveraging it for ideas about things to de-implement in your classroom. Although, here, you are less likely to follow the process end-to-end.

We also think it's important to stress that because de-implementation is so new to education—we went for a "Rolls-Royce" approach to the book. We thought it was important to summarize the totality of the research and lay out many ways that you could undertake an inquiry cycle. This means that it is (quite) a big book filled with (quite) a lot of options. While we suggest that you work through each stage and step of the *Room for Impact* cycle sequentially, the optionality comes with which (of the many) tools you use and how long you spend digging.

Suppose you are working at system or district-level, then you might spend days or even weeks on each step because you are seeking to de-implement things across many schools, with ever-compounding risk (and reward). But suppose you are working at whole-school or teaching-team level, then you might sprint through the Discover and Decide stages in a few highly focused days and press on to de-implement. Whereas if you are reading as an individual practitioner—looking for things that you can subtract on your own—then you might simply read the book for inspiration and ideas, quickly identifying one or two things that you can de-implement in your classroom and get moving at speed.

Lots of options. Lots of ways. You decide.

Finally, we end the introduction by raising the curtain on the *Room for Impact* methodology itself, which you can see in all its glory in Figure 0.2. At this stage, fret not if this looks to you like tangled alphabet-spaghetti because all will become clear as you read on.

But to give you a taste of how *Room for Impact* can work in practice, take a look, too, at Figure 0.3. This (A) introduces the 4Rs of de-implementation (i.e., whether to Remove, Reduce, Re-Engineer, or Replace current practices); it then (B) provides a high-level "shopping list" of areas that *could* be amenable to de-implementation; and, finally, it maps out some of the de-implementation options related to the example area of student homework, (C) and (D). You may find some of those options unpalatable or even shocking. But that's the point: to investigate all the options carefully before selecting the approach that has the best fit to your local context. And to then de-implement with rigor!

FIGURE 0.2   The *Room for Impact* Methodology

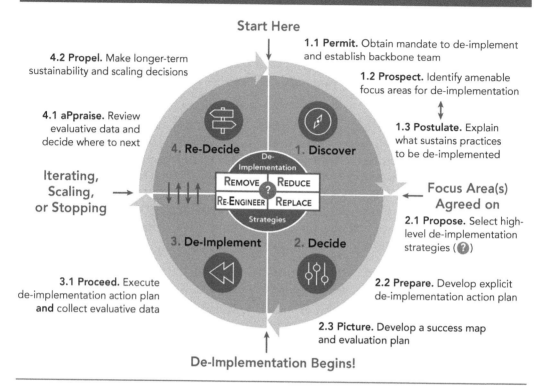

Start Here

1.1 Permit. Obtain mandate to de-implement and establish backbone team

1.2 Prospect. Identify amenable focus areas for de-implementation

4.2 Propel. Make longer-term sustainability and scaling decisions

1.3 Postulate. Explain what sustains practices to be de-implemented

4.1 aPpraise. Review evaluative data and decide where to next

4. Re-Decide

1. Discover

De-Implementation

REMOVE   REDUCE
RE-ENGINEER   REPLACE
?

Strategies

Iterating, Scaling, or Stopping

Focus Area(s) Agreed on

2.1 Propose. Select high-level de-implementation strategies (?)

3. De-Implement

2. Decide

3.1 Proceed. Execute de-implementation action plan **and** collect evaluative data

2.2 Prepare. Develop explicit de-implementation action plan

2.3 Picture. Develop a success map and evaluation plan

De-Implementation Begins!

FIGURE 0.3   From Opportunities to Actions—an Illustration

A

ROOM FOR IMPACT OPTIONS	
1. REMOVE	**2. REDUCE**
i.e., just **stop doing it** completely	i.e., **do it less** frequently or apply it to fewer people (i.e., restrict)
3. RE-ENGINEER	**4. REPLACE**
i.e., do it **more efficiently**, with fewer steps/actions	i.e., **substitute it** with a more efficient and/or effective alternative

B

ROOM FOR IMPACT TARGET-AREA EXAMPLES

- Curriculum Development
- Lesson Planning
- Homework
- Formative Assessment

B

ROOM FOR IMPACT TARGET-AREA EXAMPLES

- Timetabling
- Lesson Observation
- Data Collection, Management, and Use
- Parental Reporting
- Student Behavior Management
- Multitiered Systems of Support
- Breaktime Duties
- Professional Development
- Staff Meetings
- Out-of-Hours Working
- Wall Displays
- Co-curricular Activities
- Whole-school Programs
- Early Career Teacher Support
- Revision/Catch-up Classes
- Teacher Cover
- Administrative Activity

C

SELECTED DE-IMPLEMENTATION AREA

Current Practice	Daily Homework for All Students That Is Devised, Set, and Marked by Teachers

D

WHAT ARE OUR DE-IMPLEMENTATION OPTIONS?

1. CAN WE REMOVE IT?	2. CAN WE REDUCE IT?
• **Stop** homework completely for all (e.g., for Primary/Elementary) students	• **No setting of homework in the week before holiday breaks,** to ensure that staff do not return to a pile of marking • **Frequency of homework reduced** from twice per week per subject to once per week • **Size of homework assignments reduced** to decrease preparation and marking time (This is technically an act of re-engineering!)

(Continued)

(Continued)

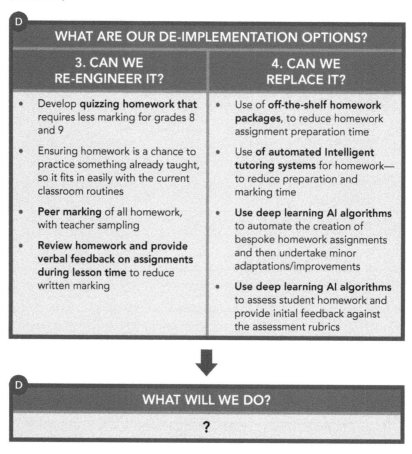

Back in 1955, the historian Cyril Northcote Parkinson famously said "that work will expand to fill the time allotted for its completion." This has become known as Parkinson's Law. Unfortunately, in our world of education, the challenge is deeper. Work is expanding *beyond* the time available with no real evidence that the additional hours are pushing the needle on student achievement, which has largely remained stagnant since the 1970s (Altinok et al., 2018).

It's time we got our lives back—but without harming student outcomes. And *Making Room for Impact* can help with that!

Part 1

The Big Picture

Why We Need to De-Implement (and Why It's Hard)

1

This chapter is for the skeptics, those of you who are perturbed or even doubtful about the value of de-implementation. Maybe you believe that pausing, stopping, or reversing is *never* something that should be considered in the fight for education improvement and equity of outcomes—that quitters are losers, and stickers are winners.

This is a reasonable gut instinct and one we held ourselves before exploring the alternatives deeply. There are, however, three baskets of reasons for de-implementation that we would like you to consider:

> **Basket 1: Arguments From Teacher Workload, Stress, and Well-being**
>
> **Basket 2: Arguments From Inputs vs. Outcomes**
>
> **Basket 3: Arguments From Value for Money**

In the sections below, we explore each of these in turn; and we hope that one or more of these arguments convinces you of the benefits of thinking about (and embracing!) systematic de-implementation. And that this, in turn, drives you to leverage the *Room for Impact* processes.

After we've completed our sales job (and at the risk of making you skeptical again), we then unpack some of the reasons why de-implementation is exceedingly hard to bring to life. We do this, not to put you off, but to illustrate the key decisions we have taken in the *Room for Impact* protocols design—so that difficult becomes possible and then probable.

Let's start first, though, with those three baskets.

The Three Baskets
Basket 1: Arguments From Teacher Workload, Stress, and Well-being

Bizarrely, there is still the misperception in some quarters that teaching is an easy number—that teachers only work until the middle of the afternoon and get long stretches of holiday or vacation.

Of course, nothing could be further from the truth. But, sadly, by some accounts, the wider public underestimates teacher workload by an average of ten hours per week (Varkey Foundation, 2018). Instead, as we illustrate in Figure 1.1, there is sometimes a significant disparity between officially contracted working time and the much longer hours required actually to perform the role.

FIGURE 1.1   Theory vs. Reality of Teacher Workload

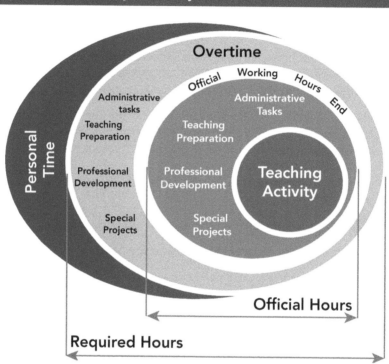

Source: Adapted from OECD (2021b).

When we zoom in and look country-by-country at teacher survey data of their working hours, the picture is (potentially) more harrowing:

- In the **United Kingdom**, educators report working an average of fifty hours a week, with 79 percent of surveyed secondary teachers and 68 percent of surveyed primary teachers saying that they "disagreed/strongly disagreed" that they had an acceptable workload (Walker et al., 2019). This figure is also relatively consistent over the past twenty-five years, although there is some counter-intuitive evidence that workload may have gone down during the COVID-19 lockdowns (Walker et al., 2020)

- In **Australia,** teachers report working an average of fifty-three hours a week, with a quarter of this spent on nonteaching and learning-related activities (Weldon & Ingvarson, 2016). More recent research suggests that this has not abated and that it is driven by the requirement to undertake compliance tasks that are perceived to have limited impact on student outcomes (Gavin et al., 2021). And a 2022 teaching survey conducted by the Grattan Institute also found that 90 percent of surveyed teachers reported that they did not have sufficient time to prepare for their classroom teaching (Hunter et al., 2022)

- In **New Zealand,** in a recent study of primary school leaders, almost half reported working more than fifty hours a week during term time, and 11 percent reported working more than sixty hours a week (Riley et al., 2021)

- For **Canada,** in some contexts, teachers report working more than fifty-two hours per week, seventeen of which are outside their regular days and/or during weekends, with 30 percent of time being expended on noninstructional duties (Government of Northwest Territories, 2017)

- And in the **United States,** international comparative data suggests the US lower secondary teachers have the third highest teaching load in the world (twenty-eight classroom hours per week), with only Chile and Alberta, Canada, coming out higher, and that US teachers work an average of forty-six hours per week (OECD, 2022). However, a recent survey by *Education Week* suggests this may be much higher, at fifty-three hours per week (Education Week, 2022).

We should stress, however, that none of these data come from rigorous time and motion or diary studies, where teachers systematically record their working hours and activities over several weeks. This kind of research is quite rare. Instead, the available data reports on educator *perceptions* or estimations of their workload. The reality *could* be better or far, far worse.

There is also a strong perception that teacher workload increased (or at least changed) during the COVID-19 pandemic with the need to pivot from face-to-face, to online, to hybrid, to running "catch-up" classes and back again. Hard data on the impact of COVID-19 on teacher workload are still a work in progress, but common sense and some emerging findings tell us to expect a significant increase in workload (DeWitt, 2022). Although, as we highlighted above, in some contexts, teachers reported working fewer hours during COVID-19 (Walker et al., 2020).

What is less contestable is that across all these jurisdictions, a relatively high proportion of teachers are exiting the profession soon after starting. In the UK, an average of 20 percent of teachers have left teaching by their second year, and almost one-third by year five (School Workforce Census, 2021). Australian data are harder to unpick, but, according to national statistics, 53 percent of people who hold a teaching degree do not currently work in education and 20 percent never entered the classroom after obtaining their licensure (ABS, 2021; Stroud, 2017).

In the United States, more than two-thirds of teachers quit before retirement, and 90 percent of teachers who join each year are replacing a colleague who left voluntarily, that is, before retirement (Carver-Thomas & Darling-Hammond, 2017). In New Zealand, however, the statistics are currently more encouraging with *only* 15.4 percent of teachers quitting within five years—down from 18 percent pre-COVID-19 (New Zealand Ministry of Education [NZ MOE], 2022). Although in the East Asian contexts where Arran works and lives, it is common for 95 percent or more of teachers to stay in the profession until receipt of their golden carriage clock. So, from this Asian perspective, even the New Zealand attrition numbers are (comparatively) high.

According to many of the analyses on teacher attrition, one of the most critical push factors is workload, stress, and burnout (Fernet et al., 2012; Hakanen et al., 2006; House of Commons, 2021; Jerrim & Sims, 2021; Kokkinos, 2007; Saloviita & Pakarinen, 2021). Teachers who feel that they have too much on their plate and that there simply are not enough hours in a day to do a good job and to maintain a work-life balance are more likely to head for the door.

This means that they need to be replaced with fresh entrants, who must in turn be trained and supported to grow their professional expertise anew. All in the hope that they, too, do not exit stage left. This systematic replacement of more experienced teachers departing, and being replaced by less experienced, and therefore, on average, less effective teachers, means that education systems have to run fast just to stay still.[1]

Of course, the reality is that there are a whole host of national, local, and individual variables that will determine whether *your* workload (and that of your colleagues) has become unmanageable. You may be reading this book and think:

> *I work a bit more than I should, but I've got everything under control,*

or you may be thinking

---

[1] Although, when we look at the workloads of teachers who leave and compare them to those who stay, there is actually little difference. The more critical factors seem to be resilience and coping strategies to withstand the pressures of the role (Gundlach, 2022).

I've got too much on my plate, and it sometimes feels like I'm trying to push water up a mountain.

There may also be just as much workload variation within as between schools and systems. For example, in the case of the latter, according to TALIS data, Japan reports the highest teacher workload in the world at a self-reported average of fifty-six hours per week, and Finland has the lowest at thirty-two hours per week (OECD TALIS, 2020). And both are high PISA performers! Something we come back to in basket two.

You may feel that your personal workload is under control, or you might have developed good coping strategies to deal with the stress (see Lazarus & Folkman [1984] for the seminal research in this area). But if you, your colleagues, and your school feel overwhelmed (or even just moderately concerned) by the plethora of programs, activities, and initiatives that are piling up, or if your mental health is at risk and you find yourself looking at career options outside education, you should strongly consider explicit de-implementation. Which means that *Room for Impact* is for you.

Now, you may be nodding in agreement that your workload is too great but also thinking that de-implementing means that you will be stopping important, positive practices that will have an impact on student outcomes. You may be thinking that if you slow down a little and stop doing some things, your students will turn into pumpkins, which brings us nicely to the Basket 2 arguments about the difference between inputs and outcomes. As we go on to suggest, it *may* be that you are actually filling your time with actions that are only weakly connected to improving student outcomes: busy work or even fake work.

Basket 2: Arguments From Inputs vs. Outcomes

Wouldn't it be amazing if there was a secret magical way that enabled you to do less and actually generate more in the process? Yes, it sounds implausible—almost like turning water into wine. But there are a lot of evidence-based reasons for thinking it is eminently possible.

In Figure 1.2 we cross-tabulate the official length of the school year for a range of countries with their results in the 2018 Programme for International Student Assessment (PISA). As you scan the chart, what do you notice?

FIGURE 1.2 Official Weeks of Schooling per Annum vs. Combined PISA Scores (Reading, Mathematics, and Science, 2018)

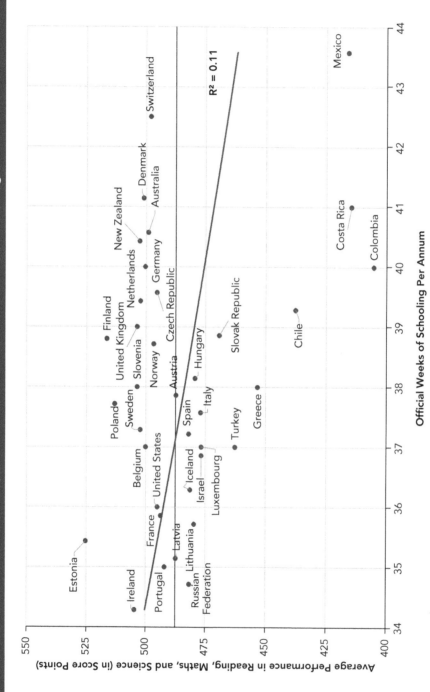

Source: Adapted from OECD (2019), PISA 2018 Database, Tables I.B1.4, B3.1.1; and OECD Indicators D1a, D1.1. This is an adaptation of an original work by the OECD. The opinions expressed and arguments employed in this adaptation are the sole responsibility of the authors of the adaptation and should not be reported as representing the official views of the OECD or of its member countries.

First, you might spot a *significant* difference in the length of the school year across these countries—almost ten weeks longer or shorter in some cases. Second, if there were a strong relationship between the length of the academic year and student learning outcomes, we would also expect to see all the top performing countries clustered in the top right of the chart (i.e., longer year = higher PISA results) and all the poorer performing countries clustered in the bottom left (i.e., short school year = lower PISA results). However, we see nothing of the sort.

When we focus on the countries that score above the OECD combined average of 488 in PISA, we see that they are spread out across the chart. Ireland, for example, scores above Switzerland but provides eight *fewer* weeks of official instruction time per annum. And Estonia scores considerably higher than the United States, UK, and New Zealand with an average of four weeks *less* instruction. The chart also shows the R^2 value, which is a measure of how much the variation in the length of the school year accounts for the variation in the PISA scores. In this case, the length of the school year accounts for only 11 percent of the variation in PISA scores.

At this juncture, it is worth pointing out that we cannot tell from such data that the length of the year *causes* changes in PISA results. It could be, for example, that countries with education systems that perform poorly, for whatever reason, compensate for that by extending the school year. There are also some oddities in the data. For example, the UK is reported as having thirty-nine weeks of school each year, but in fact in three of the four jurisdictions in the UK (England, Scotland, Wales), students attend for thirty-eight weeks; the additional five days are reserved for staff preparation and training. And in Northern Ireland, schools have to be open for two hundred days each year, but this can include staff training days where students do not attend. Yet, despite these niggles, Figure 1.2 still makes us pause for thought. Some systems seem to be doing less and achieving more.

Of course, you might be wondering whether the countries with shorter school years are making up for it in longer school days, operating like Korean *Hagwons* who teach late into the night, filling each day to the brim. Good thinking—but the data suggests this is not the case, either. As you can see from Figure 1.3, there is also a MASSIVE variation in the number of cumulative hours of instruction provided per student between systems. A gap of almost five thousand hours exists between the most and the least instruction-heavy systems across primary and lower secondary schooling. Assuming an average five hours of instruction time per school day, this translates into almost a thousand-day difference.

Yes, you read that correctly: one thousand days. And, assuming an average 180-day school year, that's the equivalent of a five-and-a-half-year difference in instructional time. Five and a half years *less* instruction in some systems and better PISA outcomes!

FIGURE 1.3 Cumulative Official Hours of Instruction per Student in Primary and Lower Secondary vs. PISA Performance (Reading, Mathematics, and Science, 2018)

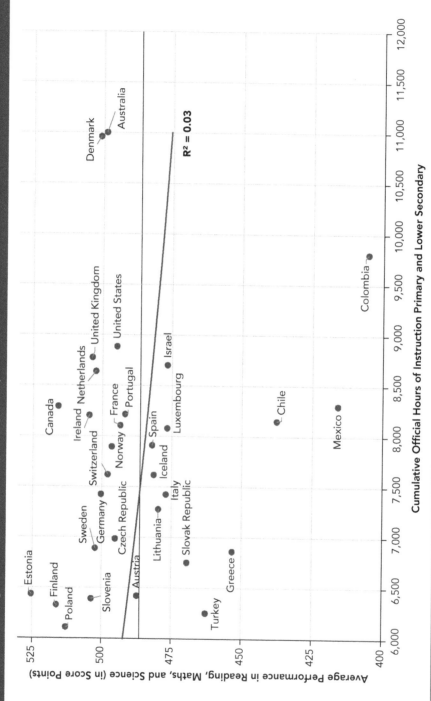

Source: Adapted from OECD (2019), PISA 2018 Database, Tables I.B1.4, B3.1.1; and OECD Indicators D1a, D1.1. This is an adaptation of an original work by the OECD. The opinions expressed and arguments employed in this adaptation are the sole responsibility of the authors of the adaptation and should not be reported as representing the official views of the OECD or of its member countries.

What sticks out most in Figure 1.3 is that Estonia, Finland, Poland, and Slovenia score very favorably in PISA with cumulative instruction hours in the 6,000–6,500 range, which is at the low end for contact time. Canada achieves a similarly favorable PISA score but with circa two thousand *additional* instruction hours. The United States and UK put even more instructional hours for a lesser return than Canada. But at the far right of the chart, we have Australia, which scores above the OECD average for PISA but by burning through circa 11,000 instructional hours.

Now part of this is explained by differences in when students start school. In the UK, many students begin primary school shortly after their fourth birthday, while in others, such as Finland, primary school starts when students are seven, although most are in some form of formal preschool from the age of two. We should also note that some countries have much broader curricula than others. In the United States, 75 percent of scheduled teaching time is typically allocated to the three PISA subjects (reading, mathematics, science), while in others, it is less than half. In some countries, art, music, dance, and drama are formally timetabled, while in others they are regarded as "extracurricular" time. But, nonetheless, these PISA data still paint a picture of a *significant* disconnect between inputs and outcomes.

Perhaps the most important feature of this graph is the extremely weak relationship between the number of instructional hours and PISA rankings. You will also notice the nonexistent statistical correlation between cumulative hours of instruction and student learning outcomes ($R^2 = 0.03$). This is about as significant as the relationship between hair color and student achievement. Not very significant at all.

Now as noted above, this doesn't mean that the number of hours of education students receive is irrelevant; as with all international comparisons, we have too many variables and too few data-points. What the data from PISA and others do show, we believe, is that *how* those hours are spent is at least as, and probably more, important than the raw number of hours students are in classrooms.

Granted, unless you are a policymaker or trade union official, you can personally do very little to reduce the length of the school day. You can't award yourself more holidays or unilaterally decide to teach fewer periods per week. However, by international averages, 50 percent or more of your time is likely spent on activities that take place outside the classroom. And the case that we want to make is that it's extremely likely that you *can* de-implement at least *some* of this—without any negative impact on student outcomes.

The UK, for example, has been implementing teacher workload reduction strategies since 2014 and Australia modified these strategies (see AITSL, 2020). While, yes, some of these have been top-down and focused on the deletion of paperwork and report generation tasks, a good deal of it has also been about schools undertaking local inquiry cycles to see what they can stop, implementing the stop, evaluating to check no harm has been done to student learning, and then repeating. Peer-reviewed evaluations of this approach are still a work in progress, and the de-implementation protocols are not yet fully codified—hence the need for this book; but the early findings suggest that British educators have managed to de-implement with success (Churches, 2020; C. Robinson & Pedder, 2018). Most of this UK action research focused on efficiencies in formative assessment (including feedback), lesson planning, and data reporting; and the findings—although small scale and short-term—report a moderate upswing in student outcomes alongside this dialing back. In other words, doing less to achieve more.

In England, partly to address the increase in teacher workload caused by pandemic-related school closures and the rapid switch to what Paul Kirschner calls "emergency remote teaching," the government also established the Oak National Academy, which provides teachers with lesson plans, printed resources, and videos that they can use in their regular teaching. While some commentators have argued that providing high-quality learning resources to teachers undermines their professional autonomy, it is worth noting that no surgeon makes her own medical equipment and that few successful actors write and perform their own screenplays. The challenge is to find a middle ground between, at one extreme, telling teachers exactly what to do via scripted lessons, and, at the other, leaving each teacher to reinvent the wheel by requiring them to develop every resource they use from scratch.

We think de-implementation that saves time and reduces teacher workload—even if student learning outcomes remain static—is a goal worth progressing. But the early findings from England tentatively suggest that the increases in teacher well-being are also being paid forward to student learning, at least during the initial months of de-implementation. Some of the reasons for this *might* be the following:

- Educators are explicitly refocusing their energies on higher-impact activities;

- Educators have more free time to reflect on where to go next, because their bandwidth is not crowded out by constant (tail-chasing) action;

- More students have increased agency, with learners taking more responsibility for their learning because their teachers are letting go of the reins;

- Use of shared teaching and learning resources, which can be more effective than the resources the teacher would have developed on her or his own. For example, a recent study by C. K. Jackson and Makarin (2018) found that giving mathematics teachers "off-the-shelf" lesson plans had no adverse impact on the most effective teachers and made average and below-average teachers more effective.

Of course, at this point the skeptical reader might point out that any improvements might be placebo effects (produced by the novelty of a different approach) or Hawthorne effects (generated by the fact that teachers know they are being observed) and are therefore unlikely to be sustainable. However, we believe that there is now enough evidence to suggest that these kinds of changes *can* be both effective and also sustainable—if they are continually attended to (see for example Ashman & Stobart, 2018; DfE, 2016a, 2016b, 2016c; Ellis et al., 2017; Featherstone & Seleznyov, 2017; Handscomb et al., 2017; Herbert et al., 2017; Kime, 2017; King et al., 2018; Protsiv et al., 2017; Qing et al., 2017; Richardson et al., 2017; Webb, 2017; White, 2017).

And, even if we are not sure whether de-implementation makes student learning go up, the evidence suggests that if the *right* areas are selected, it doesn't push student outcomes down either: that is, it doesn't *harm* learning. And that's the key!

Basket 3: Arguments From Value for Money

A third perspective on de-implementation relates to the economic efficiency of your impact. If you are working at the classroom level, this *may* be less relevant to you or at least it is something you have less influence over. However, if you are a budget holder working at school or system level, we think you should take a strong interest in the returns to student learning from every dollar, euro, or pound that you expend.

According to recent global estimates, each year, governments and citizens collectively spend more than US$4.9 trillion on education (World Bank & UNESCO, 2022). The global education sector employs more than 84 million teachers, or to put it another way, one in every one hundred people in a country are schoolteachers (World Bank EdStats, 2022). By some accounts, education also happens to be the world's second largest "industry" after healthcare. It's globally bigger than oil, insurance, automotive, banking, and tourism (IBISWorld, n.d.). And, on average, each nation expends approximately 4.6 percent of GDP on education, which works out at around 14.5 percent of total public expenditure (World Bank EdStats, 2022).

The key question, however, is whether more money results in better student learning outcomes. To help us answer this, Figure 1.4 cross tabulates country mean average PISA performances in the reading, mathematics, and science assessments, plotting these against cumulative spending per student.

FIGURE 1.4 Cumulative per Student Spending vs. System PISA Performance (Reading, Mathematics, and Science Combined, 2018)

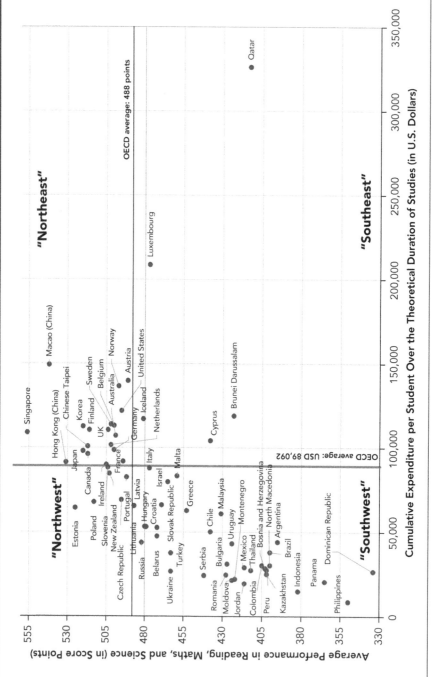

Source: Adapted from OECD, PISA 2018 Database, Tables I.B1.4, I.B1.10, I.B1.11, I.B1.12, I.B1.26, I.B1.27, & B3.1.1. This is an adaptation of an original work by the OECD. The opinions expressed and arguments employed in this adaptation are the sole responsibility of the authors of the adaptation and should not be reported as representing the official views of the OECD or of its member countries.

As you scan the chart, you may notice several systems clustered in the "Southeast" quadrant with below-average funding and below-average outcomes. Yes, money does matter. But as we shall see, only to a point. There is quite a difference between what, for example, the Dominican Republic and Ukraine can do with near identical levels of student funding (to the tune of over 100 PISA points).

When we look at the "Northern" quadrants of the chart, we see some outliers in the "Northeast" that can unlock strong PISA performances with below-average funding levels, such as Estonia, Poland, and the Czech Republic. And we see countries like the UK, United States, and Australia in the "Northwest" that are performing above average in PISA but for an equally above-average level of funding.

This doesn't mean that more money never makes a difference. Instead, it suggests, as we noted earlier, that it needs to be spent on the *right* things and that, perhaps, some systems are not doing that. Of course, the logical extension of this thinking is that money *removed* from the *wrong* things will not harm learner outcomes either. So long as you can confirm they truly are *wrong* before you get a cutting!

Now, if you are a school budget holder, you might be thinking, "I bet most of this funding goes on things that I have no direct control over—like teacher salaries and building costs." You would be right to think that. Recent estimates suggest that more than 70 percent of education budgets are spent on teacher and support-staff salaries (OECD, 2021a). We estimate that no more than 10 percent of total education spending—or around USD $490 billion—is globally available for:

- teacher professional development;
- education technology—hardware and software; and
- teaching and learning resources, such as textbooks/learning content and consumables.

But, of course, the proportion of this that ends up in your particular school and within a budget line that you have local control of will perhaps only be in the low thousands or low tens of thousands of dollars.

What is crucial is that you spend this nectar wisely—that you invest it in activities and resources that have a high probability of impact in your local contexts. It is also essential that you check that the impact is actually being realized.

It is important that you do this to confirm that you are not spending your budget on shiny (but ineffective) baubles. If, however, you find that you are, the next step is to stop, to de-implement in order to re-harvest the budgets for more impactful initiatives or even to give yourselves a rest and focus on your collective well-being.

Bringing the Three Baskets Together

Your de-implementation motivations and actions might, therefore, be guided by one or more of the following:

1. **To save time and reduce your workload:**
    a. As an end in itself (i.e., for your individual and collective well-being)
    b. With the intention of positive organic washback (i.e., the less overworked you are, being a better and more impactful teacher, because you have time to reflect, think, and improve)

2. **To save financial resources:**
    a. To reinvest in higher-probability interventions
    b. As an end in itself (more relevant during economic downturns when education budgets are sometimes reduced)

3. **To explicitly reinvest your time and energy into the highest-impact activities**; that is, you de-implement to create room for more effective impact by replacing "good" things with "better" things. However, if this is your goal, we strongly recommend you take a look at our sister book *Building to Impact* and leverage the protocols to choose those replacement actions with great care. Otherwise, you may end up replacing "good" things with "poor" things without even realizing it.

Health Warning: De-Implementation Is Hard

Now that we have hopefully made you excited about the benefits and opportunities of de-implementation, it's time for the sucker punch. We need to put our cards on the table and be up front that bringing de-implementation to life is hard. Devilishly so.

And there are nine reasons for this, which we unpack in the subsections below. We do this not to put you off. Forewarned is forearmed. For each of the nine reasons we also lay out the implications and how these feed forward into the *Room for Impact* protocols to better help you in avoiding the beartraps.

*Before we begin, some health warnings about the health warnings. The remainder of this chapter is, we think, possibly the most complex part of the book. The nine points that we will discuss were—to us— very important background considerations in framing the *Room for Impact* stages and steps. But if you would prefer not to get sucked into these detailed research considerations, feel free to skim what follows and exit at chapter 2—where things get much more practical!*

But for the Spartans among you, now onto those critical nine reasons!

Reason 1: We Are All (Probably)
Cognitively Primed for Addition

You might already be familiar with the branch of psychology research that focuses on cognitive biases. This suggests that our brains are naturally prewired to process and respond to environmental cues in certain (pre-programmed) ways (Haselton et al., 2009). For example, when we see a snake, "emergency" neurons fire in our brain and we are primed to run away. No prior learning is required. Even babies without pre-exposure to snakes seem to respond with flight (Poulton & Menzies, 2002). When we seek out information about snakes or indeed about anything, we tend to look disproportionately for data that confirms our existing beliefs (i.e., confirmation bias); and when, finally, we know the outcome of an event, we also often think we knew it all along and forget there was a time before we knew when everything was uncertain (i.e., hindsight bias). These are just some of the more than two hundred cataloged (and overlapping) cognitive biases that have been identified by psychologists (see, for example, Cognitive Bias Codex, 2016; Hattie & Hamilton, 2020).

More recent cognitive psychology research suggests that we may also be "hardwired" to have a similar bias toward addition (Adams et al., 2021). This means that when we are presented with a problem, we are more likely to explore options that involve adding new activities, initiatives, programs, resources, and time. And we are less likely to consider the converse, that by subtracting we might achieve more. Adams et al. (2021) identified this tendency across eight different laboratory studies, where they found that people prefer to add rather than subtract:

- bricks to make a wonky Lego bridge stand up without wobbling

- pixels to make a digital image symmetrical

- materials to improve a miniature golf course

- ideas for organizational improvement

when in all cases, subtraction would work just as well.

The literature also suggests that a second cognitive bias called Loss Aversion may also compound this tendency (McGraw et al., 2010). This is the idea that fear of losses (i.e., from abandoning an existing and engrained practice) is stronger than the attraction to gains (i.e., from adopting new practices). It has been suggested that this may explain why we are more likely to cling doggedly to existing ways of doing things rather than to adopt newer and more efficient alternatives or just plain *STOP* (C. Burton et al., 2019; Davidoff, 2015; McKay et al., 2018; van Bodegom-Vos et al., 2017; Willson, 2015).

Of course, we mustn't be fatalistic about this bias toward addition and toward loss aversion. As humans, we have many biases that may well have been, at some point in our evolutionary history, useful, but are useless, or even harmful, in our current environment. And so, yes, while it *might* be a hardwired predisposition to search for things to add and to be reluctant to subtract—the same research suggests that with training and priming we can all learn to investigate subtractive improvement—before we pivot to our default setting of addition (Adams et al., 2021; Klotz, 2021).

Implication: We need robust processes and ways of working to overcome our natural tendency toward addition and not letting go. We can't just leave it to chance: the whole point of *Room for Impact*!

Reason 2: There Is No Such Thing as "Unlearning"

As we learn, new information and new processes pass from our working memory and into long-term memory, where it becomes "saved" into one of our many "mental filing cabinets" (Cowan, 2014). These stored items can then be accessed easily and automatically to perform a pre-learned behavior or just to retrieve a prestored fact—like remembering who won the 1989 Super Bowl.

This model of short-term and long-term memory is a bit like the distinction between memory and storage in a computer: Data is retrieved from the storage system (i.e., the hard disk) and is manipulated in the computer's memory (i.e., the RAM or random-access memory chip). In the same way, humans retrieve items from long-term memory (such as names, dates, and multiplication facts) and process them in working memory. This is, of course, just a model, and as statistician George Box famously remarked, "All models are wrong, but some are useful," yet this distinction between working memory and long-term memory, while being a gross simplification, turns out to be extremely powerful in understanding how we think.

However, there is one key difference between humans and computers that is especially important when thinking about de-implementation. On a computer, you can delete information that is no longer needed by moving it into the trash folder and then expunging it entirely from the system. Human brains, however, don't seem to work like this. Once new information has been stored, it stays there permanently. Yes, the salience of the information may diminish if you access the "file" infrequently, but it remains (in some form) on the system forever unless our brains become physically damaged (Durst et al., 2020; Gupta et al., 2017; Visser, 2017).

A good demonstration of this "forever phenomenon" is a neuroimaging study of scientists with PhDs in physics, which found that their "naïve" (kindergarten-level) theories about physical phenomena persisted even when their advanced scientific training told them these beliefs were "wrong." New ideas did not replace old ideas, but rather the scientists learned (with effort) to select the more advanced ways of thinking once they had suppressed the "naïve" old response (Allaire-Duquette et al., 2021). But those "naïve" theories still lingered in the background, *forever*.

So, we cannot "delete." Instead, we seem to need to write a new piece of mental code (i.e., learn a new behavior) as an alternative to the existing pathway and then learn to select this rather than the earlier response.

This might be about:

- **Making alterations to the process steps in something you already do**—To look at a practical example: Maybe your routine for getting to work requires you to take Bus 12, walk a mile, then take tram line A, and then walk half a mile. But you now buy a fold-up bike that you use to cycle rather than walk the gaps between the bus, tram, and your final destination, allowing you to get to that end point much faster. In other words, you have **re-engineered** the process to insert and then prime the "bike subroutine" rather than the "walking subroutine."

- **Priming an entirely new process**—So that instead of doing A, B, C, D, you do 1, 2, 3, 4. Here, like the physicists, you are swapping one routine for another. For example, perhaps you are trying to lose weight, so you pivot from your regular diet of cheese, chips, cake, and soda (A, B, C, D) to an entirely new (fad) diet where you only consume eggs, raw seaweed, chili flakes, and water (1, 2, 3, 4). In other words, you have **replaced** the existing process.

- **Creating a Void**—So that instead of doing A, B, C, D, you default to 0, that is, you do nothing. For example, you go from smoking to not smoking, and you do so without any alternative behaviors like gum chewing or tea making to fill the void. In other words, you have **removed** (or at least quarantined) the process. Or maybe you just cut down the number of sticks you smoke, in which case you have **reduced**.

The challenge, of course, is that none of the prior behaviors have been deleted from your long-term memory. They have merely been adapted or substituted or quarantined. They remain available for reversion.

An example of this is when Arran's kitchen tap broke during the COVID-19 lockdowns. He couldn't call a plumber and needed to use another nearby sink in his house. But for about a week, he still automatically went to the broken sink, reached for the tap, and suddenly realized that it was futile. Then, finally, the retrieval strength of "go to the alternative sink" became stronger than "use the regular sink" and all was good. He had **re-engineered** the process of washing-up.

When, after several weeks, the plumber finally was allowed to come, Arran faced the same challenge in reverse. The reversion to his existing six-year habit of using the original sink was, however, far easier because that original behavior was more deeply engrained. A neuroscientist might say that over those six years, Arran had built up more myelin around the "go to the regular kitchen sink" pathway and that this increased the conductivity of the relevant neurons, upping their "broadband speed" (Dehaene, 2020), thus, making it easy to revert to those prior behaviors quickly.

Implication: Our de-implementation processes need to be aligned to what we know about habit formation and change, including how the brain works and specific behavior changes strategies.

Reason 3: De-Implementation Is Highly Context Specific

In his work on learning environments, Robin Hogarth and his colleagues distinguish between *kind* and *wicked* learning environments (Hogarth et al., 2015). A kind learning environment is one where what you learned in one situation can be easily transferred and used in another, whereas a wicked learning environment is the opposite: what is learned in one setting can be completely the *wrong* thing to do in that second, seemingly similar, situation.

The games of chess and tennis are good examples of kind learning environments. Whether you are playing chess in Kansas or Kazakhstan, the rules are the same and your learnings about chess strategy will be equally applicable. Ditto tennis—where, yes, there is some difference between clay, hard, and grass courts—but overall, the same techniques apply.

There is, by contrast, plenty of evidence that many aspects of education constitute wicked learning environments:

* Programs that "work" in one setting may be less effective or even counterproductive in other settings. A good example of this is class-size reduction, which was found to be effective in a small project in Tennessee, but which proved disastrous when implemented in places where the extra teachers recruited were significantly worse than those already employed, as was the case in many districts in California (Wiliam, 2018).

* Instructional approaches that are effective in the short term can often be less effective in the long term (Carrell & West, 2010).

* What works for younger students may be totally inappropriate for older ones (Hamilton & Hattie, 2022).

* Some studies have found extending the school day helpful (Figlio et al., 2018; Patall et al., 2010), while others have found little or no impact (Meyer & van Klaveren, 2013). Even when the effect of extending the day increases average achievement, this can mask different outcomes for different learners. For example, analysis of the effects of extending the school day in Germany found that teachers used some of this time to teach extra content rather than on consolidating children's understanding on the core curriculum; and this actually made the achievement gap larger (Huebener et al., 2017). And even if extending the day is effective, on the assumption that teachers would need to be paid for the extra hours they are

putting in, there is always the question of what else could be done with the money and whether these alternatives could be even more effective.

- Without good theories, we may also draw the wrong conclusions about "what" worked and why. When Dylan worked with Jo Boaler and Hannah Bartholomew studying the impact of ability-grouping practices on a cohort of over one thousand students in six secondary schools, they found that students placed in higher-achieving groups made more progress, and they interpreted this as an effect of student grouping. However, it has now become clear that teachers vary greatly in their effectiveness, so this effect might have been produced by the allocation of the most effective teachers to teach the highest achieving students (Wiliam & Bartholomew, 2004).

Hence, education is a wicked learning environment. What worked *here* does not (necessarily) work *there*. We think the same principles are also likely to apply to de-implementation. What is reduced, removed, re-engineered, or replaced with good effect *here* might result in calamity *there*.

So, while there are certain whole-system de-implementation actions that departments and ministries of education can (and should) consider—like decreasing the administrative burden on schools and so on—a lot of the locally appropriate action will vary from school to school. Reducing or removing homework could, for example, be a highly viable strategy for primary schools where the evidence suggests only modest returns from continuation, but it would be more unwise in secondary/high-school contexts (Cooper, 1989). Instead, in these contexts, it might be better to focus on the efficiency of homework management, to reduce the burden on teachers.

A related challenge is to identify the things that might derail any planned de-implementation activity in the local context. Here are some examples of attitudes that might act as de-implementation hinderances:

- It's normal to do it this way here.
- I have always done this.
- I swear by it.
- I like it.

And, after we identify them, we need to plan mitigations or antidotes.

Implication: Because the appropriate de-implementation actions are likely to vary by context (along with the reactions to them), it's more valuable to provide schools and systems with a framework to help them discover and implement their own strategies than simply to provide a list of recommendations or top tips.

And because there are (almost) always going to be derailers, we also need to understand what sustains those existing practices, so our local tactics are more likely to succeed.

Reason 4: There Are No Preexisting *Oven-Ready* De-Implementation Processes

Unlike the field of implementation (a.k.a. adding, growing, or expanding) where many process manuals and a range of systematic reviews and meta-analysis enable us to unpick the critical features we must attend to, no such literature on de-implementation exists. We are still, sadly, in the "Wild West" early days of de-implementation research. Hence the need for this framework, with our suggested processes for you to consider as you embark on your own personal de-implementation quests.

Now, in simple systems, it might well be the case that de-implementation can be carried out simply by reversing the process of implementation. But with complex systems, de-implementation is absolutely *not* implementation in reverse (Nilsen et al., 2020; Prusaczyk et al., 2020). As an example, consider someone with a shard of glass stuck deep in their upper thigh. Reversing the process—simply extracting the shard of glass—is likely to have serious consequences. Instead, care must be taken to understand the positioning of the shard, whether any major blood vessels are affected, and so on. The process for taking something out is not the same as for putting it in. It's a totally different thing.

In a similar way, in complex systems like schools, de-implementation requires different types of steps and actions that carefully map and attend to the behaviors that sustain inefficient practices and that enable us to prime alternative behaviors. This means that de-implementation is more like giving up smoking (i.e., removing) or dieting (i.e., reducing), or using a different kitchen sink (i.e., re-engineering), or ditching your petrol car and going electric (i.e., replacing). And de-implementation requires different processes to those used for starting and sustaining a new behavior (e.g., for things like making the commitment to go to the gym each day or to implement a blended phonics program).

However, often, in complex systems like schools, de-implementation also requires understanding what produced the apparently inefficient practice in the first place, because otherwise there is the real risk that old habits die hard. Those expunged behaviors gradually bubble back up (see discussion of "Chesterton's fence" in the next chapter).

The good news is that in some ways de-implementation is easier than implementation because it does not always require you to design, learn, and implement new replacement actions. Mostly, it's "merely" about (carefully) removing, reducing, or re-engineering an existing thing that you already do. But because of the cognitive biases discussed above—what is conceptually simple turns out to be practically difficult. You may, for example, end up feeling guilty about stopping certain actions—even if you know that those actions are exceedingly weak drivers of student outcomes. You may feel that stopping is slovenly and downright lazy. You may also believe that winners never quit and quitters never win. There might also be immense professional pressure for you and your school to conform to practices that have been branded as the "ideal standard" and seen as "required" within the teaching profession. However, we want you to question this thinking and embrace controlled, collaborative, and evaluative quitting.

Implication: We need to build those oven-ready de-implementation processes. That is the whole point of this book!

Reason 5: There Are Different Levels of De-Implementation Within Education Systems

As we unpack in the table below, these range from actions you can take at a personal or individual level to those that you can undertake locally in your teaching teams to those that can only be traversed at whole school or even system-level (DeWitt, 2022).

LEVEL	DESCRIPTION	EXAMPLES
L1 Individual	The actions you can remove, reduce, re-engineer or replace on your own—without recourse to anyone else. You can normally implement these quickly, even instantly.	Checking your emails less regularly Limiting your late-night working Sourcing pre-developed teaching and learning resources online rather than building your own from scratch
L2 Local	Actions that require cooperative engagement with your immediate teaching teams but do not require senior leadership permission. These actions can also be implemented relatively quickly, over a couple of weeks, once you have decided and agreed what you will do.	Stand-up team meetings to finish more quickly Developing more time-efficient student feedback rubrics Collectively sharing all your teaching materials to reduce preparation time Co-planning your lessons with colleagues, for example, by divvying up different areas, so that between you, you develop a single shared set of materials
L3 Whole School	Actions requiring agreement and cooperation from your school leadership team and governing body, which are likely to be implemented on a whole-school basis. The process will likely take longer—possibly several months—and involve stakeholder engagement and piloting before new and more efficient ways of working are locked in.	Changing the start and end times of the school day (or even the decision to go to a four-day week) Streamlining parental engagement processes Adjusting school-wide data collecting and reporting systems to make these more efficient Decisions about the type and frequency of teacher professional development

(Continued)

(Continued)

LEVEL	DESCRIPTION	EXAMPLES
		Altering your student behavior management policies and system for efficiency
		Decisions about adopting an "off-the-shelf" curriculum across the whole school
		Automating admin tasks and data collection for example, through better leveraging of your school's electronic management information system (eMIS)
L4 System Level	Actions that require permission from the highest levels of the school system and that likely take several years to traverse from the policy consideration stage to practical implementation across whole schools.	Reducing the length of the school day, week, and year
		Reducing national/state data reporting and administration requirements
		Streamlining national/state-mandated programs and processes that all schools must implement
		Advocating/mandating that all school adopt a *Room for Impact*-type inquiry cycle
		Providing information to schools about things they are allowed to remove, reduce, re-engineer, and replace

Implication: *Room for Impact* needs to be useful and usable at all system levels to make the most significant difference.

Reason 6: There Are Also Different De-Implementation Strategies That You Can Pursue

We have hinted at these different strategies already, and they include:

REMOVE		REDUCE	
i.e., **Stop** doing it completely		i.e., doing it less (which can also involve **Restricting** who it is done by or to)	
RE-ENGINEER		**REPLACE**	
i.e., do it more efficiently, with **fewer steps**/actions		i.e., substitute it with a **more efficient** and/or effective **alternative**	

Adapted from Hamilton and Hattie (2022); Northern Territory Government (Australia) (2020); Norton and Chambers (2020); Verkerk et al. (2018); Wang (2018).

As we shall explore, there will likely be different local trade-offs to each of these strategies in your local context. And these trade-offs may be between:

- the amount of time or other resources saved

  vs.

- the ease of de-implementation

  vs.

- the level of harm vs. benefit generated

  vs.

- the level of stakeholder perception or beliefs that the quality of service and outcomes has diminished.

Implication: *Room for Impact* needs to support you in understanding the pros and cons of different strategies in your context and then to support you in implementing, evaluating, and growing the best fit approach.

Reason 7: De-Implementation Can Increase Your Workload in the Short Term

One of the most likely reasons you are interested in de-implementation is that you feel that your workload is too high and that you want to find more efficient ways of generating (at least) the same student outcomes but with significantly less time. The risk, of course, is that you choose the wrong actions to de-implement, which ends up significantly harming the life chances of the children in your care. Or you might choose the right actions and make a collective plan to de-implement, but then you find that no one is following the plan and that old habits die hard.

To counteract these possibilities, you need a rigorous process that:

- gives everyone permission (reducing the collective shame and guilt);
- explores the highest probability de-implementation targets (reducing the harm);
- maps the behaviors that keep the existing practices alive (to prime alternatives);
- de-implements; and
- monitors and evaluates (to ensure people are de-implementing and that there is, indeed, no harm).

The purpose of this book is to give you exactly these processes.

But there is a paradox. For a short time, ranging from weeks to months, your workload may well go up (Burkeman, 2021; Klotz, 2021). This is because you will be undertaking your time-intensive, business-as-usual practices *and* also traversing our *Room for Impact* protocols alongside, to identify targets for de-implementation and build your strategy and evaluation plan. This means that before you can do less, you (may) need to do more for a short time.

Implication: No pain, no gain.

Reason 8: More De-Implementation Already Happens Than You Might Think

Yes, you read correctly, lots of de-implementation already occurs. But it tends to happen organically and at earlier stages of adoption of new initiatives or programs. You may have heard of the work of Rogers (2003) and his research on the *diffusion of innovations*, which is illustrated in Figure 1.5.

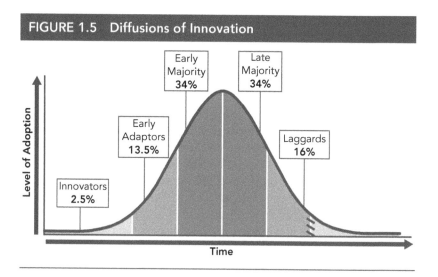

FIGURE 1.5   Diffusions of Innovation

This suggests that when people embark on new initiatives, a small number of highly enthusiastic pioneers adopt with alacrity even if there is no evidence of impact (i.e., the *Innovators*). And at the other end, there is an army of *Laggards* who are highly attuned to the opportunity cost of adopting new practices and wait until the evidence suggests it is worth their while before joining the party much later. Most real-world de-implementation occurs because new initiatives do not pass the tipping-point threshold to achieve mass adoption; and therefore, even the *Innovators* and *Early Adopters* (eventually) cease and revert back to their previous practices. Perhaps this is partly because they feel foolish for joining the bandwagon so early and adopting an untested idea that later proved superfluous.

This de-implementation—because of quiet and building resistance to adopting and scaling a practice—is relatively common. It's why so much (additive) implementation fails, because of *natural attrition*. But once new innovations get past the tipping point and become entrenched, they require a similar amount of time and effort to dig up the roots, as was required to get implementation going in the first place. Even where continuation is patently absurd.

Another cognitive bias at least partially explains this—the aptly named *Plan Continuation Bias*, a.k.a. the sunk cost fallacy (Kahneman, 2011). The research suggests that people are primed to continue and remain invested in status quo because they have already spent so much learning, implementing, and evangelizing the new approach. To suddenly admit to themselves and to others that all their work has been a complete and utter waste of time is just too difficult to contemplate.

Implication: Another reason why the *Room for Impact* processes are so necessary. We need tools for explicit de-implementation to get beyond informal natural attrition.

Reason 9: The Tendency to Expand the Work to Meet the Time Available

Back in the 1950s, Cyril Northcote Parkinson (1955) observed that "work expands so as to fill the time available for its completion." In this case he was talking about the mushrooming number of staff at the UK government's colonial office, even though the British empire had been largely dismantled and very few colonies were left for these civil servants to administer! As discussed in the introduction, this adage has since become *Parkinson's Law*.

Parkinson's Law Corollaries

If you wait until the last minute, it only takes a minute to do (Pannett et al., 2013).

Work contracts to fit in the time we give it (C. Barber, 2014).

In ten hours a day, you have time to fall twice as far behind your commitments as in five hours a day (Asimov, 1969).

Data expands to fill the space available for storage (Jansen, 2008).

The relevance of Parkinson's Law to the *Room for Impact* approach is threefold:

1. Current ways of working within your school are *likely* over-engineered. You have very likely expanded some of your work to fill the time available and then taken on new work, extending it again, way beyond that time (Womack & Jones, 2003).

2. As you work to de-implement and make room in your day, it's also *likely* that you will be tempted to fill this free time up with other activities rather than enjoy the peace and thinking time created (Burkeman, 2021).

3. However, if you really must fill that saved time with new activities, we want to make sure that those replacement actions are the strongest and most valuable things you could be doing with that time, not busywork or feel-good happy projects that make not one iota of difference to students' lives and life chances. Suppose you cannot break the addiction to addition. In that case, we suggest you leverage our sister book *Building to Impact: The 5D Implementation Playbook for Educators*, which provides a range of processes for selecting high-impact actions worth your time and energy.

Implication: We need strong processes for both addition and sub-traction. This is why *Building to Impact* and *Making Room for Impact* are sister volumes—the yin and yang of school improvement!

Health Warning Summary

These nine reasons mean the following:

1. We (probably) prefer adding to subtracting.

2. We can't purge our brains of knowledge, skills, and habits that are no longer useful—they always lurk in the background.

3. In schools, there are unlikely to be standard things that we can uniformly de-implement; the viable targets might vary across systems and schools, and the specific local strategies almost certainly need to vary too.

4. There are (relatively) limited examples of effective de-implementation protocols from other sectors that we can borrow and re-purpose for education, but there are some good leads.

5. For *you*, the areas that are amenable to de-implementation will vary depending on whether you are working on your own, within a teaching team, or at the whole school, or even at system level.

6. There are also multiple strategies that you might adopt, ranging from removal to reduction, to re-engineering, and to replacement with each having different context-specific advantages and trade-offs.

7. De-implementation is likely to actually increase your workload in the short term, as you need to set aside time to identify suitable target areas, build plans, implement, evaluate, and repeat. The flip

side of this is that approaches to de-implementation that do *not* increase your short-term workload are probably destined to fail because you are not thinking and planning deeply enough.

8. Most of the currently successful de-implementation is really failed or aborted implementation, where stakeholders refused to adopt new processes and where they fought tooth and nail against implementation. However, when something is embraced and fossilized, we confront challenges (1) to (7), above.

9. Even if you are successful, Parkinson's Law may mean that your workload slowly creeps back up unless you continually attend to de-implementation.

This in turn means that if we are super, ultra-serious about embarking on de-implementation, we need access to rigorous processes that are designed specifically to support success in schools and school systems. And this is where we believe the *Room for Impact* tool kit can help.

—

Friends, having now made the case for why we should all get serious about de-implementation and having also presented the evidence on why bringing de-implementation to life is so hard without a rigorous process, we are now ready to get to that helicopter overview of the *Room for Impact* methodology. The task of the next chapter!

Room for Impact

The Helicopter Overview

2

//

At last, we get to the good stuff: our suggested processes to de-implement with rigor. Processes that are designed to reduce your time and resourcing requirements but (most importantly) without harming student outcomes.

In this helicopter overview chapter, we:

- explain where the underlying research comes from

- unpack the *Room for Impact* stages and steps

- address a range of common "pre-liftoff" considerations.

> At the end of the chapter (and in more detail in Appendix 1) we also give you a range of practical suggestions about things you could *potentially* de-implement in your context. But choose with care, using the *Room for Impact* protocols to check and check again!

The Research

In order to identify and bundle appropriate de-implementation processes and activities into a kit of tools for impact we reviewed:

- **over thirty health and social care sector** process maps, manuals, and systematic reviews on de-implementation; and **eighteen education sector** de-implementation reviews and case studies, which is the sum total of *all* the relevant research we could find (see Appendix 2 for a summary)

- successful strategies deployed in the business and industrial sectors, including *Lean* and *Six Sigma* methodologies that are specifically focused on the efficiency/re-engineering of existing processes (see Appendix 3)

- the cognitive psychology literature on behavior change—particularly on how therapists support individuals to de-adopt addictive behaviors like substance dependency—and the literature on government-wide "nudging" initiatives (which we cite, where relevant throughout the book); and

- **over fifty implementation methodologies**. While, as we outline in the health warnings in chapter 1, the emerging consensus is that de-implementation is *not* implementation in reverse—we were still able to identify elements from some of these methodologies that were highly relevant to de-implementation (see Appendix 4 for a summary of the more than fifty methodologies).

We then identified four critical stages of activity for successful de-implementation:

1. **Discover** – where a backbone team is established, and target areas for de-implementation are prospected, agreed upon, and explained

2. **Decide** – which is about developing the overarching de-implementation strategy, the specific action plan, success criteria, and evaluation plan

3. **De-Implement** – where the plans come to life and where evaluative data is also collected

4. **Re-Decide** – where the evaluation data is reviewed to decide where to next. This phase also includes considerations about sustaining and scaling your de-implementation successes.

Nestled within the four stages are a series of steps that support you in grappling with key questions and in making locally appropriate decisions. Each of the steps starts with a "P"-word; hence they are "P-Steps" for short.

The four stages and underlying "P-Steps" are re-capped in Figure 2.1, and we need to acknowledge a learning debt to the brilliant work of Davidson et al. (2017), the main inspiration for this framework.

FIGURE 2.1   Recapping *Room for Impact*

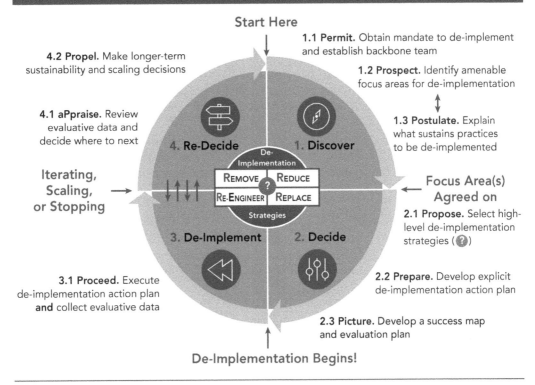

Start Here

1.1 Permit. Obtain mandate to de-implement and establish backbone team

4.2 Propel. Make longer-term sustainability and scaling decisions

1.2 Prospect. Identify amenable focus areas for de-implementation

4.1 aPpraise. Review evaluative data and decide where to next

1.3 Postulate. Explain what sustains practices to be de-implemented

4. Re-Decide

1. Discover

De-Implementation

REMOVE   REDUCE
RE-ENGINEER   REPLACE

Strategies

Iterating, Scaling, or Stopping

Focus Area(s) Agreed on

2.1 Propose. Select high-level de-implementation strategies ()

3. De-Implement

2. Decide

3.1 Proceed. Execute de-implementation action plan **and** collect evaluative data

2.2 Prepare. Develop explicit de-implementation action plan

2.3 Picture. Develop a success map and evaluation plan

De-Implementation Begins!

Unpacking the Room for Impact Protocols

The **four stages** and underlying **P-Steps** are as follows:

> # 1. Discover Stage
>
> *Where the backbone team is established and target areas for de-implementation are prospected, agreed, and explained*

Step 1.1: Permit
Obtain a Mandate to De-Implement

Given that many of us are likely to feel (professionally) guilty about de-implementing an engrained and habitual practice, we need explicit permission, a mandate, or even direct instruction from above to get serious and to proceed. The *Permit*-step is about establishing this mandate, which could involve instituting a school-level Backbone Organization that looks systematically and relentlessly at targets for de-implementation and that supports the whole school to bring the other P-Steps to life.

The great thing about the word "Permit" is that it can be read and interpreted in two ways. The first meaning is about the act of giving permission: "I permit you to de-implement." The second is about giving someone a permit—a piece of paper, a license that gives them the explicit rights to do something. In many countries, if you want to go fishing, own a hunting rifle, or keep a dog, you need a permit. And, of course, a teaching license is also a type of permit. The **(1.1)** *Permit*-**step** gives you such a permit, permission, and a mandate from your paymasters to systematically de-implement. And it enables you to set up a team to get the job done!

Step 1.2: Prospect
Identify Amenable Focus Area(s) for De-implementation

Random tugging at existing practices is likely to be highly dangerous—almost akin to indiscriminately removing wooden blocks from a Jenga tower. Within the tower, some blocks are crucial to the structure's overall stability, whereas others can be removed or hollowed with minimal risk. The **(1.2)** *Prospect*-**step** is about mapping what takes the most time and resource in your local context and the potential risks and opportunities with de-implementing each of the high-intensity areas. The outcome of this P-Step is that you will (provisionally) agree on your de-implementation focus area(s)—that is, those Jenga blocks that are more amenable to removal, reducing, re-engineering, or to replacement with a more efficient substance. And all without harm to student outcomes.

Step 1.3: Postulate (a.k.a. Chesterton's Fence)
Explain What Sustains Practices to Be De-implemented

G. K. Chesterton (1929), the author of the *Father Brown* detective series, once suggested that before you decide to take down a fence, you had better inquire into why it was put up in the first place (see Figure 2.2). You need to know the purpose it serves and the historical, cultural, and belief-oriented behaviors that sustain it. We need to know all this to reconfirm that it is a fence that we truly want to take down. This idea is often referred to as *Chesterton's Fence*, and the core principle is that change should not be embarked on until we understand the reasoning behind the existing state of affairs.

If, for example, you discover that the villagers originally put the fence up to stop the local bull from charging, you can then check whether the bull is still around, whether it is likely to be brought back, and whether there are any alternative bull-charge prevention strategies that might be more cost-effective than maintaining the fence. With that knowledge, you are in a much better place to decide whether fence removal is a wise strategy.

Chesterton's Fence applies equally to education de-implementation. To de-implement something, we first need to understand *why* it was implemented and *what* keeps it in place. We also need to pre-anticipate the consequences and the areas of school life that the removal (or re-engineering) of our chosen "fence" will ricochet into. The **(1.3) *Postulate*-step** is about undertaking this analysis and building a *theory of the present*.

We can then decide whether we still want to de-implement this specific thing. And we can also predict what might make people *creep back into the field late at night and secretly put the fence back up*. With this knowledge in hand, during the Decide stage, we can then propose better plans that are more likely to keep that fence down and make de-implementation a success!

After we have undertaken this analysis, we might well conclude that our selected de-implementation area is not, after all, a "fence" that we really want to take down. In which case we go back to **(1.2) Prospect** and select the next cab off the rank. Alternatively, if we are still convinced that this is indeed an area that is amenable to some sort of de-implementation, then we drive forward to the **Decide stage**.

FIGURE 2.2   Chesterton's Fence

Image: Sketchplanations

> ## 2. Decide Stage
>
> *Where we develop the overarching de-implementation strategy, the specific action plan, and success criteria*

Step 2.1: Propose
Select High-Level De-Implementation Strategies

This is about developing a high-level strategy about how you will undertake de-implementation, given the information you have already gathered during the **(1.2) *Prospect*** and **(1.3) *Postulate*-**steps. This includes deciding whether you will:

Remove (i.e., stop),

Reduce (i.e., cut down or restrict),

Re-engineer (i.e., streamline the processes), or

Replace (i.e., do something else instead) within targeted activity areas.

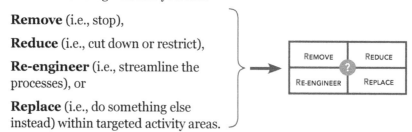

The **(2.1) *Propose*-step** also involves consideration of the behavior change strategies that will best discourage stakeholders from persisting with the identified de-implementation behavior (i.e., putting the "fence" back up). This might include social support (a.k.a. the Weight Watchers weekly weigh-in and clap model), right through to punitive sanctions—and a whole host of strategies in between. In this P-step we provide you with a menu of twenty-eight behavior change strategies for you to select from.

Step 2.2: Prepare
Develop Explicit De-Implementation Action Plan(s)

The **(2.2) *Prepare*-step** builds out the high-level de-implementation strategy you agreed on during the **(2.1) *Propose*-step** and develops this into a full de-implementation action plan—that is, a clear map of all the actions that will be undertaken from A to B to C, to de-implementation. The *what, why, when, where, how,* and *who.*

It also involves stress-testing this plan prior to activation. You do this because of what Martin Eccles calls the **ISLAGIATT** dilemma (Michie et al., 2014):

– Often, after we implement (or de-implement) a thing and find that it is not working, we end up saying "*it seemed like **a good idea** at the time*" (i.e., ISLAGIATT). And, often, the reason it seemed like a good idea, but turned out not to be, is that we spent insufficient mental energy working through what might actually happen once we have pressed "play" and brought the plan to life. If we think deeply enough, many of the barriers to success are highly predictable.

But if we have not done this thinking, we are also unable to pre-build countermeasures to these predictable eventualities, such as the secret attempts by stakeholders to "put the fence back up" and the strategies that we can have ready at hand to ensure that fence stays down!

Step 2.3: Picture
Develop a Success Map and Evaluation Plan

With your detailed de-implementation plan to hand, during the **(2.3) *Picture*-step** you will agree on your success criteria. These might be expressed in terms of one or more of the following:

- time and resources saved;
- the level of impact on student achievement;
- the benefits to staff well-being.

You will also agree on your monitoring and evaluation plan—namely, what data you will collect, at what frequency, and what exactly you will do with it.

The reason this P-step is crucial is because of *outcomes ambiguity*. We cannot know for sure whether even the most well-considered de-implementation plan will save (sufficient) time/resources, and do so without harming student outcomes, until we put that plan into action and see for ourselves. But in order to see, we need to collect data and then look at it to decide where to go next.

This evaluation planning activity is really a subcomponent of the **(2.2) Prepare-step**, but in our implementation work we find that schools and systems frequently skip developing an evaluative plan. So we see no reason why this activity skipping would not also occur for de-implementation! Hence, we have pulled it out and explicitly made it into a standalone P-Step, so that you can more fully picture your success and put plans in place to regularly measure whether you are on track to achieve it.

---

3. De-Implement Stage

Where the plans come to life!

Step 3.1: Proceed
Execute De-Implementation Action Plan
and Collect Evaluative Data

This is where you (finally) press "Play" and bring your de-implementation plan to life, so that you can make room for impact. What you do here—and indeed the quality of the outcomes—will be entirely dependent on where your analysis and thinking have taken you in relation to the preceding P-Steps.

The **(3.1) Proceed-step** is also where the majority of your activity is likely to be focused. So, if we were to rescale the *Room for Impact* methodology diagram, resizing each of the overarching stages to correspond with the likely time taken, it might look like something like Figure 2.3. But what you actually do during the *Proceed*-step is going to be a mystery or a black box to us, because it depends entirely on your local analysis and decisions during the previous P-Steps.

This step also includes the ongoing collection of monitoring and evaluation data against your **(2.3) Picture** of Success.

FIGURE 2.3   *Room for Impact* Rescaled

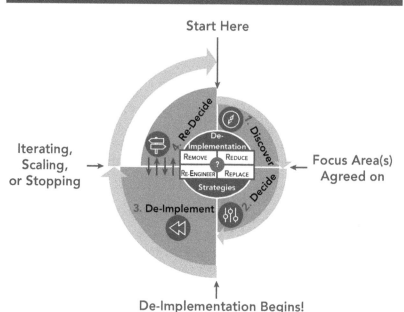

---

4. Re-Decide Stage

Where you review the evaluation data to decide where to next. This phase also includes considerations about sustaining and scaling your de-implementation success.

Step 4.1: aPpraise
Review Evaluative Data and Decide Where to Next

Here you review the monitoring and evaluation data that you collected against your **(2.3) *Picture*** of success; and you **(4.1) aPpraise** it to decide whether to:

- continue as is,

- adjust, or

- stop.

Often, the exit route from **(4.1) *aPpraise*** is back to **(3.1) *Proceed***, where you put any plan revisions into action and continue collecting monitoring and evaluation data to review (yet) again. You might "dance" back and forth between (3.1) *Proceed* and (4.1) *aPpraise* over and over as you incrementally adjust your de-implementation strategy to save more time and resources but without harming student outcomes. See Figure 2.4 for an illustration of this.

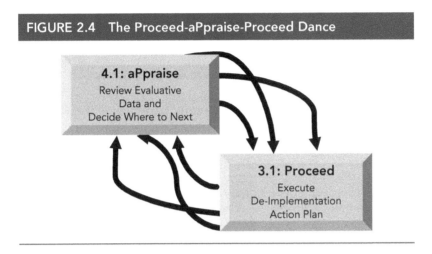

FIGURE 2.4 The Proceed-aPpraise-Proceed Dance

Step 4.2: Propel
Sustain and Scale Your De-Implementation

The **(4.2) *Propel*-step** is a strategic pause point that comes after a concerted bout of de-implementation. It's where you decide whether to keep your backbone team alive to identify and progress new target areas and also where you set out your business-as-usual transition plan for the de-implementation areas you have already progressed. This is about putting measures in place to ensure that there is neither backsliding to prior behaviors nor reversion to the mean, if your backbone team is disestablished and no longer available to monitor plan continuation.

Propelling is, therefore, both about enhancing the level of de-implementation and avoiding Parkinson's Law-related backsliding. It might also bring you back to the **(1.2) *Prospect*-step** to repeat the whole cycle; that is, to identify the next de-implementation area.

Pre-liftoff Considerations

With the helicopter overview of the *Room for Impact* P-Steps complete, let's now explore eight pre-liftoff considerations that you will want to keep in view. Some of these are provided just as clarification; others require you to make decisions as you go. Note that we also swing back to these critical eight and provide more detailed suggestions and guidance at the relevant junctures within the specific P-Step chapters. So don't worry if you struggle to take it all in!

Thing 1: There Are Multiple De-Implementation Strategies You Could Consider

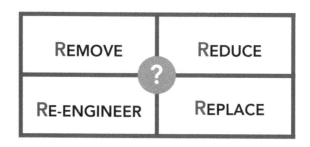

The four key strategies are illustrated at the very heart of the *Room for Impact* process diagram. You can either **Remove** the practice completely; **Reduce** how frequently you use it (or restrict who receives/delivers it); **Re-Engineer** how you implement practice you intend to maintain, rationalizing the number of steps; or **Replace** an existing practice within something that takes less time and money or that generates more impact in the same amount of time.

But, as we will go on to unpack at length, some of these strategies are easier to progress than others. For example, the research on smoking cessation and dieting helps us to see that removing something completely is likely to be more sustainable than reducing or cutting down. People who stop smoking—once they have overcome their physical dependency on nicotine—are more likely to stay smoke-free in the long term (García-Rodríguez et al., 2013). Similarly, in the case of dieting, the challenge is that you physically cannot give up food, you still need to eat; and that over time your old habits can gradually creep back (Anderson et al., 2001). Hence, so many yo-yo dieters.

We think that Replace is the hardest de-implementation strategy of all because it requires total removal of prior practices at the same time as embarking on something new. Too often, what actually happens, is that the old and the new get blended together into a hybrid practice that ends up generating less impact and/or saving less time than the status quo. Replace also happens to be the default strategy for most school improvement; that is, remove the tarnished *X-Program* and replace it with the shiny *Y-Program*. Instead, we think Remove and Re-Engineer are the easiest de-implementation strategies to progress without backsliding. We explore this and the rationale in much more detail during the chapters focusing on the *Decide Stage*.

Thing 2: It's *Not* Linear

We want to stress that while the *Room for Impact* process diagram might look linear, actual de-implementation in the real world is likely to be anything but, and as you move back and forth between the *Room for Impact* Stages and P-Steps, new information and learning unfolds. We illustrate this messy complexity in Figure 2.5.

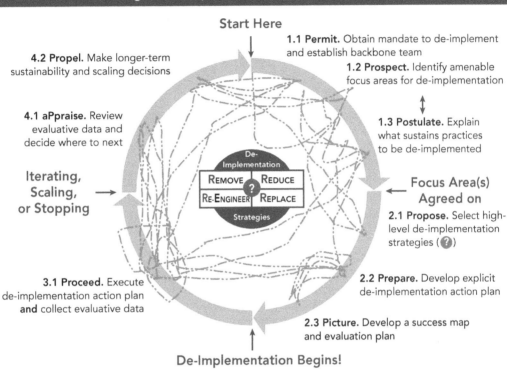

FIGURE 2.5   The Tangled De-Implementation Web

Start Here

1.1 Permit. Obtain mandate to de-implement and establish backbone team

1.2 Prospect. Identify amenable focus areas for de-implementation

4.2 Propel. Make longer-term sustainability and scaling decisions

4.1 aPpraise. Review evaluative data and decide where to next

1.3 Postulate. Explain what sustains practices to be de-implemented

De-Implementation

REMOVE   REDUCE
?
RE-ENGINEER   REPLACE

Strategies

Iterating, Scaling, or Stopping

Focus Area(s) Agreed on

2.1 Propose. Select high-level de-implementation strategies (?)

3.1 Proceed. Execute de-implementation action plan **and** collect evaluative data

2.2 Prepare. Develop explicit de-implementation action plan

2.3 Picture. Develop a success map and evaluation plan

De-Implementation Begins!

We also suggest that you follow the *Room for Impact* cycle in the order that we have laid out: moving stepwise from **(1.1)** *Permit* to **(4.2)** *Propel*, even though after having completed a step and having uncovered new information, you might need to dance back to a previous P-Step or overarching stage to revisit prior decisions.

However, you have some leeway around the exact ordering of two of the P-Steps. In the case of **(1.3)** *Postulate*, you could potentially delay this until *after* **(2.2)** *Prepare* and undertake it as part of your activity design stress testing. You also have some leeway around **(2.3)** *Picture* and you may want to bring elements of this *forward* and start to talk and think about what success looks like before you Propose and Prepare your activity design. You would then use the Picture-Step as a double-checking point to ensure that your success criteria and monitoring and evaluation plans are up to snuff before de-implementing.

But for all the other P-Steps, we advise that you traverse them in the number sequencing order. And, most importantly, that you don't miss out any.

> Don't worry if this discussion about which P-Steps can be swapped around is difficult for you to get your head around right now—we flag all this again later in the relevant P-Step chapters.

Thing 3: The Thinking Protocols

During each of the nine P-Steps, you will also traverse an aligned checking and cross-checking process as illustrated in Figure 2.6. This starts with **Divergent** thinking routines where you explore all the potential options and opportunities with an open mind. It then pivots to **Convergent** thinking where you carefully explore the risks and returns for each identified opportunity. Finally, you will **Agree on what will be done;** and then proceed to the next P-Step in the *Room for Impact* process.

For fans of *Star Trek*, you can think of this as an inversion of Mr. Spock's famous logic statement that "the needs of the many outweigh the needs of the few or the one." Instead, we start with the many (options), narrow to the few, and then select the *one*.

FIGURE 2.6   Diverge, Converge, Agree

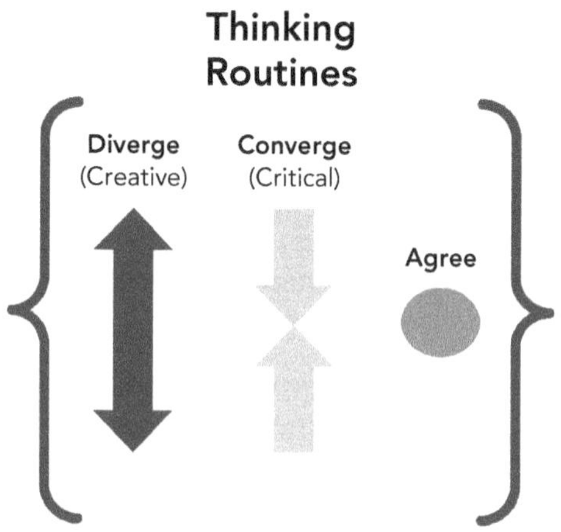

Thinking Routines

Diverge (Creative)   Converge (Critical)   Agree

Thing 4: Optimal Stopping

As you undertake this divergent and convergent thinking, you have another judgment call to make. This is about **Optimal Stopping**—that is, the length of time you spend thinking, exploring, collecting data, analyzing, and weighing up the pros and cons of different courses of action before just getting on and doing something. We confront this conundrum in many aspects of our life. For example, when we look for a new place to live, we rarely select the first place we see—because even if it's amazing, how can we be sure we won't find something better? So, we keep searching a little longer—to confirm or to dismiss our initial preference. But the key question is how long you should search for. According to mathematicians who have deeply explored this question, the optimal proportion of time spent on the searching and exploring activities is 37 percent, leaving 63 percent of your available time for implementation, iterative evaluation, and enhancement (Christian & Griffiths, 2016), although these proportions are just averages and the right balance in a particular situation might be very different.

For example, suppose you are embarking on a de-implementation initiative at a system level that involves tens of thousands of stakeholders. In that case, this magic 37 percent seems about right to us (although it is not a cast iron rule, as Christian and Griffiths did not provide a 95 percent confidence interval for this figure, so it's more a rule of thumb). But it's better to spend more time on those convergent and divergent processes before rushing in and de-implementing something that you later bitterly regret.

However, if you are working at the level of a whole school or a professional learning community (or even looking at how you can make room for impact in your individual workload), then we can see that you may want and even need to progress at a faster clip. Otherwise, you just might find that a third of the academic year has gone by and you are still talking and thinking but with little action in the works. So, your travel speed through the P-Steps is a local judgment call but one you need to think through carefully.

Thing 5: How Do You Sequence Your Inquiry Cycle?

This is connected to Optimal Stopping and is about how long you spend on each of the P-Steps and how you sequence them together. Two of the many options that you can consider are **P-Sprinting** and a **P-Marathon**. We explore each below.

P-Sprinting. A P-Sprint might involve you and a group of colleagues working together for a solid three-day *Room for Impact* "deep-dive." You would remove yourself from your day-to-day work for this solid block and spend the time vigorously focused and working all the way from **(1.1) Permit** to **(2.3) Picture**.

Before starting, you will probably already have the (1.1) *Permission* dimension covered; otherwise, getting approval to pull yourselves out will likely be challenging. You then spent those three days Prospecting (1.2); Postulating (1.3); Proposing (2.1); Preparing (2.2); and Picturing success (2.3). Then, at the end of day three, you have a de-implementation strategy that you might execute (3.1) over, say, six weeks. You then undertake weekly reviews, pivoting back and forth between Proceeding (3.1) and aPpraising (4.1). During each appraisal, you identify improvements that you then act on. And you repeat this dance again. Finally, after several dances back and forth between the (3.1) Proceed and (4.1) aPpraise P-Steps, you pivot to Propel (4.2), where you decide on your longer-term next steps.

> If you opt for a P-Sprint, you will save time by getting everyone to collect and preconsider their personal/team time-analytics data *before* you collectively put on your "running shoes" and come together for your three-day sprint.

P-Marathon. This is a more drawn-out and paced affair. It might involve setting aside some time weekly to prime actions and then to come back together to compare notes and agree on what to do next. You might start by formally seeking permission and a mandate to proceed (i.e., 1.1). Then you might develop a data collection plan and spend a couple of weeks Prospecting (1.2). And you might do this, for example, by individually collecting data and then coming together to review your collective findings and to agree on your priority area for de-implementation. You continue in this vein throughout all the other P-steps; acting and then pausing. And, during Proceed (3.1), you might even meet briefly weekly to compare notes and check that everyone is sticking to the plan.

In Figure 2.7 we illustrate some potential differences between a P-Sprint and a P-Marathon. You will notice that at the "end" of the P-Marathon, the race is still in play!

FIGURE 2.7 P-Sprint vs. P-Marathon

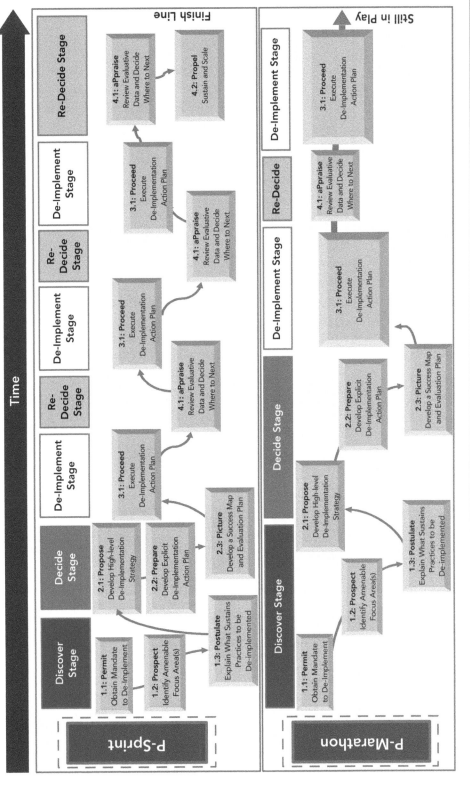

P-Sprint and P-Marathon: Advantages and Disadvantages

The advantage of P-Sprinting is that it enables you to move at greater speed. But you need to find that block of days when you and a group of colleagues can completely disconnect from your normal routines and focus. You also need to plan how you will manage each P-Step during those three days, set cut-offs for moving from Diverging to Converging, and finally reach the Agree waypoint each day. Otherwise, there is a risk that you will drift during days one and two and then in a mad rush, make bad and ill-considered decisions in the last few hours of day three.

By contrast, a P-Marathon does not require you to find and identify a large block of time. But the disadvantage is that your momentum may be slower and might fizzle out altogether unless you commit to attending regular working group meetings and publicly reporting back on the actions you also committed to undertaking. Things that get publicly committed to, and regularly reported on, are more likely to get done. This is at the heart of the Weight Watchers model of weekly public weigh-ins, group celebration, support, and making goal commitments for the next week (Wiliam & Leahy, 2016).

Thing 6: Your System-level

This is about who is involved in the *Room for Impact* cycle. And, here, some of the options include:

OPTION LEVEL	DESCRIPTION
L1 Individual Level	Here you might be focused on identifying actions that you can implement on your own and without recourse to your colleagues in order to reduce your individual workload. If you are reading *Making Room for Impact* from this perspective, you may not be able to implement all the suggested P-steps on your own, but you will still gain ideas and inspiration. We hope, too, that once you have made personal changes and seen the benefits, you will also seek to influence your colleagues and suggest that *Room for Impact* becomes a focus area for collaborative inquiry.
L2 Professional Learning Community (PLC)	Here, your Professional Learning Community commits to focusing solely on de-implementation for a period of at least one term. A year would be better, but by starting with a term, it lessens those guilt- and shame-drivers connected to stopping practices; and, we suspect you might then extend the inquiry into that full year!
	You might meet for one hour a week, with an agenda that clearly links to one of the P-Steps, although as your inquiry progresses, you can perhaps reduce to fortnightly or even monthly. And these meetings would be about (a) reporting back on what you have already committed to and (b) collectively agreeing on what you will do next and report back on at the next meeting (see, for example, Wiliam, 2011).

OPTION LEVEL	DESCRIPTION
L3 Whole School	Here, you establish a whole-school Backbone Organization with a mandate and charter to identify and implement actions that will save colleagues' time across the whole school. The cycle of meetings and actions will likely be similar to those progressed at Professional Learning Community-level, but the backbone will have the authority to explore time-intensive tasks that relate to any and all areas of school life. It will also (probably) prioritize de-implementation initiatives that generate sizable time and resource savings for as many stakeholders as possible.
L4 System-level	There are many potential system-levels—ranging from a district responsible for several schools to state/national level departments and ministries of education, with responsibility for tens of thousands of schools. However, like the whole school-level implementation of the P-Steps, this will almost certainly involve the establishment of a backbone organization.
	The key difference is that at least some of the backbone membership will likely be working full-time on de-implementation, exploring and activating initiatives that increase the well-being of teachers at scale, across many schools. Work at this level also addresses those important policy-related restrictions that the schools themselves do not have the authority to question or tinker with—like the duration of the school day/week or mandatory data collection and administrative processes. And it gives schools the confidence that it is OK for them to get serious about de-implementation, too.

Each of these system levels can be amenable to a *Room for Impact* inquiry. However, what determines most which of these levels you work at is the level that you currently sit! Suppose you are reading this as you sit at system level. In that case, you have the power to make great waves, but with less control over how those initiatives are implemented (or should we say de-implemented!) at individual school level. If, on the other hand, you are sitting at school or PLC-level, the areas that you are "allowed" to explore without getting permission from a higher system-level will be more limited, but the initiatives that you develop will have a strong local fit to your context and therefore a much higher probability of success.

Thing 7: How Many Balls Do You Juggle?

This is about whether you opt for:

1. **lots of little actions**, where you identify six to ten "bite-sized" initiatives that are easy to de-implement but with each, perhaps, only saving a handful of minutes each week;

2. **a small number of mega-actions**, where you identify one or two major activities that will require more significant habit change support and monitoring (and possibly also significant external communication to parents and students about why you are stopping) but which will save you several hours of busywork each week; or

3. **a hybrid approach**, that involves a mixture of 1 and 2.

We illustrate this in Figure 2.8.

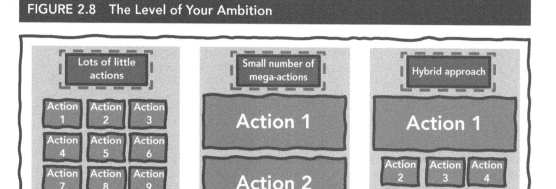

FIGURE 2.8 The Level of Your Ambition

At least partly, your ambition level will be influenced by the system level you operate within. If you are leveraging *Room for Impact* on your own, you will be limited to "little actions" (i.e., the areas you have direct control over without seeking permission from the next level of the system). And as you progress upwards, the more mega-actions you will have the authority to progress. The decision will partly be about the actions that will build momentum, confidence, and excitement; you may find that by progressing the "low-hanging fruit" of lots of little actions, you support your teams to overcome the cognitive bias toward addition. As a result, they are likely to become ever more gleeful investigators of their efficiency of impact, building up to mega-actions that require careful political management with local stakeholders.

Thing 8: What Could De-Implementation Actually Look Like?

We get that our discussion of the *Room for Impact* inquiry cycle and the opportunities for de-implementation might seem a little abstract. So, the final thing we want to do in this chapter is to whet your appetite by giving concrete examples of things that you could potentially Remove, Reduce, Replace, or Re-engineer. This list is not exhaustive and many of these suggestions simply may not work in your local context—some might even be downright dangerous. But we hope they get you thinking! In brackets, after each suggestion, we also articulate whether it is a Remove vs. Reduce vs. Replace vs. Re-Engineer-type action.

TEACHING AND LEARNING, PLANNING AND CURRICULUM	STUDENT BEHAVIOR AND EXTRACURRICULAR ACTIVITIES
• Collaborative lesson planning rather than everyone planning the same lesson from scratch (Re-Engineer) • Cloud-based resource repository where everyone places their preexisting teaching and learning materials—to stop re-inventing the wheel (Re-Engineer) • No creation of differentiated learning objectives and differentiated activity sheets (Remove) • Buying in high quality off-the-shelf curriculum and textbook packages that provide all—or at least most—of the teaching materials and learning resources, so that there is no need to develop materials at all (Replace) • Remove requirements to have a written lesson plan for each lesson (Remove) • Stop or reduce out-of-hours revision sessions: focus on high quality learning during the regular school day (Remove and Replace) • Creative timetabling so that teachers specialize in specific year groups and subjects, to reduce planning time (Re-Engineer) • Lengthen the school day and move to a four-day week, allowing staff to have a three-day weekend (Re-Engineer) • Slightly increase class size in order to reduce overall teaching hours, enabling more time for planning and preparation (Re-Engineer) • Use Deep Learning AI algorithms – to automatically create teaching and learning content, including images, which can then be quickly adapted (Replace & Re-Engineer)	• A clear behavior system and policy that is applied consistently. Students are aware of the required behaviors and the accompanying sanctions. Staff undertake quick and simple logging of sanctions applied to individual students (Replace) • Centralized after-school detention system for all behavioral issues, with one teacher on rota (schedule) to ease the burden on other teachers (Replace) • Centralized parental engagement on student behavioral issues. Teachers do not have to phone parents: leaders do this, freeing teachers to teach (Replace) • Staff do not need to do lunchtime duties. They get a break for lunch—just like the students! (Replace) • Leveraging school prefects/hall monitors to reduce the required student behavior monitoring from staff (Replace) • Stop all extracurricular activities (Remove) • Replace school-based extracurricular activities with offsite alternatives delivered by voluntary associations (Replace) • Undertake extracurricular activities during the regular teaching day (Re-Engineer)
ASSESSMENT, FEEDBACK, AND REPORTING TO PARENTS	**PROFESSIONAL DEVELOPMENT, MEETINGS, AND MISC.**
• Use of standardized self-quizzing homework for lower grades to reduce planning, task setting, and marking requirements (Replace) • Peer marking of homework for upper grades, during class (Re-Engineer) • No setting of homework the week before school holidays, so that staff don't return to piles of marking (Re-Engineer)	• Reduced number of meetings per month/year, and for those that remain, stand-up staff meetings to speed up progress (Reduce) • No out-of-hours email and no use of mobile phone to view/respond to emails (Remove) • After-school meetings rationalized: time can be repurposed for departmental planning and subject specific PD (Re-Engineer)

(Continued)

(Continued)

ASSESSMENT, FEEDBACK, AND REPORTING TO PARENTS	PROFESSIONAL DEVELOPMENT, MEETINGS, AND MISC.
• Use of online intelligent tutoring systems to further reduce homework planning, setting, marking, and feedback requirements (Replace)	• Bite-sized PD model during school hours— no more attending workshops and conferences during school holidays (Reduce/Re-Engineer)
• Parental report cards simplified to report only –, =, or + for each subject depending on whether progress is below, at, or exceeding expectations; supplemented by a single holistic report written by the form tutor/homeroom teacher (Reduce)	• Staff does not have to provide cover for absent colleagues unless they are under their allocated number of lessons (Remove)
• Whole school eMIS system, so that data is only entered once and can be used many times (Re-Engineer)	• No more wall displays in classrooms and corridors (Remove)
• Focus on feedback rather than "marking" (i.e., whole class feedback, verbal feedback, and daily quizzes). No more marking exercise books until 2 a.m. (Re-engineer)	• Centralized admin—so that teachers are not sucked into finance, data, safeguarding or reprographics—they focus on teaching! (Replace)
• Parents no longer allowed to make direct contact with teachers; instead this is triaged by a "parental coordinator" who directly handles most inquiries (Replace)	• Software system to communicate with parents and collect any payments for ancillaries (Replace)
	• Identification of pinch points during the academic year with explicit smoothing of workload across the yearly calendar (Re-Engineer)

Credits: This list is inspired by the work of King Charles I School, Worcestershire, England, and from the wider case studies in the UK Department of Education's Teacher Workload Reduction Toolkit.

This list is just a teaser. For the more comprehensive list of more than eighty areas that might be amenable to de-implementation in your local context, take a look at Appendix 1—although some of these may make your jaw drop in horror!

Conclusion

In this chapter, we provided you with a *helicopter overview* of the *Room for Impact* Methodology. We also unpacked a range of things to look for as you embark on de-implementation in your own local context. This is a chapter that you will want to return to continually as you undertake your inquiry, so that you can position the activities of whatever P-Step that you are currently working on within the bigger picture of the overall methodology.

The remainder of the book follows a remarkably straightforward path: Nine short(-ish) chapters; that is, one per P-Step. Each of these chapters follows a similar structure: providing context, processes, and tools to bring the P-Step to fruition.

Without further ado, let's get to Stage 1: Discover and the very first P-Step—*1.1: Permission.*

Part 2

Discover Stage

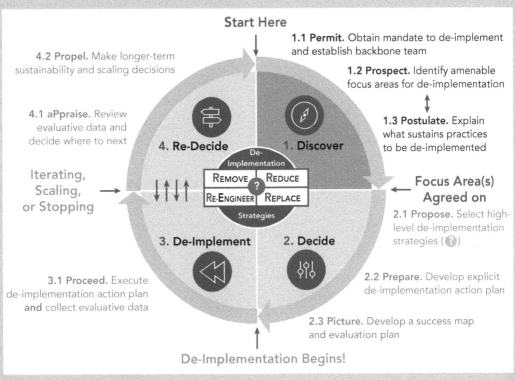

Start Here

1.1 Permit. Obtain mandate to de-implement and establish backbone team

1.2 Prospect. Identify amenable focus areas for de-implementation

1.3 Postulate. Explain what sustains practices to be de-implemented

4.2 Propel. Make longer-term sustainability and scaling decisions

4.1 aPpraise. Review evaluative data and decide where to next

4. Re-Decide

1. Discover

De-Implementation

REMOVE | REDUCE
RE-ENGINEER | REPLACE

Strategies

Iterating, Scaling, or Stopping

Focus Area(s) Agreed on

2.1 Propose. Select high-level de-implementation strategies (?)

3. De-Implement

2. Decide

3.1 Proceed. Execute de-implementation action plan **and** collect evaluative data

2.2 Prepare. Develop explicit de-implementation action plan

2.3 Picture. Develop a success map and evaluation plan

De-Implementation Begins!

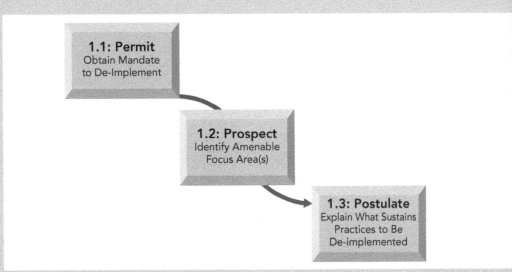

1.1: Permit
Obtain Mandate to De-Implement

1.2: Prospect
Identify Amenable Focus Area(s)

1.3: Postulate
Explain What Sustains Practices to Be De-implemented

Permit (1.1)

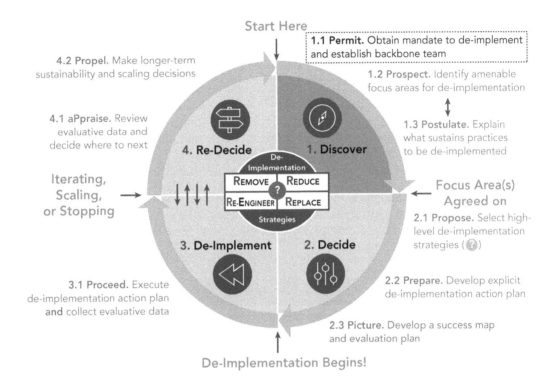

3

Start Here

1.1 Permit. Obtain mandate to de-implement and establish backbone team

4.2 Propel. Make longer-term sustainability and scaling decisions

1.2 Prospect. Identify amenable focus areas for de-implementation

4.1 aPpraise. Review evaluative data and decide where to next

1.3 Postulate. Explain what sustains practices to be de-implemented

4. Re-Decide

1. Discover

De-Implementation Strategies

REMOVE | REDUCE
Re-Engineer | Replace

Iterating, Scaling, or Stopping

Focus Area(s) Agreed on

2.1 Propose. Select high-level de-implementation strategies ( )

3. De-Implement

2. Decide

3.1 Proceed. Execute de-implementation action plan and collect evaluative data

2.2 Prepare. Develop explicit de-implementation action plan

2.3 Picture. Develop a success map and evaluation plan

De-Implementation Begins!

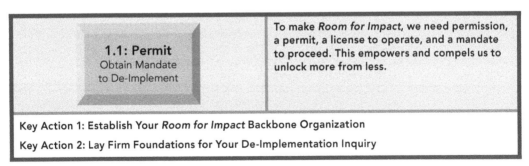

1.1: Permit
Obtain Mandate to De-Implement

To make *Room for Impact*, we need permission, a permit, a license to operate, and a mandate to proceed. This empowers and compels us to unlock more from less.

Key Action 1: Establish Your *Room for Impact* Backbone Organization
Key Action 2: Lay Firm Foundations for Your De-Implementation Inquiry

Context

We humans are inherently social animals. Usually, we want to feel part of the tribe and to feel that we are doing our utmost to further our tribe's interests. By some accounts, this tendency to form strong social groupings and to develop a shared identity, shared purpose, shared rituals, and shared practices is at the beating heart of humanity's success (McPherson et al., 2001; Singer, 1981).

When we believe that we are about to do something that goes against the norms and rituals of our tribe, we can, therefore, feel intense *shame* and *guilt*. We can feel like black sheep, pariahs, outcasts, or lepers-to-be. And that fear of being cast out from the tribe, of being ostracized and excommunicated, can rein back our more reckless inclinations. Better not to rock the boat, we think.

There is every reason to believe that these same tribal tendencies apply equally to professional groups, like educators, working in organizational settings. And that this can prime those very same shame and guilt-based inhibitors to avoid any action that goes against the grain - putting the brakes on a wide variety of actions, including de-implementation!

Although there are still skirmishes within psychology about the distinction between shame and guilt (Leach, 2017), for the purposes of *Room for Impact*, Figure 3.1 helps us to frame these two interconnected emotional states.

FIGURE 3.1   Shame and Guilt

SHAME	GUILT
A negative emotional state connected to the beliefs and opinions of *others*; that is, we feel shame when we have committed an act that brings our "tribe" (or profession) into disrepute.	A negative state of emotion and mental conflict that occurs when individuals believe they have compromised their *own* standards of behavior.
—	—
We can also feel *Pre-shame*, which is the act of anticipating, predicting, and imagining this negative state in advance, with this turn, thwarting us from proceeding.	We can also feel *Pre-guilt* and anticipate that if we fail to perform an action, we will feel that we have let ourselves down.
—	—
Shame/pre-shame is a social driver to continue with existing activities, rituals, and customs. It's about the impact on the group, the individual's role in the group, the group's identity, and conduct toward others.	Guilt/pre-guilt about the self and our self-identity, e.g., "Quitters are losers and I'm not a loser."
a.k.a. fear of letting others down	*a.k.a. fear of letting yourself down*

Source: Synthesized from Shen (2018); Elison (2005); Tangney (1998).

As educators, we can feel guilty about not maintaining our preexisting personal standards. And we can also feel shame alongside—we can worry about the reactions from our colleagues, the children, and the complaints from parents—if we are perceived to be shirking from our core responsibilities.

This combination of guilt and shame can paralyze us. Even though we *know* that we are working long hours and even though internally we may be questioning the utility of all this work—we may think that by stopping we are letting ourselves, our team, and the students (badly) down. And this can mean that we carry on with it all until we make ourselves sick from exhaustion or until we decide to leave the profession and are replaced by fresh faces who repeat the cycle again and again.

Sometimes, it's purely about the shame. Educators usually know, in their heart of hearts, that the various reports and checklists that they are spending so much time completing do not—in the slightest—push the needle on student impact. But they can often believe that they are not *allowed* to stop. That there is a directive from "on high" that requires them to collect this data, to tick these boxes, to jump through these hoops, to dot these *i*s, and to cross these *t*s. Sometimes these directives are real, but other times they are imagined or at least partly imagined and then over-engineered as each stakeholder in the delivery chain adds additional requirements before the increasingly overengineered requirement is cascaded to the frontline.

To break this shame-guilt loop:

> It's essential that the most senior levels of leadership with the school or system give their teams not just explicit **permission** but also a **mandate** to focus on de-implementation.

Everyone needs to know that it's OK to (collectively) do less to achieve more. It might even be perfectly OK to do less to achieve the same. That, in fact, it's an expectation that teams follow the P-Steps to undertake systematic and controlled de-implementation—without harming student outcomes. Ideally, you also need to establish a Backbone Organization to lead the charge. So that everyone knows this isn't just talk from the leadership but a serious hardcore endeavor—with high expectations for impact.

In some schools and systems, a version of this task force already exists. It is sometimes called "the well-being committee" and it ends up being just that: a group of people with uncoordinated ideas that pursue low-hanging fruit, like meditation sessions for teachers or the distribution of aromatherapy oils to help everyone de-stress. Of course, the trouble with these kinds of "happy projects" is that they don't get to the heart of the matter—they address the consequences of unproductive practices rather than the practices themselves. They don't break the cycle of fresh-faced teachers becoming stress-laden and reaching for the door. And the need to replace them, yet again.

So, your Backbone Organization needs to be a proper, hard, serious investigation and action group. It needs to have not just permission but a *mandate from the highest levels of leadership* to focus relentlessly on de-implementation and to do it properly, rigorously, and with enthusiasm. There also needs to be more than the expectation that the agenda will be pursued but also an accompanying expectation that this will *save serious amounts of time and without harming student outcomes*. The best outcome is that we do less and achieve more. But if we do less and it results in the same (i.e., no backsliding for the students), this *might* be perfectly OK.

Key Action 1: Establish Your *Room for Impact* Backbone Organization

Depending on where you sit within your local education system, you might be mandating the establishment of a *Room for Impact* Backbone Organization at:

- **System level** – to de-implement across many schools (this is more likely to involve full-time members who eat, live, and breathe the P-Steps for 100 percent of their working hours)

- **School level** – to progress actions at whole school level (less likely/very unlikely to contain full-time membership)

- **Within-school level** – to undertake inquiry within a subject team and/or Professional Learning Community (everyone working very part time on *Room for Impact* – juggling de-implementation with all the things they are currently implementing alongside)

Or you might be influencing upwards, seeking to convince more senior stakeholders within your organization of the benefits of systematically following the P-Steps, and seeking their permission to proceed.

Obviously, establishing a *Room for Impact* Backbone Organization involves somewhat of a chicken-and-egg situation. One of the early key tasks of the backbone team (during *1.2 Prospect*) is to systematically investigate whether your collective workloads are indeed too high. And this means that when you initially set up that backbone team, you might not (yet) have hard data in hand that shows you truly do need to de-implement. Instead, you might only have perceptions, and you might get to the (1.2) *Prospect*-step and conclude all is well—that your workloads are manageable—and then end up disbanding the Backbone.

However, our hunch is that you won't disband. Because you are not going to agree to establish a Backbone unless implicitly and intuitively you have already concluded that your team is facing significant workload stresses.

This means that your investigation is *likely* to identify work practices that are over-engineered, that are not strong drivers of student outcomes, and that *could* be dismantled if you can get past the guilt, shame, and habit-based drivers that often sustain these practices.

Your *Room for Impact* Backbone team is (probably) a temporary organization that exists only for as long as you have systemic workload management challenges and that can then be disbanded once you have these under control. Although, we should stress that actions toward de-implementation are often pendulumlike. You turn the safety value, releasing the pressure and getting workload under control. But before too long, you find the pressure building again and those guilt and shame-based drivers compelling everyone to take on more and more. Think back to Parkinson's Law, discussed in chapter 1.

One of the core roles that you will want to include in your *Room for Impact* Backbone team is that of a sponsor(s):

- This might be an individual or a group, but it is the ultimate authorizer and accountable activity owner. The sponsor(s) are likely to be the most senior stakeholders within the organization (e.g., the district superintendent or the school leadership team). The sponsor needs authority and (sometimes) budget to authorize the *Room for Impact* inquiry, establish the Backbone organization, and convey the message across the wider organization that:
  - we are 100 percent committed to de-implementation;
  - we think our processes and actions may be overengineered and this may be *significantly* harming your personal well-being;
  - you need to seriously attend to de-implementation and there is no need to feel guilty or shameful about finding things to stop; in fact,
  - you should feel guilt and shame about carrying on with ineffective practices that take lots of time but generate scant impact, because this is just wasteful busy-work, fake work; and
  - we need to focus *only* on the real work that deeply enhances student outcomes.

The sponsor(s) also need to meet with the backbone team regularly to reconvey the message that de-implementation is a good and noble cause, that it is mandated and expected, and that efficiency of impact is the "holy grail."

To maintain momentum as the team traverses the P-steps, the sponsor also needs to check on the level of progress, leverage their sponsorship authority to remove roadblocks, and stress-test the emerging thinking, planning, and doing that is underway. By keeping de-implementation as a core area of focus and personal attention, the leadership signals to the wider organization that

- this isn't a fad or fancy;

- it isn't going away;

- everyone is expected to do their part; and

- we expect to see serious savings in time—but without harming student progress.

> The sponsorship role might even be fulfilled by a school board, a governing body, a council of trustees, or guiding coalition chaired by the most senior stakeholder, and that includes wider stakeholders with resources and authority that can be leveraged at key junctures to get things done. It may well also include parent and student representatives. More on this later.

The other core roles that you will want to include in your *Room for Impact* Backbone Organization include:

- **Team Leader(s).** This critical role spans the boundaries between the strategic imperative to de-implement and the tactical implementation of the *Room for Impact* inquiry cycle. The team leader coaches and leads the other members of the backbone team to identify activities that are *not* worthy of being continued as is and then to design de-implementation strategies that have the greatest chance of recouping overextended time and resources. Most likely there will be a single team leader, but occasionally you might have co-leaders. And because they are continually pivoting from thinking strategically to tactically, your ideal team leader will be able to shift from big picture and then to getting right into the de-implementation details.

- **Investigators.** Under the coaching, guidance, and oversight of the team leader(s), your investigators will be the arms and legs of your backbone team. They will lead or contribute to specific P-Step tasks to facilitate the search for things to remove, reduce, re-engineer, or replace; develop practical strategies; bring this all to life; and collect monitoring and evaluation data to check that student outcomes have not been harmed. They will get deeply into schools and classrooms and into discussions with teachers, students, and parents about what can be de-implemented, what the side effects might be, and what can be done to mitigate these.

- **(optional) External Facilitator.** This is a de-implementation specialist who deeply understands the P-Steps and wider research and applications. They might, for example, help you to establish the backbone. They might also provide you with analytical tools. But most importantly, their key role is to coach and support *you*, for example, by warning you that you are getting sucked into the blizzard and to help you get back out and refocused on the *Room for Impact* inquiry.

We take the notion of a Backbone Organization from the work of Kania and Kramer (2011). All mammals have backbones, hard rods of calcium that house and protect the critical central communication cables of the central nervous system. They also provide a centralized piece of infrastructure, or scaffolding, that all the other parts of the body are directly attached to. Without a backbone we are literally spineless.

Your Backbone Organization gives you that spine. It acts as a central conduit that facilitates collective thinking and that turns decisions into action, and actions into impact. In this case, actions are designed to reduce future momentum, conserve energy, and keep the collective powder dry.

It may also be the case that the membership of your Backbone Organization changes or evolves as your inquiry progresses. During the early P-steps, you need your most analytical people engaged—individuals who can help you to systematically review what the wider team is spending their time on and whether it's time well spent. This is like a management-consulting mindset. But as you progress to the latter P-Steps, which are focused on implementation (or should we say de-implementation), you need the support of team members with a project management mindset—people who can turn plans into actions and drive change through.

If you are undertaking a *Room for Impact* inquiry cycle *within a subject department* or an informal teaching team, you don't need to worry so much about an explicit Backbone Organization. We see the backbone as operating more at whole-school or system level.

Within your department or teaching team, you may already have a Professional Learning Community (PLC) in place with established norms for how you work together; and you *might* decide to slot the *Room for Impact* P-steps within the work of your existing organizational structure. This can be highly effective as long as you commit to explicit actions and you meet regularly to report back on your commitments— that is, back to that notion of the Weight Watchers weekly "weigh-in"—and as long as you have explicit permission to proceed.

(Continued)

(Continued)

> If, however, you are seeking impact at a **whole-school, district, or wider system level** – having a formal *Room for Impact* Backbone Organization – with a clear purpose, with permission, with a clear mandate, and with the burning expectation that there will be de-implementation – is highly recommended. This is likely to increase the seriousness with which the wider system engages with the P-Steps; helping to ensure that they, too, come along for the ride.

It can also be helpful to give your backbone team a formal *license to operate* that outlines the purpose of the organization and the rights, duties, and responsibilities of the team.

A License to Operate

- A statement of purpose, for example, to save time, to switch to more effective strategies, and/or save money, and so forth

- A statement of what is out of scope; for example, it is absolutely *not* about staffing efficiencies to make people redundant

- A term limit

- Membership

- Roles and responsibilities

- What it is that people are committing to do

- How meetings will be organized and chaired

- How decisions will be made (e.g., voting/consensus, power of veto, etc.)

- Delegated authorities (i.e., what decisions they can make directly and what needs to be agreed on by the sponsors)

- Resources that will be made available

- The process for amending the articles of incorporation

Source: Adapted from Hamilton et al. (2022).

However, we provide you with no pre-templated *license to operate* for you to fill in the blanks, because we want you to think deeply about your inquiry's purpose and governance structure during the (1.1) *Permit*-step.

Although, there is one look-for that we highlight, particularly if you are working at whole-school or system level. And that is that you must frame the inquiry with wider stakeholders with great care. Imagine how you would feel if someone turned up at your workplace with a stopwatch and timed how long it took you to do things or asked you what activities you thought could be stopped or rationalized.

You would likely call your union representative, fearing that your job was on the line. So, it's essential that you frame your inquiry in the *right* way: that you make clear it is not a witch-hunt. That it is not about rationalizing, downsizing, or letting people go, and that most things will definitely not change. Instead, it's about giving your teams a work-life balance, so that they remain committed educators for the long haul. And it's so that they remain mentally fresh and are able to engage in deep and deliberate practice that enhances their collective impact on the kids rather than feeling continually frazzled and bedraggled.

You should also consider the pros and cons of including parent and student representatives in your Backbone Organization. Whether you do this or not is entirely a local decision and there will be a wide range of contextual, cultural, and historical factors that influence whether you involve these wider critical stakeholders within your backbone.

An advantage of including (some) parents and students, at least at some key junctures, is that it primes them to understand why these "reductions" in service are being implemented and to also understand that the reduction in inputs and outputs have been carefully selected so that they are unlikely to harm the overall level of outcomes (i.e., student progress and achievement). However, a disadvantage of including parent and student voice is that it might (initially) slow the pace of your inquiry down as you collectively traverse the storming, forming, and norming process to come to a dialogic understanding.

Key Action 2: Lay Firm Foundations for Your De-Implementation Inquiry

Now that you have agreed to establish a Backbone Organization (or decided to leverage an existing structure to undertake *Room for Impact*-focused inquiry), there are some further considerations that you should now work through to ensure you lay firm foundations for success. These are the following:

- **Consideration 1** – ensuring everyone has clear responsibilities and accountabilities

- **Consideration 2** – explicitly articulating the values that underpin your inquiry

- **Consideration 3** – reconfirming that you have a clear and shared sense of purpose; that is, a clear *why*.

We unpack each of these, in turn, in the subsections below.

Backbone Establishment Consideration 1:
Responsibilities and Accountabilities

From a whole host of research on group dynamics and social loafing, we know that where team members do not have clear responsibilities and accountabilities, the day–job blizzard often eats into the initial enthusiasm (Simms & Nichols, 2014). And that before long, everyone has totally forgotten that they were part of a *Room for Impact* inquiry.

To counteract this possibility, you might want to go as far as codifying a formal responsibilities and accountabilities matrix so that everyone in the backbone team has clarity about their role and expectations. We illustrate this in Figure 3.2.

FIGURE 3.2   Responsibilities and Accountabilities Matrix Example

CODE	STANDS FOR	THIS PERSON IS
R	Responsible	Responsible for performing the task or creating the product and/or output
A	Accountable	Accountable for and has sign-off authority for the task (e.g., the project manager, sponsor, or technical lead)
S	Supportive	Provides expertise, advice, and support to the person responsible for the task or deliverable
I	Informed	Informed of task progress or results, usually by the person responsible

TASK	PERSON 1 TEAM LEADER	PERSON 2 INVESTIGATOR	PERSON 3 INVESTIGATOR	PERSON 4 SPONSOR
Establishing the backbone team (1.1)	Responsible	Supportive	Supportive	Accountable
Agreeing on the Articles of Incorporation (1.1)	Informed	Responsible	Supportive	Accountable
Undertaking *Divergent* Prospecting (1.2)	Supportive	Responsible	Supportive	Accountable
Undertaking *Convergent* Prospecting (1.2)	Supportive	Responsible	Supportive	Accountable
Agreeing on the *Room for Impact* Focus Area (1.2)	Responsible	Supportive	Supportive	Accountable
Exploring what sustains current practices in the Focus Area (1.3)	Informed	Supportive	Responsible	Accountable
Proposing multiple viable theories of improvement (2.1)	Informed	Supportive	Responsible	Accountable
Agreeing on *the theory of improvement* (2.1)	Responsible	Supportive	Supportive	Accountable

As a rule of thumb, make sure everyone is responsible for at least *one* thing! And also make sure that the team meets regularly (probably at least weekly) to:

- **Account**—Namely, to individually report back on progress with assigned and agreed responsibilities and accountabilities

- **Clear the path**—Namely, to collectively support one another to identify strategies and tactics to traverse blocked paths

- **Commit**—Namely, to individually agree what actions you will implement during the coming week, for which you will be held accountable by the group at the next session.

We illustrate this cycle in Figure 3.3.

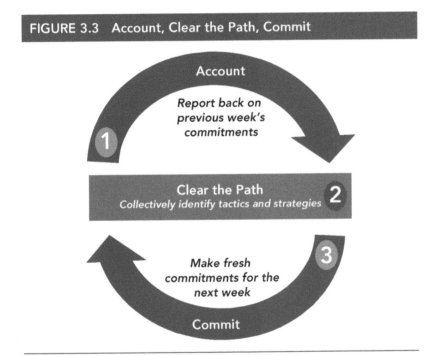

FIGURE 3.3   Account, Clear the Path, Commit

Backbone Establishment Consideration 2: Your Values

It is also worth considering and agreeing on the values that will underpin your *Room for Impact* inquiry. Some of the values that are important to us (and which we think are likely to be equally important to you) include:

- **Privileging efficiency of impact over impact at any cost:** We are more impressed and more excited when someone achieves a brilliant outcome with fewer steps, less motion, fewer resources, and *more* rest than when they are a "busy fool."

- **Privileging data and evidence over opinions and anecdotes:** We might believe that we will harm student learning through less motion and less action, but the only way to know for sure is to undertake controlled de-implementation and evaluate the impact. And the reverse also holds true, so we must test carefully!

- **Not making the facts fit the theory:** We test, test, test, and we abandon any theories and plans that don't come up to muster.

- **Respect for others at all times:** We all hold different opinions and beliefs, and we are unlikely to make progress through divisive polarized discussion. Through respectful dialogue we are better able to identify what sustains the existing practices, habits, and rituals that we are seeking to de-implement.

- **Accepting when we are wrong:** We recognize that our pet ideas, which *seem* good, do not always generate the impact we seek. So, we collect data to check; and we avoid burying our head in the sand if the data isn't positive. Instead, we say "that didn't work out as expected. What have we learned from it and what are we going to do instead?"

- **Do no harm:** We don't undertake de-implementation at any cost. An acceptable outcome is status quo in the impact on students. A preferred outcome is that less leads to more. If less is leading to less, we need to default to doing more.

We suspect these values will also likely be just as applicable to you. Some of these are connected to the Enlightenment values of rationality, reason, and empiricism; these values took us out of the Dark Ages and propelled us to the magnificent scientific and social progress that we have collectively achieved in the modern age (Pinker, 2018). Others are connected to the Japanese concept of *muda*, which is about reducing futile and wasteful endeavors, and instead privilege efficient impact—with more leverage and less motion (Womack & Jones, 2003). But there will, of course, be other values you seek to privilege alongside—or instead of those we suggest—to bring shared meaning to life in your local context.

Once agreed, your *Room for Impact* values become the critical test or bellwether for all your key decisions. So, it's worth considering these deeply and also including them in the "operating licence" of your Backbone Organization. Then, when someone new says "quitters are losers, we should never quit," your collective response can be "we privilege efficiency of impact above all else. Why take the most treacherous and long-winded path up educational Everest when smarter thinking and acting will still get you to the top with less motion and less resource expended?".

Backbone Establishment Consideration 3: Reconfirming Your *Why*

Finally, you need to think about why it is you have decided to embark on a *Room for Impact* inquiry cycle. Or rather, we should say "rethink" as we suspect you will already have given this much thought already! So, it's perhaps more about reconsidering and then confirming your collective *why.*

That *why* might be one or more of the following:

WHY	DESCRIPTION
1. **Staff Well-being**	To get your lives back: • without harming existing levels of student achievement and/or • with the expectation that this might also improve student achievement
2. **Student Well-being**	To reduce the burden of programs and initiatives on students
3. **Resource Efficiency**	To utilize public finances more efficiently
4. **Resource Reinvestment**	To explicitly reinvest the saved time and money into new and more effective initiatives—akin to the healthcare *Choosing Wisely Campaign* — If you are doing this, we strongly recommend that you leverage our sister book *Building to Impact* to help you ensure that the proposed replacement activities are *better* than the status quo. Otherwise, the risk is that you might be replacing *good* things with *average* or even *poor* things.

Depending on your local context, any and all of these *whys* can be acceptable and even noble goals. So, we express no opinion on which of these *whys* you prioritize. We just ask that you think about it deeply and that the backbone team and wider organization understand and can connect to your collectively chosen *why.*

Then you are ready to go!

Summary

The (1.1) *Permit*-step is focused on establishing an appropriate organizational structure so that you have firm foundations for your *Room for Impact* inquiry. The two Key Actions you will have undertaken are as follows:

- **Key Action 1**: Establish Your *Room for Impact* Backbone Organization.

- **Key Action 2**: Lay Firm Foundations for Your De-Implementation Inquiry.

As you establish your Backbone, don't forget to also explicitly *consider your rate of travel.* Are you going to undertake a faster **P-Sprint** or a slower **P-Marathon**? Go back to our discussion in chapter 2 if you need a recap.

1.1 Permit: Cross-Checking and Agreeing

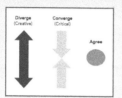

Finally, we recommend that you explicitly undertake **divergent** and **convergent** cross-checking and **agreeing** before concluding the (1.1) *Permit*-step and proceeding forward.

Here are some of the critical cross-checking questions you can consider:

1. Has permission been expressly granted at the highest levels of the organization?

2. Have we established a clear purpose for the Backbone Organization—that is, a clear *why*?

3. Do key stakeholders understand and agree with that purpose? And is it the right purpose for us?

4. Have we identified the correct people to lead and participate in the *Room for Impact* inquiry?

5. Does the team have the knowledge, understanding, and skills to implement the P-steps or could they benefit from external support?

6. Have we explicitly decided on the *speed* of our inquiry—namely, whether we are going to undertake a P-Sprint or a P-Marathon?

7. Does everyone understand their role in the inquiry and their responsibilities?

8. Have we established a clear governance structure?

9. Are we going to include parents and students within our backbone? Why or why not?

10. How do we avoid the risk that the backbone successfully "ticks off" the procedural aspects of the P-Steps but without this resulting in any actual de-implementation within the wider organization?

11. Who do we need to communicate with about our *Room for Impact* inquiry both within the organization and outside? Why do we need to communicate? What do we need to say? How and when will we say it?

12. Are we now ready to move to the next P-Step? Are we ready to (1.2) Prospect?

Prospect (1.2)

4

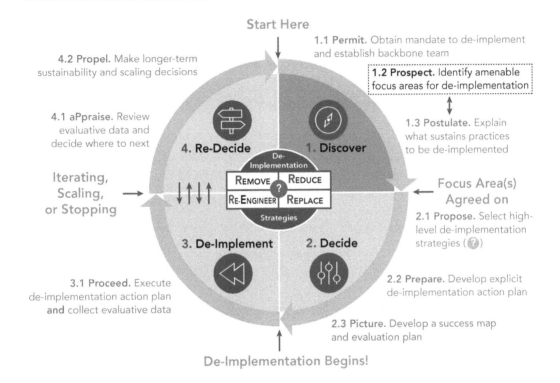

Start Here

1.1 Permit. Obtain mandate to de-implement and establish backbone team

1.2 Prospect. Identify amenable focus areas for de-implementation

4.2 Propel. Make longer-term sustainability and scaling decisions

4.1 aPpraise. Review evaluative data and decide where to next

4. Re-Decide

1. Discover

1.3 Postulate. Explain what sustains practices to be de-implemented

De-Implementation

REMOVE | REDUCE
RE-ENGINEER | REPLACE

Strategies

Iterating, Scaling, or Stopping

Focus Area(s) Agreed on

3. De-Implement

2. Decide

2.1 Propose. Select high-level de-implementation strategies ( )

3.1 Proceed. Execute de-implementation action plan **and** collect evaluative data

2.2 Prepare. Develop explicit de-implementation action plan

2.3 Picture. Develop a success map and evaluation plan

De-Implementation Begins!

1.2: Prospect Identify Amenable Focus Area(s)	To make *Room for Impact*, we need to identify all the things we *could* remove, reduce, re-engineer, or replace. We then need to agree on amenable focus area(s) for de-implementation.

Key Action 1: Collect Data on De-Implementation Opportunity Areas (a.k.a. mapping your Jenga tower)

Key Action 2: Provisionally Agree on Your Amenable Focus Areas(s) (a.k.a. picking your target Jenga blocks)

Context

We think of the (1.2) *Prospect*-step as being a lot like the game of Jenga. You probably know and have played the game, which involves stacking wooden blocks into a uniform tower and then taking turns selecting a block to remove, gently prying it out, and then carefully reinserting it at the top of the tower, growing the height. And the process gets repeated over and over until one of the players topples the now much-heightened (but more unstable) tower, losing the game.

The thing with Jenga towers is that they are overengineered.[1] In Figure 4.1 you can see this illustrated. In the picture, there are two towers made up of an identical number of blocks. But one tower is almost double the height of the other—it has used its resources more efficiently.

FIGURE 4.1   The Two Towers

Source: Hamilton and Hattie (2022).

Indeed, we can have so much fun with Jenga because there are far more blocks propping up the tower than are required. An obvious initial strategy is to take out all the middle blocks from each layer. If you do this carefully, there is almost zero risk that you will bring the tower crashing down. However, after you have extracted all these "low-hanging fruit," the game becomes dicier. You have to test each remaining block more carefully before you make your extraction decision—gently poking, prodding, and manipulating the block to see if the tower starts to wobble. And if it does, you need to carefully push it back in and search for a new target.

---

[1] This point and analogy only works within limits. The Jenga blocks are only overengineered if the context is stable. If the table is wobbly, the tower may need additional support. This is important as schools rarely operate in stable conditions. And this means that as you select "blocks" for potentially removing, reducing, re-engineering, or replacing, you need to consider the side effects with great care. We provide protocols to support this as part of (1.3) Postulate and (2.1) Propose.

What you are doing during the **(1.2)** *Prospect*-**step** is exactly like the game of Jenga. You can think of your school or system as akin to the tower and each of the blocks representing the different actions and activities that contribute to your collective impact. During this P-step, you are surveying the "blocks," testing them, to judge which ones you can remove, reduce, re-engineer, or replace without bringing the system crashing down. You are identifying amenable focus areas.

However, unlike the game of Jenga, you have more options. You can, of course, remove entire blocks; or you can hollow them out shaving some of the resource from the sides or extracting it from the middle. You can even replace blocks with a more efficient "substance" that has the same structural stability, but which is less resource intensive. And you can decide to keep the blocks (i.e., the time and/or resources) that you have saved to one side, or you can opt to reinvest these to grow the height of the tower by putting them back in. It's your choice.

What you are going to do during this P-step is as follows:

- **Key Action 1: Collect Data on De-Implementation Opportunity Areas** (a.k.a. mapping your Jenga tower)
- **Key Action 2: Provisionally Agree on Your Amenable Focus Area(s)** (a.k.a. picking your target Jenga blocks)

Key Action 1: Collect Data on De-Implementation Opportunity Areas (a.k.a. mapping your Jenga tower)

In this section, we provide you with five lenses (and accompanying tools) that you can use to map the areas (i.e., the Jenga blocks) within your school or system that are *potentially* overengineered so that you can then identify what can potentially be Removed, Reduced, Re-engineered, or Replaced.

If you are working at system level, you may wish to use all or most of these lenses to gain a deep and appreciative understanding of each of your "Jenga blocks." However, if you are working at whole-school or Professional Learning Community level, you have a local judgment call to make about (1) how many of these protocols you use and which ones; and (2) how long you spend prospecting, testing the blocks before agreeing which ones you will focus on.

Let's now look at the five lenses in turn.

Lens 1: The Policy-to-Practice Mapper

One of the common reactions when we discuss the idea of de-implementation with school-level educators is:

- We're not allowed to stop doing "X" [*insert overengineered activity here*].

- It's a [government/state/district/leadership] requirement that we do this.

- Of course, it's crazy! It's completely overengineered! And it serves *no* benefit to the students.

- If only the people upstairs understood how pointless this is!

- But as much as we would like to stop, it's simply not allowed. We would get into big, big trouble.

However, when we then go up the chain and have similar conversations with system-level leaders, we instead often hear:

- It's *not* actually compulsory—just recommended "best practice." If the school or department decides not to do it, it's completely up to them; or

- Yes, it *is* required, but if you look at the regulations, they are actually quite loose.

- There are a few different ways you can implement [*inserted overengineered activity here*].

- Some schools have a two-page policy and only spend a few hours a year looking at it. Other schools have a sixty-page policy and embed it as a key part of their day-to-day work.

- We thought the schools that were spending a lot of time on [*inserted overengineered activity here*] were doing so because they decided it was important to them in their local context.

- Truth be told, we don't even really look at the data . . .

Dylan recalls a conversation with Jon Coles, then director-general of schools in England's Department for Education, in which Coles relayed a discussion with some of the country's leading head teachers. Coles had asked the group if there was anything that the heads would like to do that would improve the quality of education in their schools but that they were prevented from implementing because of the government's regulations. Approximately 75 percent of the heads' suggestions were already actually authorized for implementation or de-implementation. The barriers existed in their minds, in their beliefs about what was written down in the rulebooks. If they actually looked carefully at the rules, they would see a world of opportunities.

Indeed, one of the reasons things become overengineered in the first place is that each layer of the educational delivery chain misunderstands or overinterprets the requirements of the level above. As a result, new ingredients get added that everyone *thinks* are required and mandatory. But when you unpick more carefully, you discover that these things are not really needed at all. Or that if they are needed, no one is forcing you to implement in the particular way they are being carried out currently.

One way to confirm that you are not overengineering the regulatory requirements is to explicitly check. In some education systems, this is easier than others—for example, at a national/state level there is a central book of regulations. In other instances, however, the various decrees and recommendations are spread across different circulars, memos, policy documents, and reference books.

> **System-level hint:** A good place to start your de-implementation journey is to review the regulations and guidelines that you circulate. Just bringing them all together in one place and condensing them into one handy quick-sheet or guide will be helpful.
>
> Obviously, even more helpful would be to *review the regulations to see which can be discarded* as well.

At school-level, you can use a **Policy-to-Practice-Mapping Tool** to check what your system-level "overlords" require and see whether what you are doing exceeds these requirements. We give you a worked example of this tool in Figure 4.2.

FIGURE 4.2   Policy-to-Practice Mapping Tool

WHAT IS REQUIRED [i.e., THE POLICY/ REGULATIONS]	WHAT WE ACTUALLY DO [i.e., THE PRACTICES]	ROOM FOR IMPACT OPPORTUNITIES?
School Operating Hours: • Regulation 12.6 states that we must provide 26 hours of instruction per week.	• School is open Monday to Friday from 9 a.m. to 3.30 p.m., with timetables providing 26 hours per week per student. • We also provide a range of co-curricular activities, e.g., sports, chess club, debate club, etc., after school hours between 3.30 to 6 p.m.	• Our operating days are not mandated, e.g., technically we *could* run a 4- or 4.5-day week – as long as we provide 26 hours contact time. • There is no regulatory requirement for us to provide this after-hours support. We could *potentially* de-implement this.
State Curriculum: • Statutory curriculum objectives are provided for each age/grade.	• Our teachers individually develop schemes of work, lesson plans and resources that they individualize for each group of students – this is linked back to the statutory curriculum objectives.	• There is no regulatory requirement to develop local curriculum materials – we could just buy into a high-quality program of study. • There is no regulatory requirement for teachers to produce a detailed lesson plan for every lesson. This could *potentially* be stopped.

(Continued)

(Continued)

WHAT IS REQUIRED [i.e., THE POLICY/ REGULATIONS]	WHAT WE ACTUALLY DO [i.e., THE PRACTICES]	ROOM FOR IMPACT OPPORTUNITIES?
Parental Engagement: • Regulation 123.7 states that we need to have at least one parent representative on the school board; and that we need a formal process to deal with any parent complaints, including escalation to the district.	• We have a separate Parent-Teacher Committee as well as parent representation on the school board. • We provide detailed reports each term to parents on their child's progress. Each subject teacher produces these.	• Technically we don't need to have this Parent-Teacher Committee at all! • Nothing in the regulations mandates us to provide any written reports to parents. While it might be difficult to stop doing this completely, maybe we could move to a single report from the form tutor, rather than a report from every teacher. Or we could invite parents to come to a one-hour class with their child presenting on their work and learning.

The above is just a *worked example to give you an idea* of what *might* be possible in your system. But it would help if you looked at your specific local regulations, which vary country by country and sometimes even region by region, to understand what you *legally* have to do versus what you are *actually* doing.

You can also do this *analysis the other way around*! Start by listing all the things you currently do that take up a great deal of your time. Then explicitly look at what the policies, regulations, and guidelines say about what you *actually need* to do. Our hunch is that once you start digging into the rule books, you will have many "aha!" moments—times where you realize that many of the things you initially believed were requirements are actually your overengineered (mis-)interpretations of those regulations.

Yet, another way of thinking about this is illustrated in Figure 4.3.

FIGURE 4.3   Policy Typology

EXTERNALLY IMPOSED	INTERNALLY INTERPRETED	INTERNALLY IMPOSED
External policy or process that must be followed to the letter	External policy or process that can be adapted to local needs and where local steps may have become over-elaborated	No external agency cares whether you do it or not—it just cares about your outcomes
Can only de-implement through complex negotiation	Many types of de-implementation possible	Everything to play for!

Lens 2: Live Initiatives Stocktaking

A second angle you can explore relates to programs and initiatives you are currently implementing. If your school is anything like the average school, at any one time you are likely to be progressing several different whole school agendas simultaneously. These might include:

> standards-based bulletin boards; project-based learning; thematic-integrated curricular; trademarked whole-school professional development programs; making a shift from whole-word reading to phonics (or vice versa); meta-cognitive strategies; collective efficacy; learning styles; trauma informed instruction; culturally relevant pedagogy; professional learning communities; graded readers/leveled texts; multiple intelligences; cyberbullying prevention; drug-abuse resistance education; growth mindset; breakfast clubs; Japanese lesson study; instructional coaching; explicit direct instruction; and the list goes on and on.

Some of the interventions in the list above are based on shaky research (bonus points if you know which ones!). Others have much, much stronger evidence of impact **but only if they respond to a need that you *actually* have in your school**. And only if you implement these initiatives correctly and collect monitoring and evaluation data to check they are working—and have ongoing iteration protocols in place to respond to the evaluation data and enhance the impact.

Therefore, you can use the Live Initiatives Stocktaking Tool in Figure 4.4 to undertake an inventory of all your live initiatives.

FIGURE 4.4 Live Initiatives Stocktaking Tool			
1. *ALL* OUR CURRENT PROJECTS	**2. PROJECTS WITH *SYSTEMATIC* EVALUATION DATA**	**3. PROJECTS WITH *REALLY* POSITIVE EVALUATION DATA**	**4. POSITIVE PROJECTS THAT *STILL* NEED PUMP-PRIMING**
In this column, you list all your active special projects and initiatives.	Here, you narrow down to those that you have bothered to collect evaluation data systematically. If you have not set up evaluation protocols, your initiative is more likely to be busywork that's not worth your time; and we recommend that you **assume that anything you are *not* evaluating is having *no* impact.**	Now you narrow down even further to the projects you are systematically evaluating and where the data show extremely strong, or at least highly cost-effective returns. The most straightforward way of doing this is to compute percentage gains (or losses!) in student achievement, using pre- and post-data and comparing these across all your initiatives; and, also, to cross-tabulate these against the cost per student of each intervention, where these data are available.	Of the positive projects that are generating profound impact, how many still need centralized support to keep them going? It may be that many of the changes have already become engrained and sustained or that the original need no longer exists. Put the projects that *still* need continuing/backbone team oversight here.

Source: Adapted from Hamilton et al. (2022).

Once you have progressed to column 4, you then go back to the longer list in column 1 and circle/highlight only the items left in column 4. These are the initiatives you should continue with. Everything else is a target that you should consider for de-implementation.

Lens 3: Time Studies

A third way of identifying areas for de-implementation is to explicitly measure what everyone is actually spending their time on and how long all of their various tasks are actually taking. One benefit of doing this is that we can sometimes misperceive the passage of time; if you ask people to give you estimates of the time it took them to undertake an activity, these often turn out not to be very accurate (Newport, 2021).

A time study enables you to collect more objective data, and you can do this by taking the following actions:

1. **Holding a focus group with your teams to list out all the categories of activity that they undertake in an average week**. You will likely identify a wide range of areas including lesson preparation, teaching, assessment, staff meetings, professional development, data-inputting, lesson observation, learning walks, student display, detention supervision, corridor patrols, parent-teacher engagement, co-curricular activities; and so on.

2. **Undertaking a time study for a period of one week**. Team members can do this manually, keeping a spreadsheet and inputting the number of minutes for each activity category per day. However, there are also a number of smartphone apps (some even free) that enable you to key in all the activity areas and then log the start and stop times for each activity type—at the press of a button. We provide a time study illustration of this in Figure 4.5, below.

An aligned type of tool that you could also use is a time-anticipation study, where you seek to identify and map out the peaks and troughs in workload over the course of the academic year. While this is just an estimate, it is useful to do this because no two weeks are exactly alike. See Figure 4.6 for an illustration.

The value of this type of analysis is that there are often non-negotiable things that you are required to do at some point during the school year but where we have some degree of flexibility about *when* you do them, and when you schedule the task. So, it may be that this analysis helps you to identify those traditionally quieter times and to reschedule activity to smooth out the ebbs and flows.

FIGURE 4.5   Time Study Illustration

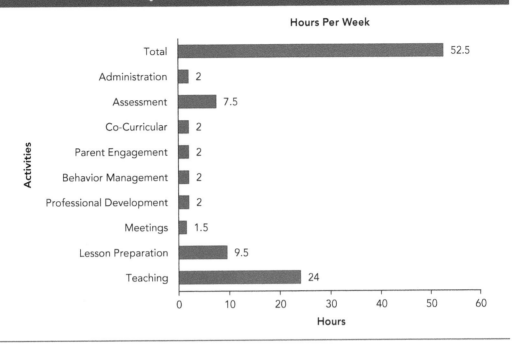

FIGURE 4.6   Time Anticipation Study

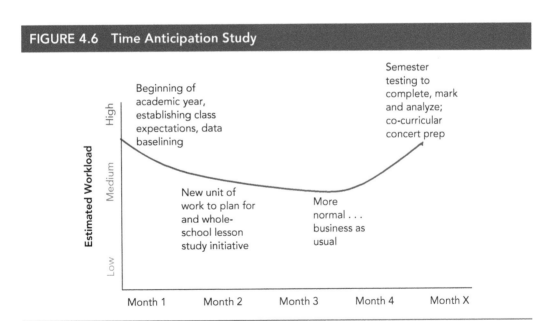

Source: Adapted from UK Department for Education School Workload Reduction Toolkit (Department for Education, 2019).

Lens 4: Cost-Benefit Analysis

Suppose one of the reasons that you have embarked on your *Room for Impact* inquiry cycle is that you are seeking to save financial resources. In that case, you will also want to undertake a formal cost-benefit analysis of each of your programs/initiatives. A way of doing this is illustrated in Figure 4.7.

FIGURE 4.7   Cost-Benefit Analysis Worked Example

PROGRAM	TOTAL COST PER ANNUM	NUMBER OF DIRECT BENEFICIARIES	COST PER BENEFICIARY	STATUTORY REQUIREMENT?	IMPACT DATA Y/N	WHAT DOES IT SHOW?
Intelligent Tutoring System	$3,255	217 targeted students	$15.00	N	Y	8% learning gain per student per annum
Whole School Metacognition Program	$22,780	1,226 students	$18.58	N	N	N/A

Here, you list out each of your special projects or programs that incurs financial expenditure, particularly those that involve payments to third parties outside your school or organization. You then tabulate the cost per annum, the number of direct beneficiaries from that expenditure, and the cost per beneficiary. All of this should be relatively straightforward to calculate—some of your programs might be intended to benefit all students, whereas others might have a more targeted audience. In the worked example in Figure 4.7, for example, you can see that the Intelligent Tutoring System is being targeted at a narrower cohort of students, whereas the Metacognition Program is being leveraged across the whole school.

Next you confirm whether there is a statutory requirement that you incur this expenditure. Of course, even if it is a requirement, this does not necessarily mean that the program, activity, hardware, or subscription that you are purchasing is the most *cost-effective* way of meeting the regulatory requirement.

Finally, you list out whether you are collecting impact data and what these data are showing. And you use this cost-benefit analysis table to then make decisions about what to keep, drop, or substitute with a more cost-effective alternative.

Obviously, all sorts of considerations will come into play as you make your decisions. For example, it may be that the Intelligent Tutoring

System also saves teacher time in setting and marking homework and that there is significant evidence that it supports children in accelerating their learning—and that, perhaps, you should use it even more widely. Maybe the whole school metacognition program is being implemented without parallel evaluation and you have no idea whether it is making any difference or even whether it responds to a priority education challenge that your school genuinely has. For other items of expenditure, however, the data might not be so clear cut.

Lens 5: Staff Voice

Our final suggested lens focuses on gathering perception data from your teams about their respective workloads and their ideas about what can be de-implemented and with what cost. Two ways you can collect staff voices are *interviews* and *pulse surveys*, and we provide you with tools that you can adapt, below.

Interviews

Some of the questions that you can ask, include the following:

1. How many hours do you think you are working on average per week?

2. Do you feel your workload is manageable/sustainable?

3. What are the most significant contributors to your workload that you also feel have minimal impact on student learning outcomes?

4. What would you change that you feel would reduce your workload but without it harming student outcomes?

5. If you could only implement one of these ideas, which one would you prioritize and why?

6. How would you implement this change?

7. What do you think the risks might be with implementing it?

8. How might you overcome those risks?

9. If you could make changes at the whole-school level, what are some things you feel would be effective for workload reduction?

Pulse Survey

You can also use one of the many free online survey tools to build, distribute, and then analyze responses from your teachers. Some of the questions you could ask include those illustrated in Figure 4.8.

Bringing It All Together

To reiterate, you might not use all these five lenses to divergently explore and map all the potentially amenable "Jenga blocks" in your context. You might just use one or two, selecting the ones that are the quickest and easiest to collect data for. But you should think carefully

FIGURE 4.8   Teacher Workload Pulse Survey Example

Teacher Workload Pulse Survey

This is a short survey to learn more about your workload and improve your well-being. Your response will help us review and streamline school processes—to help reduce your workload.

We will also survey you again in the future to measure our collective progress in teacher workload reduction.

It should take you no more than 5 minutes to complete the survey. All responses are anonymous. If you have any questions about the survey, please contact XXX.

1) In your most recent full working week, was the time spent on each of the following activities, too little, too much, or about right—when considering the impact/returns it had on student outcomes?

	TOO LITTLE	ABOUT RIGHT	TOO MUCH	N/A
Individual planning and preparation of lessons				
Teamwork and collaboration with your colleagues				
Assessing student work				
Student counseling				
Student supervision and tuition outside of timetabled lessons (including break time and lunch supervision)				
Student behavior management including detentions				
Participation in school management processes				
General administrative work (including email, telephone, paperwork, and clerical tasks)				
Engagement with parents/guardians				
School extracurricular activities (e.g., sports, clubs, societies, and cultural activities)				
Providing cover for absent colleagues during the timetabled day				
Coaching, mentoring, training, monitoring, and/or appraising other staff				

	TOO LITTLE	ABOUT RIGHT	TOO MUCH	N/A
Engagement with people and organizations outside the school, other than parents				
Organizing resources and premises				
Setting up wall displays and/or setting up/tidying classrooms				
Team/staff meetings				
School policy development and financial planning				
Recording, monitoring, and analyzing data on student performance and for other purposes				
Other activities (you may wish to specify)				

2) To what extent do you agree or disagree with the following statements?

	STRONGLY DISAGREE	TEND TO DISAGREE	NEITHER AGREE NOR DISAGREE	TEND TO AGREE	STRONGLY AGREE
My workload is acceptable					
I achieve a good work-life balance					
The majority of activities I undertake in my work have strong and direct returns to student learning					

3) What changes do you think could be made to further improve your work-life balance that will not negatively impact student achievement?

Source: Adapted from UK Department for Education School Workload Reduction Toolkit (Department for Education, 2019).

about which ones are likely to give you the *best* data sources before you proceed—the best leads on the Jenga blocks that might be amenable to removal, reducing, re-engineering, or replacing.

> You might also be able to *shortcut your investigatory process* (to some degree) by looking at the shopping list of more than *eighty de-implementation opportunities* that we present in Appendix 1. You could, for example, work through these as a group and simply circle those that *could* be viable in your local context. And then proceed to Key Action 2!

Key Action 2: Provisionally Agree on Your Amenable Focus Area(s)

Once you have selected your inquiry tools and gathered your data, the outputs might look something like Figure 4.9. This is simply a long list of potential de-implementation areas, with the average time spent per teacher clearly listed.

FIGURE 4.9   The Long List of De-Implementation Prospects – Worked Example

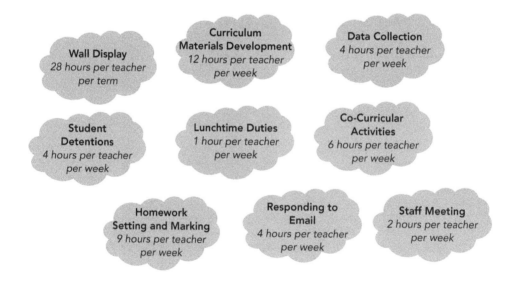

During your prospecting (undertaken during Key Action 1), you will likely have identified many areas that you could *potentially* de-implement. But you cannot progress them all simultaneously: there just aren't enough hours in the day. And obviously, if you de-implement too much too soon, there's a risk that you might bring your whole Jenga tower crashing down.

Therefore, you need some rules-based processes to help you weigh the pros and cons of each de-implementation opportunity and then to vector in on those with the highest probability of impact. We illustrate this in Figure 4.10.

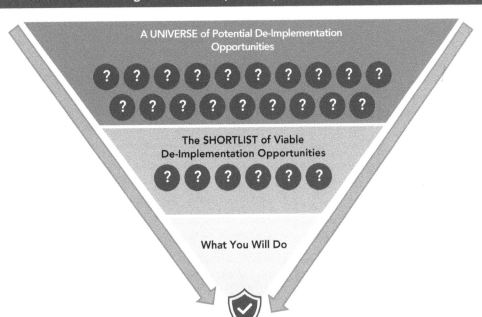

FIGURE 4.10   Vectoring in on Your Top De-Implementation Opportunities

A UNIVERSE of Potential De-Implementation Opportunities

The SHORTLIST of Viable De-Implementation Opportunities

What You Will Do

Source: Adapted from Hamilton et al. (2022).

You are now going to make a provisional agreement about which ones you want to explore more deeply, with the aim of undertaking some form of de-implementation.

Suppose you are working at system-level with lots of resources at your disposal. In that case, you might choose to investigate and build plans for every single one of the identified de-implementation prospect areas and to hold off on taking any off the table until you know much more about the opportunities and costs of proceeding. This means that you will put *all* of them through the **(1.3) Postulate** and (possibly) also the **(2.1) Propose-steps** (covered in the next two chapters) before agreeing on the actions you will take.

However, suppose you are working at school or Professional Learning Community level. In that case, it is very unlikely that you will have the resources to investigate and build plans for all your potential de-implementation opportunities at the same time. Instead, you need to make a judgment call about which two or three you will carry forward to explore and plan for in more detail. And, if, later on you find that these are not going to fly—you can always come back to this original list and select some of the others that you initially decided not to progress. Indeed, at the Professional Learning Community level, you might be better off just selecting one thing to inquire into at a time. Then, if you decide later that it will be too difficult to bring that thing to life and de-implement, you can return to **(1.2) Prospect** and select the "next cab off the rank."

You are looking for the hottest prospects, so we give you the HEAT criteria to help you make that decision, as illustrated in Figure 4.11.

FIGURE 4.11 The HEAT Criteria	
DOMAIN	**DESCRIPTION**
Harm	• Is this an area with a high probability of negatively impacting student achievement if we de-implement?
Ease	• Do we have the authority to make changes in this area? • Do the various ways we could make changes require a lot of work or will it be easy?
Acceptability	• Are stakeholders going to be open to making changes in this area?
Time Saved	• What maximum amount of time *could* be saved if we undertake de-implementation in this area? • Also consider resource savings here too.

Let's now unpack these considerations in a little more detail:

1. **The likely level of *harm* to student outcomes in making changes in the target area** – you can't (yet) quantify the likely level of harm until you have decided (later) whether your strategy is to Remove, Reduce, Re-Engineer, or Replace within the target area. Each of these will generate different levels of harm. But you can speculate that things that are only tangentially connected to teaching and learning are less likely to generate harm if they are de-implemented. So, changes to email management, staff meetings, lunchtime duties, and corridor wall display are likely to generate less potential for harm than poking around in the curriculum materials, homework, and possibly also the co-curricular domains.

2. **Whether it is *easy* to make significant changes in the target area** – here, one consideration is whether (or not) you have the authority to make any changes at all. For each potential target area, you can start by going back to the rules, regulations,

and policies to confirm what you are and aren't allowed to do. Things that are totally within your local control will be easier to progress.

3. **How *acceptable* it is to make changes in the target area** – that is, acceptable to educators, students, and parents. This one is harder to unpick until you have decided what the exact change is. For example, in the area of curriculum materials—asking teachers to share their materials on a cloud drive, so that their colleagues can adapt them—is likely to be more acceptable than to ask them to all pivot to a scripted instructional approach. So, you can't have a particularly good sense of acceptability until you know what your exact de-implementation strategy is going to be, which does not come until **(2.1) Propose** and **(2.2) Prepare**. But nonetheless, you can still have some sense that, say, making changes to staff meetings is going to be less contentious than anything you might plan in, say, curriculum materials development.

4. **The total amount of *time* that theoretically *could* be saved** – a good place to start is by looking at the average hours per teacher per week (or per term) currently expended on each task. Those things you are spending the most time on (theoretically) have the most potential for savings.

We want to reiterate, though, that it is difficult to make definitive judgments about any of these four HEAT domains at this stage. Much depends on the type of de-implementation strategy you decide to progress, a decision you will make in later P-steps. And this is a decision about Removing vs. Reducing vs. Re-Engineering vs. Replacing—and each of these options comes with different potential time savings, different potential levels of acceptability, different levels of ease, and for some you will have the authority to make the changes but for others you may not.

This means that your decisions about which areas to progress are going to be provisional. You may well end up back in the **(1.2) Prospect-step** again, if later on you decide that your initially selected areas are going to be too challenging to take forward and de-implement.

But, right now, we simply want you to come to judgments for each de-implementation opportunity against the HEAT criteria. And as you do so, you will also want to think carefully about the quality of evidence that you are leveraging to make this judgment:

- Is it a hunch, an inkling, or an opinion?
- Is it based on peer-reviewed evidence?
- Is any peer-reviewed/systematic evidence from a context that is similar to your own?

You can then use the HEAT Scoring Matrix, illustrated in Figure 4.12, to score and rank the various de-implementation opportunities that you have identified.

FIGURE 4.12   HEAT Scoring Matrix

DE-IMPLEMENTATION OPPORTUNITY	HARM 1–5 1 = VERY RISKY	EASE 1–5 5 = VERY EASY	ACCEPTABILITY 1–5 5 = VERY ACCEPTABLE	TIME SAVED 1–5 5 = LOTS OF TIME SAVED	TOTAL
Student Detentions	4	4	3	2	13/20
Wall Displays	5	3	4	4	16/20
Parental Reporting	4	4	2	2	12/20
Curriculum Development	2	2	2	5	11/20
Data Collection	4	3	4	2	13/20
Lunchtime Duties	5	4	5	1	15/20
Staff Meetings	5	5	5	2	17/20
Email	5	4	5	2	16/20
Homework	2	3	2	5	12/20
Co-curricular Activities	3	2	2	5	12/20

And if you are struggling to see a clear delineation between the various runners and riders, you can also experiment with changing the weightings. For example, you could give double the weight to time saved—so this would mean that something that had the potential to save *lots* of time would be weighted much higher even if it scores much lower on Ease and Acceptability. After all, no pain no gain!

An alternative Four-Quadrant Scoring Framework is also provided in Figure 4.13.

This approach privileges speed over rigor and enables backbone teams to hold quick brainstorming workshops with stakeholders to quickly come to a holistic consensus judgment—based on the trade-off between the **Positive Impact** of de-implementation (i.e., time & resources saved without harming student outcomes) and **Perceived Difficulty** (i.e., whether stakeholders will agree to de-implement, how easy it will be to implement, and the perceived level of risk).

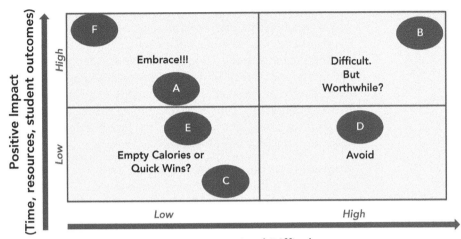

FIGURE 4.13   Four-Quadrant Scoring Framework

Our sister book *Building to Impact* contains a similar protocol to help you vector in on the highest priority areas for implementation, which respond to what we call Education Challenges. These are big, meaty, important goals that just can't be left alone. In *Building to Impact* we made the strong case that you should only seek to progress *one* or two Education Challenges at the same time. However, our *Room for Impact* advice on de-implementation is a little different. It all depends!

The number of de-implementation actions you can attend to and progress toward simultaneously depends on how easy they are to progress. We re-illustrate the three main approaches that you can adopt in Figure 4.14.

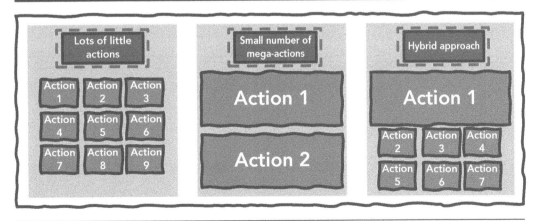

FIGURE 4.14   Recapping Approaches to De-Implementation

To unpack this in more detail, you can progress:

- **Lots of Little De-Implementation Actions**. These are likely to be low-hanging fruit initiatives like stand-up meetings, removing the requirement to have a lesson plan for every lesson, and prohibiting the sending or checking of emails after working hours and on weekends. While these are likely easy to implement, they each generate limited time savings, and there is a big difference between mandating something and people putting it into practice. So, it may require significant follow-up, monitoring, and support for relatively little returns in freed time and resources.

- **A Small Number of Mega Actions.** These are going to be bigger, meaty things that save much more time. But they are also likely to come with higher levels of risk and lower levels of acceptability. You may find that your teams don't actually want to make the changes and/or that parents and students generate resistance that blows you off course. Examples of mega actions might be removing all extracurricular activities or introducing a third-party scripted instructional program. Both have the potential to save lots of time, but both are also likely to be highly divisive.

- **A Hybrid Approach.** Where, perhaps, you decide to progress one big, meaty de-implementation goal and a handful of smaller activities alongside that will take less time and effort to bring them to fruition. Here, the risk is that you end up giving up on your big, meaty thing and focusing on the "successes" of your smaller initiatives—like turning the email server off after 5 p.m. and over the weekend, even though the impact of this is that everyone becomes stressed when one hundred emails land in their inbox at 7 a.m. on Monday morning. And this stress has been building up over the weekend, as staff are already beginning to fret about what will be awaiting them on Monday.

But of course, you cannot know for sure where you are likely to land at this stage because you will only decide in later P-steps what your actual de-implementation strategy is for each target area. This might end up being a small change like introducing quizzing homework (a.k.a. Re-Engineering) or a big change like Removing homework altogether.

P.S. Don't Forget to Think About "Buy-in"

As you provisionally agree on the de-implementation areas that you most wish to progress, you may also want to start thinking about the critical question of "buy-in." Often, when initiatives are cascaded down from "on high" these fail to gain traction because staff at the front line neither understand the rationale nor agree with what they are being asked to do (or to stop doing). And they then (understandably) reject the initiative and maintain the status quo.

There are actually two schools of thought on buy-in (Hamilton et al., 2022):

- **School 1: The Centrality of Buy-in.** This is the belief that you categorically need to get buy-in before you proceed and ideally co-construct the proposed interventions with the affected stakeholders. Then people will be more willing to engage; and, in turn, this will result in behavior change and impact. **In other words, belief change must happen *before* change and impact can occur.**

- **School 2: The Myth of Buy-in.** The counter-perspective that a lot of time gets wasted in seeking buy-in and that this often generates poor returns because it's very difficult to change people's beliefs (the *backfire effect*). Instead, according to this school of thought, a better approach is to carefully support stakeholders to make a change without getting too deeply into debates about whys and wherefores. Then, once those stakeholders see the impact with their own eyes, their implicit beliefs will change too. **In other words, belief change only comes *after* making the change and seeing the impact.**

The jury is still out on which of these two approaches works best:

- **School 2: The Myth of Buy-in** saves a lot of time in staff consultation but has a higher probability of leading you to

(Continued)

(Continued)

unworkable initiatives because you haven't checked with the front line on what the *real* implications might be. And if you do decide to foist things on people, you need to be sure that they actually "work" and also have plans alongside to monitor closely, because no one will be very motivated to do what you are asking without this oversight.

- **School 1: The Centrality of Buy-in** is almost the polar opposite in pros and cons. You will need to spend much more time collecting staff voice and may be dragged into the quagmire of belief-wars—with folk (sometimes) being unwilling to abandon their pet preferences no matter how good the evidence you present (and sometimes they may actually be right to hold firm). But you will be better able to stress test your proposed initiatives to build approaches that have a higher probability of success. And your teams will be more motivated to progress these without strong oversight.

Note, too, that whichever approach you adopt to the question of buy-in, we have included explicit processes in *(1.3) Postulate*, *(2.1) Propose*, and *(2.2) Prepare* for you to:

- understand what sustains the existing practices you are seeking to de-implement, including habits and beliefs (i.e., Chesterton's Fence);

- identify countermeasures or "antidotes" to these identified habits and beliefs;

- stress test your proposed initiatives before you get going, so that you can preempt and mitigate the potential derailers.

Summary

The **(1.2) *Prospect*-step** is focused on surveying the landscape to identify the "Jenga blocks" that *might* be amenable to de-implementation and to agreeing on the ones that you will investigate and plan for in more detail. By the end of this P-step you will have:

- **Key Action 1:** Collected Data on De-Implementation Opportunity Areas and

- **Key Action 2:** Agreed on Your Amenable Focus Areas(s).

1.2 Prospect: Convergent Cross-Checking and Agreeing

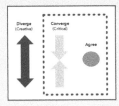

We also recommend that you undertake explicit convergent cross-checking before concluding the **Prospect-step** and proceeding forward.

Here are some of the critical cross-checking questions you can consider:

1. Have we used the right tools and processes to identify de-implementation prospects (i.e., balancing speed of inquiry with accuracy and validity of findings)?

2. Have we identified a range of potentially suitable prospects for de-implementation?

3. Have we used the HEAT criteria to sift, sort, and rank the viable de-implementation prospects?

4. Do we now have a shortlist of agreed upon de-implementation areas ready to carry forward to the next P-step?

5. Are we (relatively) confident in the quality of data that we have used to make decisions or do we need to dig further?

6. Have we thought deeply about the critical question of buy-in and made our choice in relation to School 1: The Centrality of Buy-in vs. School 2: The Myth of Buy-in? What did we decide? And what risks will we now face going forward?

7. Are we now ready to move to the next P-step? Are we ready to **(1.3) Postulate**?

Postulate (1.3)

5

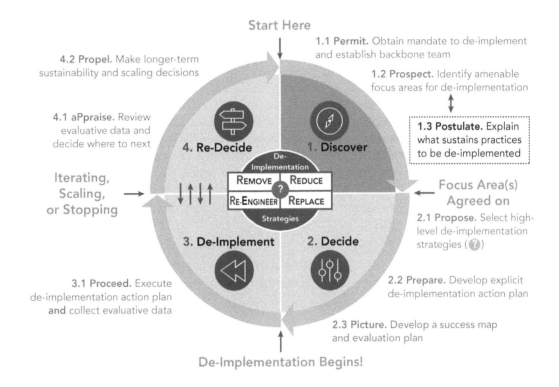

Start Here

1.1 Permit. Obtain mandate to de-implement and establish backbone team

1.2 Prospect. Identify amenable focus areas for de-implementation

1.3 Postulate. Explain what sustains practices to be de-implemented

4.2 Propel. Make longer-term sustainability and scaling decisions

4.1 aPpraise. Review evaluative data and decide where to next

4. Re-Decide

1. Discover

De-Implementation
REMOVE | REDUCE
?
RE-ENGINEER | REPLACE
Strategies

Focus Area(s) Agreed on

Iterating, Scaling, or Stopping

2.1 Propose. Select high-level de-implementation strategies (?)

3. De-Implement

2. Decide

3.1 Proceed. Execute de-implementation action plan **and** collect evaluative data

2.2 Prepare. Develop explicit de-implementation action plan

2.3 Picture. Develop a success map and evaluation plan

De-Implementation Begins!

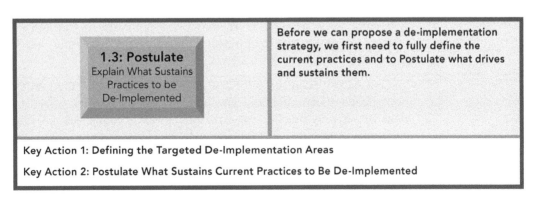

1.3: Postulate
Explain What Sustains Practices to be De-Implemented

Before we can propose a de-implementation strategy, we first need to fully define the current practices and to Postulate what drives and sustains them.

Key Action 1: Defining the Targeted De-Implementation Areas

Key Action 2: Postulate What Sustains Current Practices to Be De-Implemented

Context

To successfully de-implement in the future, you first need to:

- **define** the practices that you seek to change; and

- **postulate** what it is that currently sustains them (to confront "Chesterton's Fence").

The definition bit almost goes without saying. If you do not have a shared understanding of what constitutes the target area(s), you will busily rush around de-implementing different things in different ways, while collectively believing that you are pursuing the same agenda. You might even be working at cross purposes!

The postulate bit is also very important but often gets missed out. Or at best it gets cursory attention because everyone is itching to get straight into the action. But, as we already discussed in chapter 1, de-implementation of already deeply ingrained habits is fiendishly difficult. By directly confronting "Chesterton's Fence" we are explicitly inquiring into why the "fence" (or school improvement initiative) was erected in the first place—the backstory, the rationale, and the things that sustain it. And with that information, we are better able to:

- confirm that it is a good idea to take down the "fence" (or not as the case may be), and

- identify all the potential derailers—that is, the beliefs and engrained habits that might result in everyone sleepwalking back into the field to put the fence back up again. Forewarned is forearmed.

It was engrained habits that explain why Arran kept going to the wrong kitchen sink and why 22 percent of the global population still smoke cigarettes, despite knowing the impact on health and longevity and in spite of many wanting to give up (Our World in Data, 2022). Indeed, with smoking, it seems to be the habit and ritual drivers that thwart attempts to quit rather than physical dependency on nicotine, which generally diminishes within a week.

The reason that postulation (or explanation) is so crucial before putting de-implementation intentions into action is that by knowing what sustains the existing practice, we can better propose counteractions that circumnavigate these habit-sustaining drivers. Understanding what sustains the present helps us build a stronger bridge to a future in which we successfully de-implement those target behaviors.

So if, for example, you postulate that you smoke because (1) you have easy access to cigarettes; (2) it's common within your social group; and (3) you have particularly strong cravings after meals and stressful meetings, then you are better able to propose a de-implementation strategy that will be effective. This might involve considering the following counteractions or "antidotes":

HABIT DRIVER	COUNTERACTIONS (a.k.a. ANTIDOTES)
Access to Cigarettes	• Destroy all your smoking materials and equipment • Tell your local retailers *not* to sell you anymore, even if you beg • Restrict access to discretionary funds to buy cigarettes
Social Setting Triggers	• Stop hanging out with the smoker set • Fill social time with solitary exercise in the woods where there are no shops to buy cigarettes • Tell everyone about your quitting goal • Make an expensive public bet that you write up as a contract and sign. For example, "If I take up smoking again, I will pay $200 to each of my ten close family members and friends."
Cravings	• Take medication that makes you feel sick if you smoke • Make and drink a cup of tea every time you want a cigarette • Avoid stressful meetings (wishful thinking?)

While it is unlikely that anything you de-implement in schools will make you grumpy because of withdrawal symptoms from physically addictive chemicals, human brains are not wired to simply "delete" prior behaviors. So, there is a constant risk that no matter how logical and reasonable your de-implementation intentions, you'll find yourself back on autopilot or back justifying why you should abort your quest to make room for impact. But by covering these bases in advance, we are more likely to develop a plan that we can stick to.

In the **(1.3) Postulate-step**, we are not (yet) exploring or suggesting the potential counteractions that might result in successful de-implementation. That comes in a later P-Step. We are, instead, focused on:

- **Key Action 1: Defining the Targeted De-Implementation Areas**

- **Key Action 2: Postulate What Sustains Current Practices to Be De-Implemented**

Let's now look at each of these in turn.

Key Action 1: Defining the Targeted De-Implementation Areas

Before you get busy postulating, you need to start by explicitly defining your proposed de-implementation area. During the (1.2) *Prospect*-step, you will (likely) have already collected much of the information you need to lay out this definition. And in Figure 5.1, below, we provide a template with a partially completed worked example to illustrate how you can formalize your definition.

FIGURE 5.1   Defining Your Targeted De-Implementation Area(s)

TARGET AREA FOR DE-IMPLEMENTATION			
Overarching Description of De-Implementation Target Area	Development of Bespoke and Localized Teaching, Learning, and Student Assessment Materials by Our Teaching Teams		
SUBCOMPONENTS	**WHEN/WHERE DOES THIS OCCUR?**	**WHO DOES THIS?**	**HOW MUCH TIME IS SPENT?**
1. **Development of Overarching Scheme of Work**	Usually prior to the start of the academic year and it is reviewed and refined at the start of each term	Head of department, with input from all teachers	40 hours per term × 3 people
2. **Development of Detailed Lesson Plans**	On a daily/weekly basis and mostly out of school during evenings and weekends	All teachers and mainly independently (i.e., without sharing materials with each other)	Average of 5 hours per week per teacher
3. **Development of Student Activity and Resource Sheets**	As above	As above	Average of 3 hours per week per teacher
4. **Development of Student Assessment Tools**	As above	As above	Average of 2 hours per week per teacher

Suppose you undertook a time study as part of the (1.2) *Prospect*-step. In that case, you will also have a good estimate of the number of hours that team members spend on the overarching de-implementation target area and on the subcomponents. This information is useful, because when (later on) you progress to exploration of the most viable de-implementation strategies, you might decide that not all of the subcomponents require the same strategy. You might even decide to continue with some subcomponents, remove or reduce others, and re-engineer yet others.

You need to apply this definition Key Action to every de-implementation area that you decided to progress during the previous P-step. So, if you selected four areas, you need to lay out four definitions. If two, then two. And so on.

Key Action 2: Postulate What Sustains Current Practices to Be De-Implemented

Now that you have defined your de-implementation target areas, the next important action is to postulate (or explain) what sustains current practices. By understanding why people adopted the practice in the first place and why they are persisting with it, you are able to:

- confirm that it is indeed a good target for de-implementation; and

- identify the likely barriers to de-implementation (e.g., that risk of everyone creeping back into the field at night to put the fence back up again).

Two of the ways that you could gather this data are *inductively* and *deductively*.

Inductive

The inductive approach starts with no preconceptions. Instead, you go out and gather data and then look for the patterns in that data. You can do this by interviewing a cross-section of educators and by asking them the following questions:

1. Is "X" something that you usually do? [Probe on when, where, and how "X" is performed]

2. Why did you start doing "X" in the first place?

3. How much do you want to stop doing "X"?

4. What do you think would happen if you stopped doing "X"?

5. How easy or difficult do you think it would be for you to stop doing "X"?

6. Are there any incentives that make you continue to do "X"?

7. What emotions do you feel when you think about stopping "X"?

8. Does the social/organizational environment help/hinder you in stopping "X"?

9. Does the physical environment help or hinder you in stopping "X"?

10. Is stopping "X" in alignment or in conflict with your professional standards and/or professional identity?

11. What strategies could the *organization* leverage to help you stop "X"? [Probe on Remove vs. Reduce vs. Re-Engineer vs. Replace strategies]

12. What are the pros and cons of these "X"-stopping strategies?

Here is a worked example where X is the development of *bespoke and localized teaching, learning, and student assessment materials* by our teaching teams:

---

1. **Is X something that you usually do?** [Probe on when, where, and how X is performed]

   Yes, it probably accounts for half my workload. I sort of feel that I have two jobs. The first is teaching and the second is as a teaching materials and resource developer. Although I am now spending less time developing teaching and learning materials, because I am a few years into my teaching career, I am still spending ten to fifteen hours a week tweaking and improving the resources I have already developed and building new and better stuff.

2. **Why did you start doing X in the first place?**

   Because it's what we are supposed to do. We should develop localized materials that directly connect to the specific interests of the children we teach. It's also important that we have a fully written up lesson plan for each lesson, with a range of personalized and differentiated activities.

3. **How much do you want to stop doing X?**

   It would save me a lot of time. But I'm not sure I'm allowed. I would like the extra time, but I'm *really* worried about the impact on the kids.

4. **What do you think would happen if you stopped doing X?**

   I'm not sure. I'm worried that the students would seriously fall behind if I stop making the effort. But if they don't, I'd then feel stupid for spending so much time on this over the years.

5. **How easy or difficult do you think it would be for you to stop doing X?**

   For me, slightly easier than for a newly qualified teacher, because at least I have all my core teaching materials and

---

resources predeveloped. I'd need to focus on resisting the urge to keep polishing and adapting it for each new cohort. I think it would be much harder for new teachers, because they need to develop their materials in the first place. And that takes a lot of time.

6. **Are there any incentives that make you continue to do *X*?**

   It is in the professional standards for teachers that we develop high-quality learning experiences. It has an impact on my performance review and potentially on whether I get my increment.

7. **What emotions do you feel when you think about stopping *X*?**

   Fear. It's a big part of my job. I fear that I'll be letting down the students. I also fear that stopping makes no difference to the kids and that I realize I've been wasting my time.

8. **Does the social and organizational environment help or hinder you in stopping *X*?**

   I think it currently hinders. Everyone develops their own materials. It's a badge of honor. An expectation. If I used some third-party content and admitted to it, I think the other members of my teaching team would look down on me. They'd maybe see me as just an actor that follows the script. Not the script writer and performer. Not a true professional.

9. **Does the physical environment help or hinder you in stopping *X*?**

   I'm not really sure. Easy access to the photocopier does help me to print off my self-developed worksheets for the kids, as and when I need to.

10. **Is stopping *X* in alignment or in conflict with your professional standards and professional identity?**

    It definitely makes me feel queasy. Teachers are supposed to develop their own materials. It's an expected professional practice.

(Continued)

(Continued)

---

11. **What strategies could the organization leverage help you in stopping X?**

I think they would need to do quite a few things:

- Explicitly ban us from developing our own materials
- Give us evidence that whatever the alternative strategy is, that it works just as well or better. But it would need to be really strong evidence
- Maybe make us sign a "behavioral contract"
- Give us access to alternative resources. Maybe a good quality off-the-shelf program
- Or maybe by encouraging us all to just pool our materials and put them on a shared drive

12. **What are the pros and cons of these X-stopping strategies?**

I'm really not sure. I like the idea of pooling resources, but I'm not sure how workable it is. People tend to be quite protective of their own content. And I'm not sure how easy it would be to use or follow anyway. Even when people write up detailed lesson plans, these often contain personal shorthand terms that I don't fully understand. I end up just looking at their material for inspiration and then still building my own stuff from scratch. Sometimes it takes longer to adapt other plans than creating your own.

I guess a fully built and easy-to-follow off-the-shelf program could work. I've seen examples of these before. Some are even fully scripted. But I think there would be a lot of skepticism. People would worry about the erosion of their professional autonomy and would also have concerns about whether these prebuilt programs properly catered to the needs of their specific kids.

Of course, I'd be fine with it, but I'm pretty sure others wouldn't.

What you are doing is collecting all this rich testimony to look for commonalities, so that you can better postulate what it is that sustains the current practices. However, as you undertake these interviews you need to be mindful that:

1. Sometimes people are reluctant to give the real reasons and state their true preferences, for fear of being judged. So, instead they might give what they think is a more socially acceptable (a.k.a. "sugar-coated") response. Social psychologists have identified this trend when, for example, people are asked about their number of previous romantic partners. Men, apparently, tend to round up and women, apparently, round down—possibly to conform with social expectations.

2. Sometimes people have just not thought that deeply about your identified inquiry area prior to you asking them your probing questions. It can also be a little disconcerting (or even generate existential angst) when educators, or indeed anyone, is asked why they do the things that they do. Sometimes it sparks wider thought processes that make us question literally *everything*. And while this can be good, it's wise to frame this dialogue with great care, especially in contexts where you are engaging with overworked and frazzled educators who may already be considering leaving the profession. The sweet spot is the Goldilocks questions that enable everyone to think about how professional life *within* teaching can be made more rewarding and much less stressful. We want to love and nurture the ones we're with rather than push them back outside.

And, after you have collected all these rich insights, you need a way of synthesizing and consolidating the key messages, so that you can vector in on the signal in the noise. The subsection below on deductive postulation introduces some useful tools that you can also use to harvest that signal—so read on!

Deductive

The deductive approach works the postulation process the other way around. Rather than going out, talking to people, and looking for patterns in the data, the backbone team builds a hypothesis about what *could* be sustaining existing practices and then checks to see whether this holds water. So they develop a theory first and then they go out and test it.

In Figure 5.2, below, we provide you with six categories of (potential) reasons for why existing (but unproductive) behaviors are sustained to help with that theory-building process. We call this the Six Buckets, for short.

FIGURE 5.2   Six Buckets Framework

1. REGULATIONS	2. HISTORY	3. BELIEFS
The legal, procedural, and regulatory requirements that shape, influence, and reinforce the behavior	What is known about how, when, and why the organization adopted the behaviors in the first place	Beliefs about the purpose, benefits, and costs of the behavior
4. STRUCTURES	**5. CONSEQUENCES**	**6. INCENTIVES**
The systems, processes, resources, and environmental factors that prime continuation and/or discontinuation of the behavior	Beliefs about what will happen (to self and others) if the behavior is discontinued	The pull-push incentives to continue and/or discontinue the behavior

These are just examples of *potential* explanatory buckets. They are a good place to start, but as you explore you might find that you have identified very little that fits into some of these and that one or more of the others are overflowing. If that is the case, you can take the less relevant categories off the table, replacing them with others that are more pertinent to your local context.

You might also, for example, break out categories that have lots of items listed under them into two or more additional or alternative categories. Maybe, for example, you have identified that leadership, educator, student, and parental beliefs all contribute in different ways and that these need to be unpacked in more granularity. Maybe you also identify that teachers in different departments or stages of their careers have different beliefs. You might want to map and tag these, because it might subsequently mean that you will need a range of strategies that address these drivers.

One way of bringing all these insights together is in a Fishbone Diagram, which we illustrate in Figure 5.3. At the head of the "fish" is your working definition of the agreed upon de-implementation area. Then, protruding from the "spine" of the fish are six "bones" that relate to your six categories (or buckets). Of course, you can add more than six if you need to but be mindful of the optimal stopping problem: you need to balance the amount of time that you engage in analysis with the amount that you just get on and do something—even if you are not completely sure that it will generate impact—to avoid the potential for analysis-paralysis.

The "right" amount of analysis and exploration time is a local judgment call only you can make. But attached to each "bone" is a "sub-bone" with a concise description of the contributing factor. You will also notice that some "bones" have more "sub-bones" than others.

FIGURE 5.3 Fishbone Worked Example

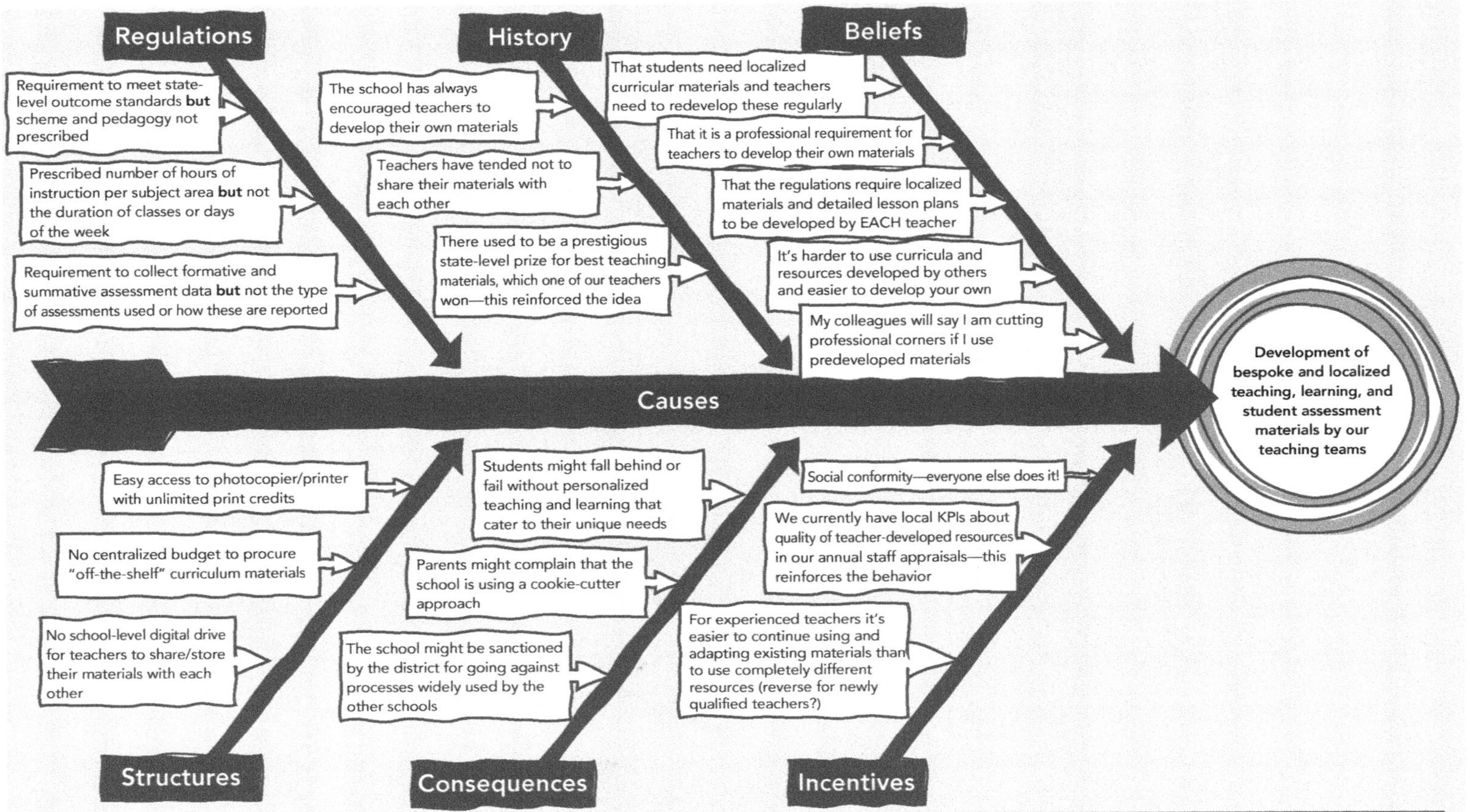

Development of bespoke and localized teaching, learning, and student assessment materials by our teaching teams

Regulations

Requirement to meet state-level outcome standards **but** scheme and pedagogy not prescribed

Prescribed number of hours of instruction per subject area **but** not the duration of classes or days of the week

Requirement to collect formative and summative assessment data **but** not the type of assessments used or how these are reported

History

The school has always encouraged teachers to develop their own materials

Teachers have tended not to share their materials with each other

There used to be a prestigious state-level prize for best teaching materials, which one of our teachers won—this reinforced the idea

Beliefs

That students need localized curricular materials and teachers need to redevelop these regularly

That it is a professional requirement for teachers to develop their own materials

That the regulations require localized materials and detailed lesson plans to be developed by EACH teacher

It's harder to use curricula and resources developed by others and easier to develop your own

My colleagues will say I am cutting professional corners if I use predeveloped materials

Causes

Structures

Easy access to photocopier/printer with unlimited print credits

No centralized budget to procure "off-the-shelf" curriculum materials

No school-level digital drive for teachers to share/store their materials with each other

Consequences

Students might fall behind or fail without personalized teaching and learning that cater to their unique needs

Parents might complain that the school is using a cookie-cutter approach

The school might be sanctioned by the district for going against processes widely used by the other schools

Incentives

Social conformity—everyone else does it!

We currently have local KPIs about quality of teacher-developed resources in our annual staff appraisals—this reinforces the behavior

For experienced teachers it's easier to continue using and adapting existing materials than to use completely different resources (reverse for newly qualified teachers?)

Comments

113

If you are working at the system level, you might also want to delve deeper still into some of the "sub-bones" to go down the rabbit hole and understand the underlying causes, and whether these, too, might need to be tackled to generate more complete de-implementation.

Another lens that you can use alongside the Fishbone is, therefore, the Sub-Bone Tool. This is illustrated in Figure 5.4, and it centers on using your three-year-old brain to keep asking those (annoying) *why?* questions. Within the context of *Room for Impact*, the reason we call this the Sub-Bone Tool is because we are literally using it to delve deeper into the sub-bones within our fishbone!

FIGURE 5.4   The Sub-Bone Tool

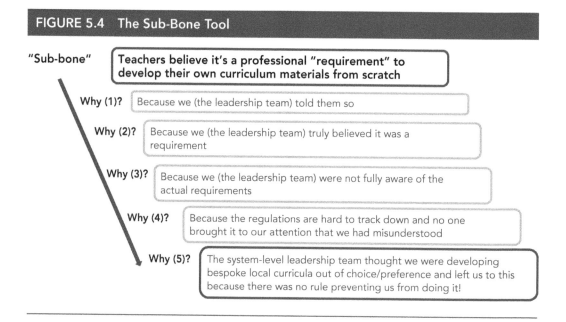

"Sub-bone"   **Teachers believe it's a professional "requirement" to develop their own curriculum materials from scratch**

Why (1)?   Because we (the leadership team) told them so

Why (2)?   Because we (the leadership team) truly believed it was a requirement

Why (3)?   Because we (the leadership team) were not fully aware of the actual requirements

Why (4)?   Because the regulations are hard to track down and no one brought it to our attention that we had misunderstood

Why (5)?   The system-level leadership team thought we were developing bespoke local curricula out of choice/preference and left us to this because there was no rule preventing us from doing it!

Hint: You can also use the Six Buckets, Fishbone, and Sub-bone tools to help you sift the signal from the noise, if you undertook your inquiry inductively and have collected lots of rich data from stakeholder interviews or focus groups. In this case, you would take all the variables you identified in your ideation sessions and place them within the Six Buckets, or more (if you have additional ideas) to help you identify the signal in the noise.

Thinking Like a Police Detective: The Sherlock Holmes Strategy

If you have taken the deductive path, you will have:

1.   postulated local reasons about what sustains existing behaviors that you wish to de-implement, using, for example, the Six Buckets Framework;

2. revised the Six Buckets to remove categories that don't make sense to your de-implementation area and to add others that do; and

3. used tools like Fishbone and Sub-Bone to delve deeper and build a more comprehensive understanding of what sustains the present.

However, while all of this is good, necessary, and important, it is just a hypothesis. You and the other members of the Backbone team have merely sat in your de-implementation cupboard and thrown some ideas up on the board. These ideas could be *true*, *false*, or *something in between*.

What you have done is not dissimilar to what a police detective (initially) does. In the TV shows they often have a giant whiteboard in the middle of the room, which is known as the evidence board or the "crazy wall." And what they do is lay out hypothesis chains with different suspects and their respective means, motives, and opportunities. But because, in most countries, courts of law presume that suspects are innocent until proven guilty, it is incumbent on police detectives to build a case that sticks.

This means that they need to gather evidence through interviews, forensics, CCTV, and all the rest. And they use this evidence to confirm or disconfirm aspects of their hypothesized causal chain. So, when they provisionally hypothesize that "it was Professor Moriarty in the Bank of England vault pilfering the gold" and they subsequently gather credible witness testimony that he was actually vacationing in the French Rivera, they can discount him from their inquiry and explore alternative explanations. The case won't stick in court. It won't pass the "beyond reasonable doubt" threshold.

Our work consistently finds that this detective-like thinking is often missing from educational inquiry. All too often, everyone jumps from problem (or need) to solution (or they start with a solution regardless of diagnosing the problem) without seeking to map and explain what drives or causes the problem in the first place. And they do so without checking that this explanation of the causes passes the "beyond reasonable doubt" giggle test.

But you really do need to check. That checking process enables us to disconfirm faulty beliefs like the "fact" that people who wear pointy hats are actually witches or goblins bestowed with magical powers, that the earth is flat, or that the harvest failed because we didn't sacrifice enough goats.

One way to put your claims to the test is to use an evidence checker, where you list out all your claims, specify where you will search for data, list your findings, and then close the loop by deciding whether the claim holds water—that is, the outcome. We illustrate this in Figure 5.5.

FIGURE 5.5   The Evidence Checker Worked Example

CLAIM	SOURCES OF DATA	FINDINGS	OUTCOME
Our teams hold the local belief that students need localized curricula and materials, and teachers need to redevelop these regularly	Interviews and focus groups with a cross-section of our teachers	75 percent of our teachers strongly indicated that they hold this belief	**Claim stands**
It is a fact that students need localized curricula and materials, and teachers need to redevelop these regularly	Visible Learning Meta[X] Data	Within the Visible Learning Meta[X] there were a number of standardized programs that generate effect sizes above $d = 0.40$, including Explicit Direct Instruction, Response to Intervention, and repeated reading programs	**Claim rejected.** Children need to understand the curriculum, but there is no strong evidence that it needs to be individually tailored or linked to the local community or that teachers need to develop materials themselves

One thing you might notice in our Evidence Checker illustration is that the same *claim* is repeated twice—that is, "that students need localized curricula and materials, and teachers need to redevelop these regularly."

But there is a subtlety. The first version of the claim we were testing was whether people actually *held the belief*. And the second version we tested was *whether the claim itself was empirically true*. This is like the difference between *believing* witches and goblins with magical powers exist and capturing them on CCTV flying through the sky on their broomsticks. We can believe things that are not true, and we can also disbelieve things in spite of strong evidence to the contrary.

However, as you search for data to verify or falsify each claim, watch out for the *confirmation bias*. This well-documented cognitive bias refers to the tendency to only search for data that agrees (or conforms) with your existing belief. To put this in context, if you believe that corporal punishment is not harmful for child outcomes, you will be able to find *some* research that is (sort of) in agreement with this claim (e.g., Baumrind, 1997 & Larzelere, 2000). But if you search for evidence against this claim, you will find a *much wider* body (e.g., Gershoff, 2008; Paolucci & Violato, 2004) that supports this alternative claim. The key is to search for *disconfirming evidence*, too, because in education you usually can find some research that supports even the most wacky and dangerous ideas. So, the more important question is what does the totality of the evidence suggest—overall?

Optimal Stopping

As you apply your police detective-like thinking to test your deductions, you have another optimal stopping decision to make. You need to decide whether you are going to:

- slowly and carefully gather evidence to explicitly cross-check each "sub-bone" in your fishbone; and/or

- collect inductive data via focus groups and surveys using the questions that we have already suggested; and/or

- just ask for a second opinion by showing your Postulations to selected stakeholders outside your Backbone team to see if they intuitively *feel* that it looks "about right," "bang on," or "not very convincing."

Which of these strategies you chose (and the amount of digging that you do) will depend on the following:

- **Your system level**—For example, if you are working at the district level (or beyond) and you are seeking to develop viable de-implementation approaches that could work across many, many schools, you are likely to dig, search, and postulate much longer than if you are working at, say, the Professional Learning Community level where you might want to get to de-implementation more quickly.

- **The size of de-implementation** you are aiming for. If, for example, you are planning to de-implement several small things like long team meetings and weekend emailing that each chisel away a handful of minutes, you might not want to Fishbone, Sub-Bone and Think Like a Police Detective for each and every one of these. But if you are

(Continued)

(Continued)

> seeking to de-implement a whale (i.e., a big fat area of activity that pervades every aspect of school life and that requires much spaghetti to be untangled to make room for impact), then we strongly recommend that you Postulate deeply, before getting motoring.
>
> In Chapter 6—which covers the (2.2) *Prepare*-step—we illustrate the "fast way" to postulation in an example related to removing a wall display. Here, the backbone team simply undertakes a quick brainstorming session and cross-checks their thinking. And they do this because they deem the risks of removing a wall display to be fairly low. They believe the reasons for the maintenance of a wall display are not that complex and therefore do not require the boiling of the ocean to get to a sufficient level of understanding to design an appropriate de-implementation strategy.

Summary

The **(1.3)** *Postulate*-**step** is focused on explaining what sustains the practices you are seeking to de-implement. By knowing, you confront Chesterton's Fence head on and can develop plans to mitigate the risk that everyone creeps back into the field late at night with carpentry equipment in hand to put the fence back up.

The two key actions that you have undertaken during the **(1.3)** *Postulate*-**step** are as follows:

- **Key Action 1:** Defined the Targeted De-Implementation Areas

- **Key Action 2:** Postulated What Sustains Current Practices to Be De-Implemented

These insights now lead you in two possible directions—backwards or forwards! If, after having explained what sustains the existing practices that you are seeking to de-implement, you conclude that the roots that keep them in place run too deep and that they are too difficult to dig up, then your next step would be to go back to **(1.2) Prospect** to select the next cab off the rank. Whereas, if after prospecting you conclude that the target area is indeed viable to de-implementation, then you path is forwards to the Decide-stage and **(2.1) Propose**.

(1.3) Postulate: Convergent Cross-Checking and Agreeing

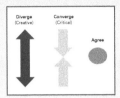

We also recommend that you undertake explicit convergent cross-checking before concluding the (1.3) *Postulate*-step and proceeding forward.

Here are some of the critical cross-checking questions you can consider:

1. Did we ensure that we defined *each* of our target de-implementation areas? And did we do so with sufficient detail?

2. Have we made an explicit decision to Postulate via inductive *or* deductive inquiry? And why did we select the approach that we used?

3. Did we use a structured approach to gather data and interpret our Postulate data, including use of the Six Buckets, Fishbone, and Sub-Bone tools, as appropriate?

4. Did we act like a "police detective" to critically check our interpretations and to converge on the highest probability explanations? Or did we conclude that this was "overkill"?

5. Does this postulation activity give good leads and ideas about viable de-implementation strategies?

6. Are we now ready to move to the next P-step? Are we ready to (2.1) *Propose*? Or has it sent us back to (1.2) *Prospect* because we have concluded that the things that sustain the present might be too complex to unravel?

Part 3

Decide Stage

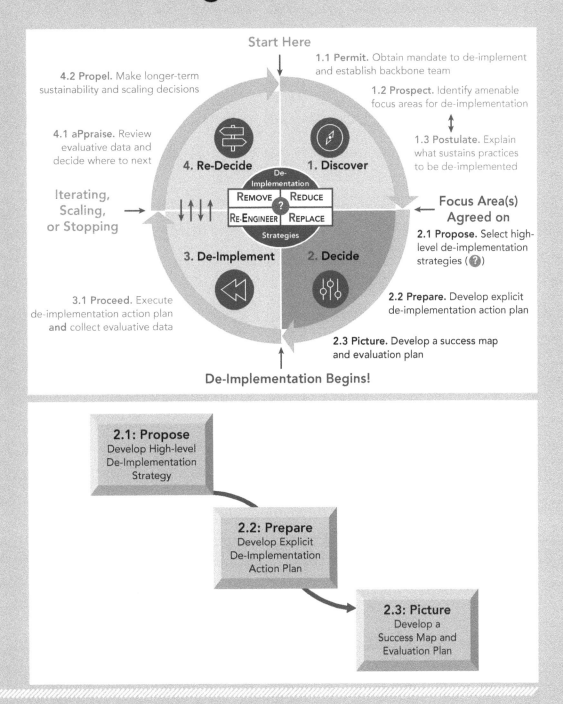

Start Here

4.2 Propel. Make longer-term sustainability and scaling decisions

1.1 Permit. Obtain mandate to de-implement and establish backbone team

1.2 Prospect. Identify amenable focus areas for de-implementation

4.1 aPpraise. Review evaluative data and decide where to next

1.3 Postulate. Explain what sustains practices to be de-implemented

4. Re-Decide

1. Discover

De-Implementation
REMOVE | REDUCE
?
Re-Engineer | Replace
Strategies

Iterating, Scaling, or Stopping

Focus Area(s) Agreed on

2.1 Propose. Select high-level de-implementation strategies (?)

3. De-Implement

2. Decide

3.1 Proceed. Execute de-implementation action plan and collect evaluative data

2.2 Prepare. Develop explicit de-implementation action plan

2.3 Picture. Develop a success map and evaluation plan

De-Implementation Begins!

2.1: Propose
Develop High-level De-Implementation Strategy

2.2: Prepare
Develop Explicit De-Implementation Action Plan

2.3: Picture
Develop a Success Map and Evaluation Plan

Propose (2.1)

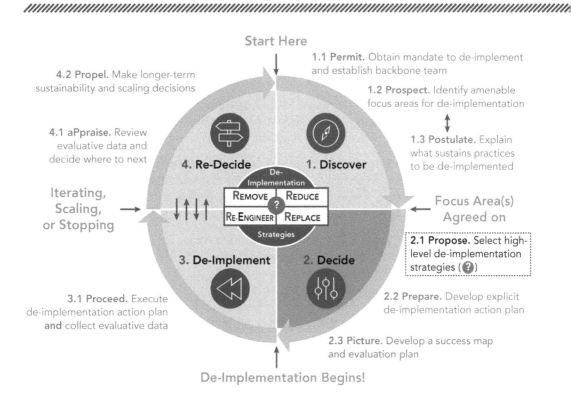

6

Start Here

4.2 Propel. Make longer-term
sustainability and scaling decisions

1.1 Permit. Obtain mandate to de-implement
and establish backbone team

1.2 Prospect. Identify amenable
focus areas for de-implementation

4.1 aPpraise. Review
evaluative data and
decide where to next

1.3 Postulate. Explain
what sustains practices
to be de-implemented

4. Re-Decide

1. Discover

De-Implementation

REMOVE | REDUCE
RE-ENGINEER | REPLACE

Strategies

Iterating,
Scaling,
or Stopping

Focus Area(s)
Agreed on

3. De-Implement

2. Decide

2.1 Propose. Select high-
level de-implementation
strategies (?)

3.1 Proceed. Execute
de-implementation action plan
and collect evaluative data

2.2 Prepare. Develop explicit
de-implementation action plan

2.3 Picture. Develop a success map
and evaluation plan

De-Implementation Begins!

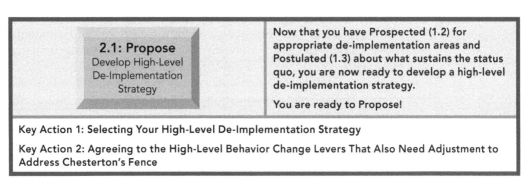

2.1: Propose
Develop High-Level
De-Implementation
Strategy

Now that you have Prospected (1.2) for
appropriate de-implementation areas and
Postulated (1.3) about what sustains the status
quo, you are now ready to develop a high-level
de-implementation strategy.

You are ready to Propose!

Key Action 1: Selecting Your High-Level De-Implementation Strategy

**Key Action 2: Agreeing to the High-Level Behavior Change Levers That Also Need Adjustment to
Address Chesterton's Fence**

Introduction

Back in 1961, when President John F. Kennedy famously declared America's intent to get a man on the moon (and back) before the end of the decade, there was much to be done at NASA. One of the most important early questions was about the *strategy* for achieving this. While, yes, there was broad agreement that rockets were the only game in town, different scientists within NASA had very different ideas about the best proposition for impact. And they needed to come to an agreement before they could even get to designing machines and then to liftoff (Neuman, 2019).

Within NASA, three camps or factions formed among the esteemed scientists (B. R. Brown, 2019):

- **Camp 1: The Build-a-Giant-Rocket Brigade.** This group suggested a very, very large rocket that would take off from Earth, fly all the way to the moon, land, and then fly back home.

- **Camp 2: The Space-Assembly Advocates.** This faction suggested a similar large rocket that would be assembled in space (at a space station, which also needed to be built!), flown from space to the moon, landed, and then flown to the Earth.

- **Camp 3: Lunar Orbit Rendezvous.** This involved the use of a significantly smaller rocket, which would take off from Earth carrying a command module and a small lunar module. The lunar module would detach from the command module and descend to the moon and then fly back up and reattach to the command module for the return journey home.

In the early days of the analysis, most scientists were firmly in Camps 1 and 2. Almost everyone thought Camp 3 was too risky, because it involved too many moving parts—namely, that a detachable lunar module that descends from and then reattaches to a command module had major risks, and misalignment could leave astronauts stranded. Although rendezvous and docking are now considered fairly standard space maneuvers, back in the early 1960s, these were totally untested ideas. However, JFK's hard deadline made the large rockets required for the proponents of Camp 1 and 2 unworkable—it would simply take too long to build and test something at the size and scale required. So, it was Camp 3 or bust.

This story illustrates that after you have agreed to your goal (e.g., getting to the moon and back or de-implementing something in your school/district), there is a lot of subsequent devil-in-the-detail just to get to the high-level strategy. And, of course, without that strategy in place, the danger is that you will get busy down the wrong path—burning lots of time, resources, and goodwill in the process.

Of course, the moon landing is about implementation not de-implementation. It's about moving forwards rather than backwards.[1] But the same principles apply just as much to the latter. If you have a goal to de-implement (say) cigarette smoking, there are many ways you could approach it. You could opt to:

1. quit completely (i.e., **Remove**),

2. cut down your consumption (i.e., **Reduce**),

3. inhale less or move to low-tar products (i.e., **Re-Engineer**), or

4. vape or suck on hard candy instead (i.e., **Replace**).

Of course, not all these options (or camps) are available for every type of de-implementation. For example, if you decide that you need to lose weight, you cannot "remove eating." You need food. However, the other three strategies are still open to you.

But much like the moon landings, you need to *propose* and agree on your high-level strategy before you get anywhere near fleshing out a detailed plan of action. And the whole point of the **(2.1)** *Propose***-step** is to support you to carefully make the same high-level decisions as NASA did, ensuring that you don't commit to something you bitterly regret later.

During this P-step, we are doing two things:

*   **Key Action 1: Selecting Your High-Level De-Implementation Strategy (**i.e., Remove vs. Reduce vs. Re-Engineer vs. Replace**)**

*   **Key Action 2: Agreeing to the High-Level Behavior Change Levers That Also Need Adjustment to Address Chesterton's Fence**

Let's explore each now, in turn.

Key Action 1: Selecting Your High-Level De-Implementation Strategy

One way of identifying all your de-implementation options is to leverage *The Four Rs of De-Implementation*, as illustrated in Figure 6.1, and which you have already seen in earlier parts of the book and as part of the overall *Room for Impact* methodology diagram.

---

[1] There was also some de-implementation occurring as well. The scientists were shedding their prior beliefs and preferences about (Camp 1) building a giant rocket and (Camp 2) Space-assembly. And we bet that this generated one hell of a tug of war!

FIGURE 6.1 The Four Rs (4R) of De-Implementation	
1. COULD WE REMOVE IT?	**2. COULD WE REDUCE IT?**
i.e., could we just **stop doing it** completely? – And HOW could we do this?	i.e., could we **do it less** or could we apply it to fewer people (i.e., **Restrict** it)? — And HOW could we do this?
3. COULD WE RE-ENGINEER IT?	**4. COULD WE REPLACE IT?**
i.e. could we do it **more efficiently**, with fewer steps/actions – And HOW could we do this?	i.e., could we **substitute it** with a more efficient alternative — And WHAT would this be?

Source: Adapted and extended from Hamilton and Hattie (2022); Northern Territory Government (Australia) (2020); Norton and Chambers (2020); Verkerk et al. (2018); V. Wang et al. (2018).

The idea is that for each of your agreed upon de-implementation areas, you identify as many opportunities as possible under each of these four categories.

There are lots of ways that you can gather ideas, including:

- **Brainstorming** – bringing your backbone team and wider colleagues together to ideate (but be careful of group think and being swayed by the opinion of the most powerful person in the room!)

- **Brain writing** – getting people to reflect quietly on their own and to collect ideas in advance before coming to the meeting

- **Delphi Method** – getting people to anonymously complete 4R Sheets (see figure 6.2) and then come together to sift, sort, and extend the lists of ideas (this is good for overcoming the authority bias, as no one will know which ideas have come from the most or least powerful people in the room)

- **Second Opinion** – asking colleagues in other schools and wider system experts for their ideas (but don't treat these as any better or more worthwhile than your own locally generated ideas; instead, see them as additional points of reference)

- **Worst possible idea** – getting people to devise as many bad ideas as possible for each 4R category. There are two benefits to this:

  1. People often feel less self-conscious when asked to contribute bad ideas than when they are asked to contribute good ideas that they fear may subsequently be shot down by others.

  2. Sometimes a good idea is simply the reverse of a bad idea, so if you map all the bad ideas it can help you identify the good!

Optimal Stopping Decision

Suppose you are working at a Professional Learning Community (PLC)/Teaching Team level. In that case, it may be sufficient to bring your colleagues together for a short brainstorming session and to complete this ideation process over the course of an hour or so.

But if you are working at a whole-school or system level, we recommend that you take longer to gather as many ideas as possible and, where possible, to use multiple ideation techniques.

If you have decided to progress multiple de-implementation initiatives, then you will need to repeat each process.

We provide a worked example of how you might undertake this analysis for one de-implementation initiative in Figure 6.2. As you scan the worked example, you can see that it relates to the same curriculum and assessment materials case study that we have been following across the previous P-steps. However, we want to be clear that this worked example is not exhaustive. And we are sure that if you put your minds to it, you could think of many more potential ideas under each of the 4R categories.

FIGURE 6.2   The 4Rs Sheet Worked Example

4RS ANALYSIS	
Overarching Description of De-Implementation Target Area	Development of Bespoke and Localized Teaching, Learning, and Student Assessment Materials by Our Teaching Teams

COULD WE REMOVE IT?	COULD WE REDUCE IT?
Can we: • Stop developing schemes of work/lesson sequences – we just fly by the seats of our pants • Stop writing lesson plans • Stop giving children homework • Stop creating differentiated activities	Reduce by: • No longer making it a requirement that teachers have a full lesson plan for every lesson—i.e., **shorthand lesson planning** • Prohibiting teachers from continually tinkering with their preexisting (and presumably) high-quality materials from previous years—i.e., **no improving the wheel** • Assigning teachers to teach multiple parallel classes so that they teach the same lessons two, three, or even four times in the same day, reducing lesson preparation time • Reducing the frequency of formal reporting on student assessments
COULD WE RE-ENGINEER IT?	**COULD WE REPLACE IT?**
Re-engineer it by: • Getting everyone to put their materials on a **shared drive**, so that autonomous teachers can save time by drawing on their colleagues' resources to more quickly create bespoke materials for their own learners • Implementing **collaborative lesson planning**, where subject teams divide up the curriculum and each take the lead in producing fewer plans, assessments, and activity sheets for specific lessons that they then all adopt/adapt	Replace it with: • A third-party **off-the-shelf curriculum**, with integrated scheme of work, lesson plans, resources, student activity sheets, and so forth • An **intelligent tutoring system** that is used for (automatic) formative assessment generation, administration, and reporting (as well as for student homework) • An **intelligent algorithm** (e.g., a Chatbot) that can be tasked with developing base versions of teaching and learning materials that teachers can adapt/extend

Some of the ideas listed in Figure 6.2 are really, really bad ideas; for example, it's never going to be a good idea to stop planning lesson sequences and to just fly by the seat of your pants! And AI Chatbots are so new to education that we do not (yet) know whether we can trust the outputs and we do not yet have good safeguards in place. For many of the others—they may (or may not) be suitable depending on your local context.

Converging and Agreeing

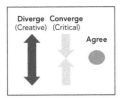

Now that you have a long list of *potential* de-implementation strategies, the next critical step is to converge and agree on the one(s) that are the most viable. Two ways you can do this are via **Deliberative Dialogue** and the use of a **Formal Scorecard**. Let's look at each in turn.

Deliberative Dialogue

This is the art of having a discussion to:

- Check that all the (obvious) 4R options have been identified

- Weigh up the pros and cons of each option

- Consider the quality of evidence supporting those pros and cons

- Propose and agree on your high-level theory of action (i.e., what you will do)

In the textbox below, we illustrate a deliberative dialogue between Rohit, Samantha, and Eddie, who are working through the opportunities and obstacles related to the ideas outlined in the 4Rs Worked Example, in Figure 6.2.

Rohit:	So, do we think we've thought of all the options under each of the 4Rs?
Samantha:	I'm pretty sure we haven't, but I can't think of anything else.
Eddie:	I also can't think of anything else. I'll take it as an action to ask around for second and third opinions from the wider group. But in the meantime, we may as well discuss the options we've identified.
Rohit:	That sounds good. Shall we start with the "Remove" quadrant? What do you both think of the ideas we identified?
Eddie:	To be honest, I don't think that any of them are viable. We can't stop doing lesson sequence planning or individual lesson plans and the children do need differentiated activities. Although, maybe the degree of differentiation could be reduced.

(Continued)

(Continued)

Samantha:	I totally agree. There's no question that our teaching materials need careful preplanning. If *someone* isn't doing this, we are literally all going in and winging it. And that's bad news.
Rohit:	I also agree. We can't "remove" the planning and preparation activity. But the real question is whether we need to do it ourselves. Whether we know our students best and only we can produce the materials—with all those materials looking different, from teacher to teacher across the school. Or whether we could just buy in a third-party package that's been built and evaluated by experts. The "Replace" Quadrant.
Eddie:	You're right, Rohit, but even discussing this can be a bit like a red rag to a bull. Maybe we should look at some of the other quadrants first and come back to "Replace" at the end?
Samantha:	I agree. I think some of the "Reduce" options could work. We all tend to overengineer our lesson plans and write them out in full, in case the leadership or district want to view them. But we've already been told we don't need to do this and that short-hand plans are fine—as long as they make sense to us.
Eddie:	Yeah, but I'm not sure how much time we would really save. Maybe ten minutes here and twenty minutes there. And it might add up, but I can't see it significantly reducing our workload if we are still doing all the planning ourselves. Oh, and I'm also not convinced that if we ask our colleagues to stop tinkering with their materials, they will actually stop.
Rohit:	Agreed. And we've already reduced the formal recording of student assessment. I don't think we can take that one down any further without serious questions and pushback from the school board and parents. So, what about the "Re-Engineer" Quadrant?
Samantha:	We could easily set up a shared drive and ask our colleagues to put all their existing materials up.
Eddie:	I'm skeptical. Yes, it's easy to set the cloud drive up. But it will end up being like a rummage sale and people will end up taking even more time to wade through it all than if they had just continued using their own materials.

Rohit: Also, I remember the time that Samantha let me use her teaching materials for covalent bonding because I didn't have anything. It actually took me more time to decipher it than if I'd just done it myself from scratch.

Samantha: Hey, those materials are really good! But I get your point. And, the more I think about it, I'm not sure everyone will want to put their stuff on a shared drive anyway. Some of our colleagues can be a bit reluctant to share their resources.

Eddie: OK, so what about a shared curriculum where we all come together and build something from scratch that everyone can use?

Rohit: That sounds like us *adding* to everyone else's workload—not *subtracting*. And how can we be sure that what we have quickly "cobbled together" will be profoundly better than a third-party program developed and evaluated by experts?

Eddie: But doesn't a third-party program undermine our professionalism and the professionalism of our colleagues?

Rohit: I'm just saying it as it is. Anything we develop is going to be quicker and undergo less testing than something developed by an expert. That doesn't mean it will necessarily be less good, but I'm not convinced.

Samantha: So, we're in the "Replace" quadrant. The red rag to a bull.

Rohit: I really think we should consider it. We have the budget to buy something in. Why are we all sitting up every night like some cottage industry, continually reinventing the wheel when we could just do our work with high quality off-the-shelf resources and go home?

Eddie: I have to say, it is worth considering. It would definitely save the most time if we could get it going. It's the attitudinal barrier that we would have to confront the most—we recorded this in our Fishbone diagram. I'd probably feel guilty if I wasn't sitting at home putting together my own specific local examples that I know my kids will get. If I was just using the cookie-cutter pack. I know everyone will feel the same.

(Continued)

(Continued)

> **Samantha:** I know there are off-the-shelf programs that *apparently* work. I was listening to a podcast about this a few weeks ago. Honestly, I don't think the parents or kids would notice if we changed our materials. It's more about us and our sense of professionalism. Assuming we could agree on a program that really does have strong evidence.
>
> **Eddie:** And a lot of them have really detailed scripts and scaffolds, so they are probably not as hard to pick up and use as when Rohit used Samantha's materials.
>
> **Rohit:** So, are we kind of agreeing that the off-the-shelf curriculum is the way to go?
>
> **Eddie:** Yes, but with lots of caveats. We need evidence it is *likely* to be at least as effective as our current locally developed materials. And we need to think through how we convince everyone else to get on board.
>
> **Samantha:** We already have some good leads about how we could convince people. We did the Six Buckets Fishbone—so we understand the culture, history, and beliefs about why everyone is developing their own bespoke materials. We should look at how we could tackle some of the critical bones on that Fishbone next!

You might have noticed that Rohit, Samantha, and Eddie have not (yet) come to a firm conclusion about which of their 4Rs ideas to take forward. Part of the reason is that through their dialogue they are gradually being drawn toward actions in the "Replacement" quadrant. And these are the hardest of all to progress, because they involve both de-implementation of existing (inefficient) actions *and* their substitution with more effective practices.

If this is not enough to contend with, there is also an additional challenge: confirming that the "Replacement" action is truly more effective. You will be able to find tools and processes in our sister book *Building to Impact* that are explicitly designed to enable you to find and then evaluate high-probability additions, prior to implementation. However, in the textbox on Pareto analysis, we also provide a shorthand thinking tool that you can also use if you are unfamiliar with *Building to Impact*.

Pareto Analysis

In addition to the Replacement action selection protocols that we provide in *Building to Impact*, another suggestion is that you can undertake Pareto analysis. This is a short-hand strategy to confirm that you are swapping one set of actions for another that generate genuine improvement vs. the status quo.

Perhaps the best illustration of Pareto analysis is presented by Stephen Covey (1989) in his book *The Seven Habits of Highly Effective People*. A man is sawing through a big log of wood with a blunt saw. Someone asks him, "Why don't you sharpen the saw?" The man replies, "I haven't got time." The important point here is that Pareto analysis goes beyond stopping doing things that are ineffective or counterproductive. It is about stopping doing good things to create time to do even better things. If you want to cut through the log, then sawing is good, but stopping sawing to sharpen the saw is better. And, possibly better still: get a chain saw!

Here's a protocol that is useful for getting people started with Pareto analysis:

1. Ask people what they would do if there were one more hour in the day. Call this X.

2. Ask people what they would do if there were one less hour in the day. Call this Y.

3. If X and Y are not the same, substitute X for Y. When X and Y is the same, you have reached Pareto optimality.

Another reason that Rohit, Samantha, and Eddie may be finding it difficult to come to a firm conclusion is that dialogue without pre-agreed upon criteria can sometimes result in you going round and round in circles. So, onto the Formal Scorecard, which provides an alternative and more formalistic approach to 4Rs selection.

Formal Scorecard

A second approach you can use to review your 4R options is a formal rubric. In Figure 6.3, we provide what we call the **AGREE Criteria**—a range of questions about whether people are likely to find the action **A**cceptable, whether it has a strong **G**oal fit, how much **R**isk it generates, how **E**asy it is to do, and how much **E**xpenditure (i.e., funds) are required to make it all happen. These build on and extend the HEAT criteria that we introduced in (1.2) *Prospect*.

FIGURE 6.3   The AGREE Criteria

DOMAIN	CRITERIA
Acceptable?	• Is it acceptable to *all* stakeholders, e.g., ○ Will teachers be prepared to do it? Will they buy in? ○ Will students, parents, and the community accept it? ○ Will system-level stakeholders allow us to do it? Do we have permission?
Goal fit	• Will it help us achieve our *Room for Impact* goals, e.g., ○ Will it save time and how much? ○ Will it save resources or money and how much? ○ Will it do so without harming learner outcomes?
Risk	• Will there be any negative side-effects from de-implementing, e.g., ○ Will it reduce overall student learning outcomes? And what evidence do we have to support this? ○ Will it widen any equity deficits that exist in our school or system? ○ Will it demotivate our teachers?
Ease	• Will we be able to do it, e.g., ○ How easy will it be to de-implement? ○ Will it be behaviorally difficult for our teams to stop or reduce the activity? ○ Will it take a long time? ○ Can we do it by ourselves or do we need external support?
Expenditure	• Total cost ÷ Total number of *Direct Beneficiaries* **Note:** You also need to factor *in recurring costs*, not just the initial setup and also subtract any resource savings

You can then come to judgments for each de-implementation opportunity against each of the AGREE criteria. And as you do so, you will also want to think carefully about the quality of evidence that you are leveraging to make this judgment:

- Is it a hunch, an inkling, or an opinion?

- Is it based on peer-reviewed evidence?

- Is any peer-reviewed/systematic evidence from a context similar to yours?

You can then use the AGREE Scoring Matrix, illustrated in Figure 6.4, to score and rank the various de-implementation opportunities that you have identified. Note that these scorings are about the local fit; they do not represent universal judgments that you can plug-in-and-play within your school or district. You have to ask these questions within your local context, and your scoring outputs are—therefore—likely to be very different, even from the school across the road. It's

FIGURE 6.4 AGREE Scoring Matrix

DE-IMPLEMENTATION OPPORTUNITY	ACCEPTABLE? 1–5 5 = VERY ACCEPTABLE	GOAL FIT 1–5 5 = HIGH GOAL FIT	RISK 1–5 5 = LOW RISK	EASE 1–5 5 = VERY EASY	EXPENDITURE 1–5 5 = LOW EXPENDITURE	TOTAL
Stop developing schemes of work	1	2	1	2	5	11/25
Stop developing lesson plans	1	3	1	2	5	12/25
Build a shared curriculum	4	5	4	1	4	18/25
Get everyone to put their materials on a shared drive	2	5	4	2	5	18/25
Shorthand lesson planning	5	2	3	4	5	19/25
No more tinkering rule	2	3	3	2	5	15/25
Buy in off-the-shelf curriculum	2	5	3	2	1	13/25
Buy in intelligent tutoring system	4	3	3	3	2	15/25

about identifying the conduct that is most appropriate and fits your local context best. You might also wish to play around with the weightings for each category area depending on what you privilege the most.

You can also use the Impact vs. Difficulty Matrix, as illustrated in Figure 6.5, to quickly sift and sort your proposed de-implementation ideas.

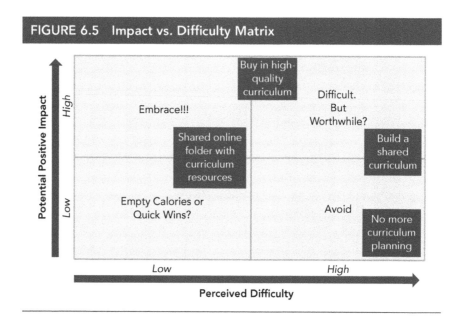

FIGURE 6.5   Impact vs. Difficulty Matrix

After undertaking this analysis, and traversing through Divergent and Convergent thinking approaches, Rohit, Samantha, and Eddie have concluded that:

> a third-party *off-the-shelf curriculum,* with an integrated scheme of work, lesson plans, resources, and student activity sheets

is their *best option for impact.* They believe that it will save significant teacher preparation time and that it might also increase student outcomes. This is provided that the expert curriculum developers have carefully evaluated the selected material for success in contexts similar to the teachers' own. It's interesting that they come to this conclusion—even though other options scored much higher in the Figure 6.4 AGREE table. But as they engaged in deep dialogue, the rich discourse led them in a different direction from the raw numbers.

They then went on to review different off-the-shelf curriculum options and visited two schools to see their preferred curriculum in action. The important point here is that even if the "off-the-shelf" curriculum isn't as good as the curriculum the teachers would have prepared themselves, the difference in quality between a bespoke curriculum and an off-the-shelf curriculum may not be great enough to justify the extra time it would take. That time might be better spent elsewhere!

However, Rohit, Samantha, and Eddie are under no illusions. They know that taking forward a third-party curriculum is going to be hard. Because as well as implementing a new initiative, they are simultaneously seeking to get everyone in their school to stop their existing practices of sitting at home at night and developing their own bespoke materials from scratch. Old habits can die hard. Like Chesterton's Fence, without careful pre-planning everyone may creep back into the field late at night and put the fence back up again. And for Rohit, Samantha, and Eddie, this would represent the worst of all worlds: buying a new, expensive curriculum and training everyone to use it—while everyone just continues to do what they did before.

High-cost and *no* de-implementation impact!

Key Action 2: Agreeing on the High-Level Behavior Change Levers That Also Need Adjustment to Address Chesterton's Fence

Now that you have:

- prospected and agreed on your de-implementation priority areas (1.1)

- postulated what maintains status quo (you did this during 1.2, using e.g., Six Buckets, Fishbone, and Sub-bone)

- proposed a de-implementation strategy (i.e., one or more of the 4Rs) during this P-step

you now have everything you need to confront Chesterton's Fence.

Your understanding of what maintains the status quo (in the form of your Six Buckets; Fishbone; and/or Sub-bone analysis—developed during 1.2) gives you a local map of all the possible reasons that you and your colleagues might (consciously and subconsciously) resist de-implementation of your engrained existing practices. And, having now selected your preferred de-implementation strategy, you are better able to visualize which of the drivers on that Fishbone are likely to come into play.

Figure 6.6 recaps the Fishbone that Rohit, Samantha, and Eddie sketched out during (1.3) *Postulate*. Another, more readable, version of this diagram is available on page 113.

Now that they have decided on a "Replacement" strategy, in the form of an off-the-shelf curriculum package, they can return to this Fishbone and

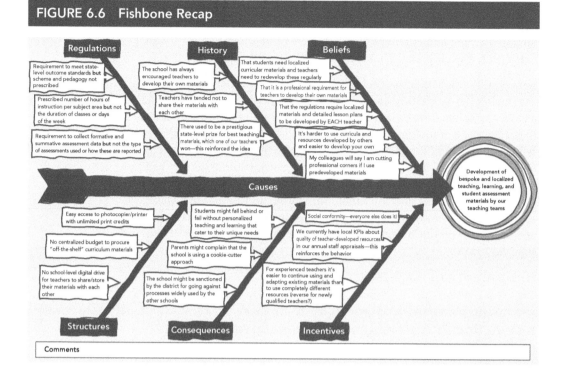

FIGURE 6.6   Fishbone Recap

consider the elements that are likely to generate the greatest resistance to de-implementation of everyone developing their own bespoke and localized teaching and learning materials. We pick up their dialogue again in the text box below:

Rohit:	Looking back at our Fishbone, what elements do we think are most relevant given that we have now opted for a strategy in the "Replace" quadrant?
Samantha:	I don't think it's the regulations. We can put that to one side. The curriculum we are planning to buy in covers all the policy requirements.
Eddie:	I agree. It's more about the engrained culture of it being a badge of honor to develop your own resources, or the belief that it's a "requirement" to do this . . .
Rohit:	And the belief that locally developed resources will always be better than third-party materials?
Samantha:	Yes! Plus the fact that we make it easy for teachers to print and photocopy their own resources and that our staff performance appraisals currently have objectives around teachers developing their own resources.

Eddie:	So, let me write this up on the whiteboard as a summary list of bullets:

- belief that it's a requirement to develop your own +
- belief that it's better to develop your own +
- habit of doing it over the years +
- performance objectives that reinforce the practices +
- the physical environment of the school allowing teachers to easily print off their own resources

Rohit:	Great summary! So, what can we do about it?

The question, now, is how do we use this knowledge to identify appropriate countermeasures? The good news is that our friends in the healthcare sector, particularly those focused on stopping people from engaging in addictive behaviors, have already developed a typology of behavior change strategies, which we have adapted and extended in Figure 6.7.

This typology outlines nine countermeasure domains ranging from policy change, monitoring, rewards, and sanctions to restructuring the physical environment. Under each of these nine domains are between two to four actions that *could* be implemented, and the final column gives some generic examples of what each *might* look like. Some of these examples relate to the de-implementation of bespoke materials development by teachers (i.e., the de-implementation initiative being undertaken by Eddie, Rohit, and Samantha), and some relate to other case studies that will be introduced later in the book. So you might want to come back and review Figure 6.7 again once you have reached the end of the book!

However, the basic idea is that you connect one or more of these "Domains" and "Actions" to specific areas in your Fishbone. They then act like "antidotes" neutralizing the impact of those specific "bones" and "sub-bones."

The next step is for Rohit, Samantha, and Eddie to use this Behavioral Change Countermeasures Map to identify all the potential actions and then agree on the ones they will take forward. Figure 6.8 illustrates how this analysis can be done. In the left column, each of the relevant Fishbone nodes are listed. In the second column all the relevant "antidote" options are outlined, drawing on the Behavior Change Countermeasures Map for ideas. Then the agreed upon "Antidote Actions" are listed along with (in the final column) an explanation—that is, *the why*? You can also use the AGREE criteria, detailed in Figure 6.3, to help you get your agreed upon Antidote Actions.

FIGURE 6.7   Behavior Change Countermeasures Map

DOMAIN	ACTIONS	EXAMPLES
Policy Change	Amend policy to *discourage* the behavior	• School policy changed to discourage teachers from developing their teaching and learning materials from scratch
	Amend policy to *prohibit* the behavior, or at least to make it difficult or impossible	• School policy changed to ban teachers from checking their emails during evenings and weekends
Goal Setting and Planning	Informal agreement on de-implementation goals	• Verbal agreement to share teaching resources with colleagues to reduce planning time
	Formal behavioral change contract	• Colleagues jointly sign a behavioral change contract and commit to sanctions if they break it, e.g., providing lesson cover or playground duty for a week, etc.
	Individual action planning	• Educator makes a personal de-implementation plan in writing
	Gap analysis between agreed goals and current behaviors	• Educators review monitoring data against their implementation of an agreed upon centralized detention system to compare their intended progress with their actual level of progress
Monitoring	Monitoring by others without feedback	• Spot checks by school leadership team
	Monitoring by others with feedback	• Spot checks with private 1:1 feedback; or spot checks with a public scoreboard
	Self-monitoring	• Maintaining a habit journal and recording every instance where you failed to de-implement and the environmental cues and triggers
Social Support	Informal self-help support	• Encouraging—but not mandating—colleagues to form a buddy system
	Formal self-help group meetings	• A formal self-help group is established, with educators attending and reporting on their progress and next steps
	Social comparison of outcomes	• A scoreboard of success is publicly maintained, i.e., chalking up and celebrating the wins
	Comparative imagining of future outcomes	• Educators collectively imagine what they will do with the personal time saved from, e.g., reducing the quantity of student assessments

DOMAIN	ACTIONS	EXAMPLES
Providing Information	Information on the consequences of not de-implementing	• Providing comparative data from other education systems that, e.g., have shorter school days/years
	Information from a credible authority	• Research/insights from a credible education researcher about the opportunity-costs of de-implementation
Restructuring Physical Environment	Adding prompts to physical environment	• Placing a sticker on the photocopier to remind teachers to use centrally developed materials rather than to develop their own
	Adding environmental frictions	• Switching the email server off at 5 p.m. or moving the photocopier to a more remote part of the building
	Removing behavioral cues	• Removing requirement for, e.g., subject teachers to attend parents meeting, to reinforce that they no longer need to write individual student reports—because the homeroom teacher now takes care of this
Habit Re-Engineering	Instructions on how to perform the new behaviors	• Providing training on alternative actions
	Providing Prompts/Cues	• Providing WhatsApp reminders *not* to perform an activity; and sending these at the times of day when the activity is usually done
	Behavioral rehearsal and repetition	• Rehearsing the new behavioral routine during formal social support sessions
Identity	Reframing group identity	• "We care most about our efficiency of impact"
	Reframing individual identity	• "Work-life balance is important to me"
	Cueing incompatible beliefs	• "The highest quality teaching and learning resources have undergone comprehensive evaluation" vs. "I like developing my own resources but don't have the time to evaluate them rigorously"
Rewards and Consequences	Material incentive	• Provision of treats/vouchers for highest performing de-implementors
	Social incentive	• Weekly team review of the scoreboard and public praise from senior leadership to highest performers
	Material sanctions	• Not receiving annual increment; receiving a fine/penalty
	Social sanctions	• Being rotated for special duties that are unpopular such as litter patrol

Source: Adapted and extended from Michie et al. (2014); Atkins et al. (2017); and Farmer et al. (2021).

FIGURE 6.8   Antidote Actions Framework

FISHBONE NODE	ANTIDOTE OPTIONS: WHAT *COULD* WE DO?	ANTIDOTE ACTIONS: WHAT *WILL* WE DO?	WHY?
Teacher Habit/ "Muscle Memory"	• Send WhatsApp reminders to staff in evening when they usually do their curriculum development work • Formal behavioral change contract • Social sanctions	WhatsApp reminders	Other approaches seem too "Orwellian" to start with. But we will consider them later.
Belief that teachers should always develop their own materials	• Reframing group identity • Cueing incompatible beliefs	Both of the identified strategies—in particular we could cue/seed the incompatible belief that teaching materials need to have undergone rigorous evaluation to verify their effectiveness, prior to use	It will be challenging for our teachers to "rigorously" evaluate their own materials. The new belief primes everyone to adopt third-party materials that have been carefully tested in a wide range of similar contexts to our own.
Belief that locally developed materials are always better	• Information from a credible authority to debunk this belief, or at least frame it in terms of costs and benefits • Information on consequences of maintaining status quo	Information from a credible authority to debunk this belief	The researcher team that developed the curriculum package has agreed to present their evaluation data to our teaching teams.
Staff performance objectives reinforce the practice	• Amend local policies to *prohibit* self-developed materials • Amend local policies to *discourage* self-developed materials	Amend local policies to *discourage* self-developed materials	We don't want to dictate, as we don't know for sure that the new curriculum will be effective until we implement it and then evaluate the results.
Physical environment enables status quo	• Move photocopier to distant location • Put sign above photocopier reinforcing use of the new curriculum • Prompts and cue posters in staff room	All of these	They are all very easy to implement.
Support required to implement replacement actions, i.e., use of new external curriculum	• Training in new use of new curriculum materials • Social incentives, e.g., scoreboard • Social support network, e.g., embedding review and self-help cycles within team PLC meetings	• Training in new use of new curriculum materials • Social support network embedded in existing PLC meetings	We need to provide training in the new curriculum anyway. Embedding social support in existing PLCs will take less time than establishing new structures.

With their high-level de-implementation strategy agreed upon and their Chesterton's Fence "antidotes" mapped out, Rohit, Samantha, and Eddie are now ready to build this out in a more detailed de-implementation plan.

Summary

During the **(2.1)** *Propose*-**step**, like Rohit, Samantha, and Eddie, you will have undertaken the following Key Actions:

- **Key Action 1:** Selected Your High-Level De-Implementation Strategy (i.e., Remove vs. Reduce vs. Re-Engineer vs. Replace)

- **Key Action 2:** Agreed to the High-Level Behavior Change Levers That Also Need Adjustment to Address Chesterton's Fence

You are now ready to work these high-level ideas into a more detailed plan of action, which takes you to *(2.2) Prepare*!

(2.1) Propose: Convergent Cross-Checking and Agreeing

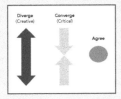

Before you get to (2.2) Prepare, here are some of the critical cross-checking questions for you to consider:

1. Have we used the right tools and processes to map and identify our 4Rs options?

2. Are we sure we have identified *all* the viable 4Rs opportunities?

3. Have we carefully considered all the pros and cons of each option?

4. Do we now have a strong consensus within the Backbone group and the wider organization?

5. Have we gone back to our Fishbone map from **(1.3) Postulate** and explicitly connected it to our proposed de-implementation strategy?

6. Have we identified and cross-checked the key de-implementation derailers?

7. Have we mapped, cross-checked, and agreed upon appropriate "antidote" countermeasures?

8. Are we confident in our "antidotes"?

If so, we are now ready to progress to (2.2) *Prepare*!

Prepare (2.2)

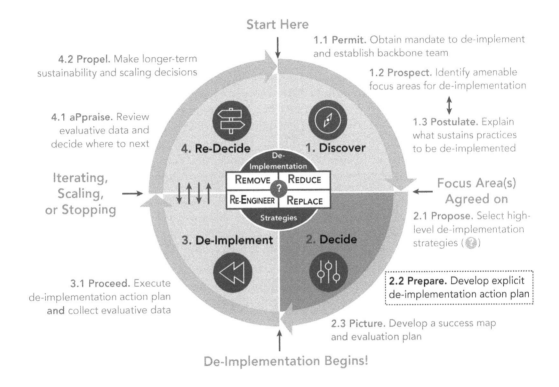

Start Here

1.1 Permit. Obtain mandate to de-implement and establish backbone team

4.2 Propel. Make longer-term sustainability and scaling decisions

1.2 Prospect. Identify amenable focus areas for de-implementation

4.1 aPpraise. Review evaluative data and decide where to next

1.3 Postulate. Explain what sustains practices to be de-implemented

4. Re-Decide

1. Discover

De-Implementation

REMOVE | REDUCE

RE-ENGINEER | REPLACE

Strategies

Iterating, Scaling, or Stopping

Focus Area(s) Agreed on

2.1 Propose. Select high-level de-implementation strategies

3. De-Implement

2. Decide

2.2 Prepare. Develop explicit de-implementation action plan

3.1 Proceed. Execute de-implementation action plan **and** collect evaluative data

2.3 Picture. Develop a success map and evaluation plan

De-Implementation Begins!

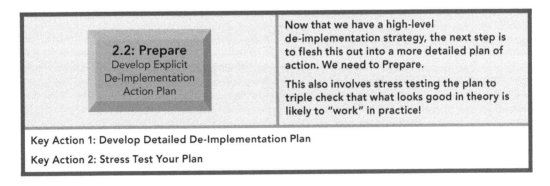

2.2: Prepare
Develop Explicit
De-Implementation
Action Plan

Now that we have a high-level de-implementation strategy, the next step is to flesh this out into a more detailed plan of action. We need to Prepare.

This also involves stress testing the plan to triple check that what looks good in theory is likely to "work" in practice!

Key Action 1: Develop Detailed De-Implementation Plan

Key Action 2: Stress Test Your Plan

Introduction

The world's (currently) tallest building is the Burj Khalifa—a tower that is a jaw-dropping 828 meters in height. It comprises 163 floors, 57 elevators, 3.33 million sq. ft. of floor space, 24,348 windows; involved 22 million person-hours to build; and had a construction cost of US$1.5 billion (Dupré, 2013). The vision was that the Burj Khalifa would be the centerpiece of a much wider redevelopment of downtown Dubai in the oil-rich United Arab Emirates. And, boy, does it stand out.

But there was a lot of subsequent devil-in-the detail from the broad-stroke vision of constructing the world's tallest building to "making it happen." This did *not* start with hiring a construction team and allowing them to iteratively build level upon level, learning, adapting, tinkering, and reversing as they go.

Instead, the process started with mapping the contours of the land, drilling boreholes 140 meters down to plot the subterranean rock, and determining the types of foundations that would be needed to make the tower stable. It also involved being aware of local environmental factors, for example, by identifying building materials that could uniformly tolerate temperatures that rise to over 50 degrees Celsius in the summer months and the extreme pressures of the high-building weight.

The highly detailed architectural designs were prepared by Skidmore, Owings, & Merrill, the Chicago-based team that also designed the Sears Tower (renamed the Willis Tower in 2009). These plans were then tested on small scale models and computer simulations long before any diggers and cranes arrived on site to break ground. The designs mapped out what was to be done—inch-by-inch—from the steel superstructure to the concrete, the glass, the cladding, the piping, the electrics, the lift mechanics, the internal zoning, and the external connection with the wider redevelopment of downtown Dubai. Thousands of pages of designs and technical specifications were provided to the construction teams to follow step-by-step.

This all had to happen in advance of the construction, because with building projects, once you break ground and begin the construction process, the cost of reversing back or iterating when the building is already several floors up is eye wateringly prohibitive. And this is why you have to carefully design and cross-check each inch of floor space before the people in hard hats get anywhere near a concrete mixer.

What you are going to do during **(2.2)** *Prepare* is similar to what Skidmore, Owings, & Merrill did (and indeed all architects have to do). You are going to do the following:

- **Key Action 1: Develop Detailed De-Implementation Plan**. This involves mapping out the precise (step-by-step) actions that are required to bring your 4R strategy to life, including the activities linked to your behavioral change levers (a.k.a. Chesterton's Fence).

- **Key Action 2: Stress Test Your Plan.** You are doing this to make sure that what seems like a good idea on paper has the highest chance of generating impact in reality by predicting the likely derailers and adjusting your plan to include countermeasures to defend against their negative impact.

Of course, one of the critical differences between your plan and that of Skidmore, Owings, & Merrill is that you are seeking to de-implement, to remove an object or activity from your environment rather than add one. Another key difference is that what you are planning to de-implement is (likely) a lot less complex than the Burj Khalifa. And, depending on whether your strategy involves Removing, Reducing, Re-engineering, or Replacing, we think that you might find different tools and different amounts of planning more (or less) useful.

In this chapter, we are going to illustrate the planning process from the perspective of each of the 4Rs, recapped in Figure 7.1.

FIGURE 7.1   Recapping the 4Rs of De-Implementation

1. CAN WE REMOVE IT?	2. CAN WE REDUCE IT?
i.e., could we just **stop doing it** completely? — And HOW could we do this?	i.e., could **do it less;** OR could we apply it to fewer people (i.e., **Restrict** it)? — And HOW could we do this?
3. COULD WE RE-ENGINEER IT?	**4. COULD WE REPLACE IT?**
i.e., could we do it **more efficiently,** with fewer steps/actions? — And HOW could we do this?	i.e., **substitute it** with a more efficient alternative? — And WHAT would this be?

Source: Adapted and extended from Hamilton and Hattie (2022); Northern Territory Government (Australia) (2020); Norton and Chambers (2020); Verkerk et al. (2018); V. Wang et al. (2018).

The approaches to preparing and planning (and the likely derailers) vary significantly across those 4Rs. So, in the text that follows, we provide a range of tools that you can leverage, and we illustrate these across several de-implementation case studies.

Preparing to REMOVE case study

When Sizewell High established their *Room for Impact* Backbone Organization, they decided to focus on the "low-hanging fruit" that they could quickly tackle to build their confidence and generate quick wins.

The backbone team felt that quick, easy, and immediate impact would build everyone's confidence to then tackle bigger (and more contentious) de-implementation projects down the line.

Their list of "low-hanging fruits" included:

- Stand-up team meetings to shorten meetings (*re-engineering* the meeting process)

- *Reducing* the number of lesson observations

- *Removing* the need to write lesson plans of any kind, or in any detail

- *Removing* wall displays from classrooms and corridors.

For each one of these de-implementation initiatives, the *Room for Impact* backbone team:

- Postulated (1.3) to understand what sustained existing practices;

- Proposed (2.1) a high-level de-implementation strategy; and then

- Prepared (2.2) a more detailed de-implementation action plan.

Let's now follow this process for **Removing display from classrooms and corridors**.

The backbone team started by defining this specific target area for de-implementation, as illustrated in Figure 7.2.

FIGURE 7.2   Sizewell High—Defining the Target Area

TARGET AREA FOR DE-IMPLEMENTATION			
Overarching Description of De-Implementation Target Area	Development of Wall Displays for Classrooms, Corridors, and Public Areas of the School		
SUBCOMPONENTS	WHEN/WHERE DOES THIS OCCUR?	WHO DOES THIS?	HOW MUCH TIME IS SPENT?
1. Development of classroom displays	Usually at the start of each term on the display boards that are located on the walls in each classroom	The teacher who "owns" the specific classroom; sometimes as a class project with one or more of their student groups	20 hours per term, per teacher

SUBCOMPONENTS	WHEN/WHERE DOES THIS OCCUR?	WHO DOES THIS?	HOW MUCH TIME IS SPENT?
2. **Development of corridor displays**	Also usually at the start of each term, with adjustments/additions being made for Christmas, Easter, and other special festivals – on the display boards on the walls and corridors throughout the school	The subject teams that "own" specific corridors, usually working collaboratively to agree on the theme for each board and then to produce the displays	8 hours per term, per teacher

Using the AGREE criteria, the Backbone team and their wider colleagues in the school concluded that the production of wall displays was disproportionately time intensive for little discernible impact on student outcomes. Their rationale was the following:

1. While the global literature suggested a strong relationship between a school building's level of heating, lighting, acoustics, and security, they could not find convincing evidence that the presence or absence or quality of wall displays made a significant difference to student outcomes.

2. There were no schoolwide programs currently being implemented that explicitly leveraged wall display as a critical active ingredient in the theory of improvement. This meant that there was minimal risk of harming an important part of an existing initiative—that is, the existing wall display was, in Lyn Sharratt's framing, "pretty" rather than "pretty useful" (Sharratt, 2019).

3. When students were asked in voice groups to recall the displays on the wall in their homerooms, they really struggled. Generally, they remembered the colors, less often the topic or project areas, and many admitted to looking at the displays once or twice (often for less than thirty seconds). Then the displays "just faded into the background." They were like "wallpaper."

Once it was agreed that wall displays were a suitable target area for de-implementation, the Sizewell High Backbone Team used the 4R framework to map their options, as illustrated in Figure 7.3.

FIGURE 7.3   Sizewell High 4Rs Analysis

4Rs ANALYSIS	
Overarching description of de-implementation target area	Development of wall displays for classrooms, corridors, and public areas of the school

CAN WE REMOVE IT?	CAN WE REDUCE IT?
• **Stop** doing wall display completely	• Do/refresh wall display **less frequently**, e.g., once-per year, rather than once per term • Have **less wall display**, e.g., take down some of the display boards in classrooms and corridors

COULD WE RE-ENGINEER IT?	COULD WE REPLACE IT?
• Have the **students take total ownership** for wall display, so that staff don't have to get involved • **Make wall display more useful**, e.g., by introducing a "Bump-It-Up Wall" approach that uses wall display to track student progress	• **LCD screens** that display generic content • **Generic and subject-specific posters** that we buy, laminate, and put up once in each area of the school and (hopefully) don't need to replace again for at least 5 years. • **Lockable display boards** so that teachers cannot easily swap over the content

During sessions with the wider teaching faculty, the backbone team explored each of these options in turn. The general consensus was that if there was no discernible impact on student outcomes of the current approach to wall displays, there was no point continuing with wall displays but just refreshing it less. There was also no point in getting the students to take responsibility for it. This would require teacher coordination and supervision that would actually take more time. What skills would the students be learning? How to cut, glue, and cooperate? These skills and dispositions were already being covered in other areas of the curriculum. There was, however, much deeper discussion on the possibility of making wall displays more useful. But, in the end, the backbone team discounted this because it would require *more* time and effort, whereas their quest was to find things to de-implement!

The LCD screens were also discounted because of the high cost and low returns. And while everyone agreed that the generic posters were lower cost, there would still be an upfront time investment to agree where to get the posters from and which ones should go in which parts of the school. So, the (gung-ho) conclusion was that everyone should just stop doing wall display completely.

This brought the backbone to the **Chesterton's Fence discussion** to the process of understanding *why* everyone started putting up wall displays in the first place and the drivers that sustained it. They decided not to use the Fishbone tool for this de-implementation area because they felt that wall-display behaviors were perhaps not that complex to explain. So, instead, they held an ideational session with a flipchart and came up with the ideas illustrated in Figure 7.4.

FIGURE 7.4　Sizewell High's *Postulate* Analysis

WHAT SUSTAINS WALL DISPLAYS IN OUR SCHOOL?

- Belief that they make school more welcoming for students
- Belief that they help students to learn
- Belief that they are a professional requirement—i.e., we have to do them to be good educators
- Many teachers like doing them—i.e., the fun art and craft dimension
- Competition between teachers and teaching teams—i.e., who can make the best wall display
- Display boards line all the corridors and classrooms—i.e., the physical environment encourages the behavior
- Availability of colored A3 backing paper in the stationary cupboards to easily decorate the boards

The Backbone team then explored the "antidotes" for each driver, using the Behavior Change Countermeasures Map as a source of inspiration. Again, because wall display was considered a relatively simple de-implementation area to tackle, they did not explicitly use the Antidote Actions Framework. Instead, they opted to ideate the options on a flip chart and to annotate the agreed upon strategies with an asterisk. This analysis is illustrated in Figure 7.5.

FIGURE 7.5　Sizewell High Antidote Options

ANTIDOTE OPTIONS

- Briefing session by the leadership team that unpacks the (limited) research evidence on the returns to student achievement from wall displays—i.e., tackles the belief drivers*
- Remove the display boards from the corridors
- Social contract with teachers *not* to produce wall displays
- Change school policy to ban teachers from developing wall displays
- Weekly monitoring of wall displays by the vice principal/assistant principal, with feedback to "offenders"*
- No longer stocking the stationary that is only used for wall display creation, e.g., the A3 colored backing paper*
- Lock the existing display boards with keys to stop staff from being able to access them
- Material incentives – the stationary savings spent on a team lunch*

* = agreed upon "antidotes" for implementation.

With this all complete, the Backbone team at Sizewell High is now ready to work this up into a full de-implementation plan that records the key activities, who will undertake them, and by what deadline. Their first cut of this is illustrated in Figure 7.6, and you can see that it also includes a column that can be used to record progress against each key task.

FIGURE 7.6   REMOVE De-Implementation Plan (What, Who, When)

TARGET AREA FOR DE-IMPLEMENTATION	
Overarching Description of De-Implementation Target Area	De-Implementation of Wall Displays for Classrooms, Corridors, and Public Areas of the School

NO.	TASK DESCRIPTION	OWNER	START DATE	END DATE	PROGRESS
1.	**Whole School Communications Session** Vice principal (VP)/assistant principal briefs all colleagues on the (limited) research evidence on benefits of pretty vs. pretty useful wall display and primes behavior change. This also includes information on material incentives, i.e., the team lunch from stationary budget savings	VP	1/10	1/10	
2.	**Subject Team Communications** Each head of department (HoD) reinforces VP messages at their weekly team meeting	HoDs - Arts - Science - Sports	2/10	10/10	

NO.	TASK DESCRIPTION	OWNER	START DATE	END DATE	PROGRESS
3.	**Removal of Display Wall Stationary** This will be locked away in the principal's private storage closet	VP	2/10	2/10	
4.	**Monitoring Walks** Weekly monitoring walk to review all wall space and ensure no new materials have been pinned. VP feedback discussion with colleagues from any areas of the school where new wall displays are pinned.	VP	15/10	Ongoing	

With their plan now developed, the next step for the Sizewell High team is to conduct a stress test making sure that any identified derailers are fed back into a revised (and improved) version of the plan. In the subsection below, we describe some of the many approaches you *could* take to do stress testing. Again, we do not advocate any particular technique: what's more important is just that you take the time to think critically about the plan you have developed before you speed on to implementation and find yourself wondering what went wrong.

Stress Testing the Plan (Key Action 2)

We are sure that if you think deeply, you can remember many times when you developed well-thought-out plans that later turned out to be fanciful, based on faulty assumptions, and that just did not work when put into practice. As we noted in Chapter 2, Martin Eccles calls this the **ISLAGIATT principle**: an acronym for *it seemed like a good idea at the time.*

All too often, those things that seem like really, really good ideas turn out to be full of holes that derail them. Back in the 1890s, Prussian field marshal Helmuth von Moltke the Elder said, "No plan of operations extends with certainty beyond the first encounter with the enemy's main strength," which has become more famously popularized as "No plan survives contact with the enemy" (Kenny, 2016). And, while the world of schooling could not be further removed from the world of the military, the principle of plans unraveling at first contact with reality sure does travel.

There are, however, things that we can do to minimize the probability of that unravel, including:

Pre-Mortem

You have undoubtedly heard of a post-mortem—that macabre thing that medical examiners do *after* people have died. The autopsy that *explains* the cause of death after the fact. A pre-mortem is a little bit like this except you do it in advance (Klein, 2007). You ask, "in one year from now, the patient *is* dead: what are the most likely causes of death?"

Obviously, when you use the notion of pre-mortem within the context of *Room for Impact* you are imagining the death of your de-implementation initiative rather than a person, but the principle is the same. You are explicitly imagining that your initiative has been a complete, utter, and total failure, and you are asking why.

But for avoidance of all doubt, you are *not* doing this to be fatalistic and to identify reasons *not* to bring your plans to life. Instead, you are doing it to better preempt the *likely* causes of failure *before* you get going and to plan countermeasures that address these identified derailers explicitly. By doing this, you radically increase your chances of success.

You can use the 4-Quadrant tool in Figure 7.7 to help you to both map the likely sources of de-implementation failure and then to plan countermeasures.

FIGURE 7.7   Pre-Mortem Planning Tool

1. POTENTIAL CAUSES OF DE-IMPLEMENTATION FAILURE	2. MOST IMPORTANT CAUSES TO REMEDIATE
Your long list of all the reasons that the project *could* fail include: • Teachers simply continue putting up wall displays • Wall displays are removed, and school is unwelcoming for students, who drop out • Wall displays are removed, and prospective parents decline to enroll their children because they feel the school is unwelcoming • Teachers use the saved time on other low-impact activities	Your shorter list of the causes of failure that *seem* to be the most important to address, based on their severity/risk and the degree to which you can address these
3. POTENTIAL SOLUTIONS	**4. AGREED UPON REVISIONS TO ACTIVITY DESIGN**
Ideating *all* the potential countermeasures or antidotes to the issues you have highlighted in quadrant 2	The countermeasures you will include in your revised activity design to increase the probability of success

Delivery Chain Mapping

Another stress testing approach is to use Delivery Chain Mapping. This involves explicitly setting out in flow diagram form each of the moving parts in your activity plan. You can do this using Post-it notes or even in cartoon format.

You might remember the "Dave Diagram" (a form of Rube Goldberg/ Heath Robinson Machine) from our sister book *Building to Impact*, which we have included as Figure 7.8. Here, Dave's goal is to change the TV channel without leaving his seat and the diagram maps out a set of interconnected actions from (A) to (I) that are designed to achieve the outcome.

FIGURE 7.8   The Dave Diagram/Rube Goldberg Machine

Source: Hamilton et al. (2022)

The idea is that by mapping out the delivery chain in as much detail as possible—in the form of that "Dave Diagram"—you can then start to ask questions like:

- Can we assume the pineapple (A) always makes it through the basketball hoop (B)?

- What happens if the mouse (D) happens to have jumped off the conveyor belt?

- What if the dog (H) does not wake up or it wanders off in the wrong direction?

By using similar thinking, you can question every link in your delivery chain to decide:

- Whether it is needed at all or whether it is a "redundant" link

- Whether it is designed in the right way

- The probability that it will effectively "speak" to the next link in the chain and, in turn, propel this into action.

And you can use this thinking to decide what alterations need to be embedded in your activity design.

Bodystorming

We are sure that you have heard of Brainstorming, that act of coming together as a group to ideate around a flip chart. But you might not have heard of Bodystorming. Originally developed by choreographer Carl Flink in partnership with biomedical engineer David Odde (Flink & Odde, 2012; Oulasvirta et al., 2003), it involves literally "acting out" the process of implementing your activity design—with your bodies!

So, you might imagine you are one of the educators in the room hearing the message from the vice principal/assistant principal about the (current) lack of strong peer-reviewed research evidence for wall display enhancing student achievement and then say:

> Well, if I was really into wall display, I'm not sure my opinion would be changed by one twenty-minute talk from the vice principal/assistant principal. I might even get defensive and want to justify my time on wall display over the years.
>
> We need to think more about this. We could either put more sessions in to convince people to stop or accept that some people will be resistant and focus on the monitoring processes instead. If we get these right, it might not matter if people initially disagree.

You might then act out the process of the vice principal/assistant principal going around the school on her weekly monitoring walk and then say:

> Hang on, we didn't take the preexisting wall display down. Unless the vice principal/assistant principal has made a very careful note of what the existing display looks like, she might not notice if people slowly slip back into their old habits and change the wall display.
>
> You know, it would actually be easier for the vice principal/assistant principal to monitor if we also took down all the existing wall displays—she only has to see whether the walls are bare or whether someone has put something up.

The idea, of course, is that you use the insights from your playacting to identify areas where de-implementation might fall down and to then agree on preventative steps. And you can see this starting to take shape in the dialogue above, where one of the backbone team has identified that it will be far easier for the VP to monitor compliance if all the pre-existing wall displays are removed.

Variant Analysis

Yet another technique that you can use was devised by Arran and John (Hamilton & Hattie, 2022; Hamilton et al., 2022). This is called variant analysis and it involves listing out all key design features of your de-implementation plan and then, for each of these, identifying all the different ways they could be varied, which we call the setting levels.

You can see a partially completed example of this for wall display in Figure 7.9. By laying out *all* the options as clearly and systematically as possible, you are more likely to select the optimal ones. This process also helps when you, later, come to evaluate. If, for example, you decide that you need to iterate or tweak some aspects, you already have a map of all the possible tweaks laid out!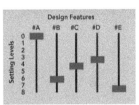

FIGURE 7.9 Variant Analysis				
SETTING LEVELS	**DESIGN FEATURES**			
	EXISTING WALL DISPLAY	**DISPLAY BOARDS**	**MONITORING**	**REPLACEMENT OPTIONS**
1.	Removed Entirely	Removed from the walls	No monitoring	No Replacement
2.	Partially Removed	Remain but kept locked	Self-monitoring	Replace existing wall display with generic posters/art
3.	Left on the walls	Remain and kept unlocked	Leadership Monitoring	Replace existing wall display with curriculum-specific posters/art
4.				Replace with LCD Screens

Side Effects Analysis

A further perspective that we strongly suggest you think from is that of "side effects." You will, no doubt, at some time during your life, have been prescribed some medicine from a physician. After you got home and opened the box, you might have found a leaflet inside—printed on thin paper and in small lettering—that lists out all the *potential* side effects of taking the medicine and what you should do if you experience these.

Zhao (2018) exported this notion of side effects from medicine to education in his book *What Works May Hurt: Side Effects in Education*. His basic premise is that all actions come with an opportunity cost: They may help you achieve a goal, but there is always the question of whether the time could have been spent more effectively. A second, related, issue is that there are always trade-offs in any complex social system. Actions that are intended to be positive may have unintended consequences or "side effects."

To be fair, you are not always going to know all the possible side effects in advance, but you can anticipate some of them. A good way to surface these issues is to ask two questions:

- What will be **better** if we implement these changes?
- What will be **worse** if we implement these changes?

If the answer to the second question is "nothing," then it is likely that further, deeper analysis is needed. Many examples of what are called "unintended consequences" could with careful analysis have been anticipated and prevented, or at least ameliorated.

Of course, ultimately, you can only know after you have taken your de-implementation "medicine" and carefully observed the effects whether there were any unintended consequences, but it is helpful, as you undertake your stress test, to think explicitly from the perspective of side effects and derailers. Your initiative might "work" but at an unacceptable cost.

Some of the side effects of removing wall display *could* include the following:

- **The school feels less welcoming to early-grade students, who have higher levels of anxiety and lower attendance.**
  - *Possible countermeasures:* collect student voice data to see if this is the case; if it is, put up some nice prints chosen by the students in the lower-grade classrooms

- **In contexts where parents have a choice about which school to enroll their child at, they might not like the "vibe" of the bare-walled school and choose to register elsewhere**
  - *Possible countermeasures:* explicitly explain to parents why your school has no wall display. Make a virtue or unique selling point out of it during your parental tours

- **Teachers might spend the time saved on wall display on other low-value activities that do not push the needle on student outcomes—that is, replacing one busywork activity with another**
  - *Possible countermeasures:* continue the *Room for Impact* inquiry cycle over successive terms, to ensure educators remain focused on their efficiency of impact, and that the potential for backsliding is mitigated.

Of course, the potential side effects might not materialize, so you might want to monitor while having the countermeasures in your back pocket for later.

Preparing to REDUCE – key look-fors (and a warning)

In the previous subsection, we worked through a REMOVE example: (1) identifying the target de-implementation area (wall display); (2) postulating what sustains the present; (3) identifying and agreeing on the most appropriate de-implementation strategy, including linked behavioral countermeasures; (4) developing a more detailed action plan (i.e. what, who, when); and (5) stress testing this plan before implementation.

Only items 4 and 5 in this "shopping list" above explicitly fall into the (2.2) *Prepare*. The rest are things that you already need to have done prior to the *Prepare*-step. But we wanted to give you a case study linked to a (relatively) simple de-implementation action—removing wall displays—so that you could see how all the prior P-steps build into this (2.2) *Prepare* activity. We also wanted you to see that although the P-steps look complicated, it's perfectly possible to work through them during a few ideational sessions over a day or two.

If, during your working through of those P-steps, you come to conclude that the most viable de-implementation strategy is to REDUCE rather than REMOVE, you will still be going through the same processes, using the same tools, and developing the same kind of "what, who, when" action plan. The only difference is that the purpose is to REDUCE—that is, do it less and/or apply it to fewer people.

There are lots of things that you could theoretically REDUCE in your school, including:

- Homework

- Data collection

- Staff meetings – frequency and/or duration

- Amount of detail required in lesson plans

- Co-curricular activities—that is, the time allocated and/or the number of co-curricular offerings

- Parental reporting—that is, frequency and/or required level of detail

- Number of lesson observations

- Teaching load via creative timetabling.

These are just examples of things that you *could* reduce. We are sure you can think of many more and you can also look at Appendix 1 for further ideas. And we are also sure that for some of those listed above your reaction might be that "reducing this wouldn't fly in our school." There might also be very good local reasons for you to come to this conclusion: What's good for the goose isn't always good for the gander. The whole point of the *Room for Impact* protocols is to support you in identifying de-implementation actions that are amenable in your context—and without harming student outcomes.

A REDUCE strategy is likely to work best in contexts where you need to keep doing the thing but where you might be doing too much of that thing. To give you a noneducational example, think about the following two unhealthy habits: smoking cigarettes (which we have already discussed) and eating to excess.

With smoking, a REMOVE strategy is perfectly feasible and desirable: you can go cold turkey and just stop smoking: you don't need cigarettes and your life is better without them. But the same is categorically not the case with eating. You can't stop eating. You need a certain number of calories per day to remain healthy. So, you need to REDUCE what you eat rather than REMOVE food from your life.

But here comes the rub. REMOVE is more sustainable than REDUCE. Think back to your friendship and family groups. We bet you know people who have REMOVED cigarettes (a.k.a. quit smoking) and others who have REDUCED food (a.k.a. gone on a diet). Out of all the people you know who quit smoking and those who went on a diet, which ones had the highest relapse rates? Was it the smokers or the overeaters?

If your social circles are aligned with international averages, the dieters were the most likely to revert to their habits in the long term. The research tells us that for smokers there is a 50 percent chance of relapse during the first year and that after this, the rate falls radically year-on-year to a 10 percent probability of relapse in the longer term (García-Rodríguez et al., 2013). But with dieting, it works the other way around. In the short-term, a high proportion of dieters can maintain their reduced calorie intake but generally rebound over time. Anderson et al. (2001) in their meta-analysis of 29 longitudinal weight loss tracking studies found that, on average, dieters had regained more than half of their lost weight within two years and more than 80 percent within 5 years. Other studies have corroborated this finding (K. D. Hall & Kahan, 2018; Loveman et al., 2011; Wu et al., 2009).

REDUCE is so hard because you are still engaging in the behavior, just to a lesser extent. And the risk is that over time you creep up and up, particularly after you have stopped actively monitoring and thinking about the area in question. Imagine, for example, someone who opts to cut down their cigarette intake (i.e., REDUCE). It's obvious that as a standalone strategy, this will rarely work in the long term. While we bet you know many people who successfully removed cigarettes from their lives, we doubt you know many who successfully cut down from, say, twenty-a-day to ten without their consumption gradually (and inevitably) creeping back up over time.

We suspect the same applies equally to any form of REDUCE strategy in education. With great willpower and careful monitoring, you will be able to generate short-term success. But in the longer-term you are highly likely to backslide. **Therefore, REDUCE is our least recommended of the 4Rs.**

If, despite this forewarning, you find yourself going down the REDUCE path, you need to carefully select your behavioral change countermeasures, deeply stress test your activity designs, and assume that you will need to monitor *forever*. Much like dieting, if you stop getting on the scales, the weight slowly creeps back up as you regress to the mean. There is, to our knowledge, no way around this. Sorry.

Preparing to RE-ENGINEER – Case Study

The third type of de-implementation strategy that you could be prepping for is RE-ENGINEER. Here, you are opting to continue with the existing activity, but you are looking for ways to make that existing process more efficient, so that it takes less time and effort.

Let's say, for example, that you have decided to RE-ENGINEER your school's behavior management system so that teachers are no longer spending an hour or more at the end of the school day supervising students that they have put into detention. Instead, a new centralized system is proposed where one teacher stays behind on a rota (schedule) and all students on detention that day go to an allocated room for supervision by that one teacher.

For this case study, we will not go back through the definition of the de-implementation target area, the 4Rs analysis, or the Chesterton's Fence and antidote mapping. Instead, we want to focus on the aspects of Preparing to RE-ENGINEER that are different.

What you are doing when you develop a RE-ENGINEER plan is very similar to the Lean methodology, which is commonly used in manufacturing to make processes more efficient (Womack & Jones, 2003). This type of thinking started in Japan and the whole focus is on *muda* (the Japanese word for waste). The idea is to reduce *muda* by identifying all excess time, motion, resources, steps, and processes that can be removed to simplify an existing process without impact on the quality of the outcome. In Lean manufacturing, this is usually about improving a car or a widget, but we think that the thinking can be applied equally to education. In other words, it is process simplification that results in less time, motion, and energy being expended *but* without harming student outcomes.

A common starting point for Lean RE-ENGINEERING is to map the existing process. You can do this with Post-it notes, with one note for each step. You then put this in sequence, with arrows coming in and out of the Post-it-note (boxes) to show how the steps link together into a full process. You can also undertake some time and motion analysis alongside to understand how long it takes to implement the existing process.

Then, as a group, you build as many alternative processes as possible and map whether these would save time. You also stress test each of these alternatives to check that it is implementable, that people can and will follow it, and that the side effects of adopting this new and more efficient way are not harmful to student outcomes.

In Figure 7.10, we illustrate what this could look like for RE-ENGINEERING of a school's behavior management system from a decentralized to a centralized approach. Look at this figure carefully before reading on.

FIGURE 7.10   Re-Engineer De-Implementation Plan

1. TARGET AREA FOR DE-IMPLEMENTATION

Overarching Description of De-Implementation Target Area	Decentralized Student Detention System With Teachers Supervising Their Own Detentions

2. "AS IS" PROCESS: DECENTRALIZED DETENTIONS — TIME EXPENDED

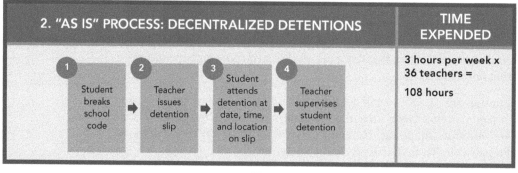

	TIME EXPENDED
1. Student breaks school code → 2. Teacher issues detention slip → 3. Student attends detention at date, time, and location on slip → 4. Teacher supervises student detention	3 hours per week x 36 teachers = 108 hours

3. "TO BE" PROCESS: CENTRALIZED DETENTIONS — TIME SAVED

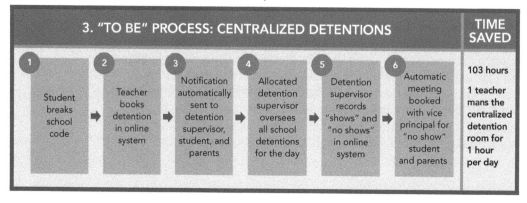

	TIME SAVED
1. Student breaks school code → 2. Teacher books detention in online system → 3. Notification automatically sent to detention supervisor, student, and parents → 4. Allocated detention supervisor oversees all school detentions for the day → 5. Detention supervisor records "shows" and "no shows" in online system → 6. Automatic meeting booked with vice principal for "no show" student and parents	103 hours 1 teacher mans the centralized detention room for 1 hour per day

	4. DETAILED TASK LIST				
NO.	**TASK DESCRIPTION**	**OWNER**	**START DATE**	**END DATE**	**PROGRESS**
1.	**Activation and testing of behavior management module in school online management system** School IT manager activates system module, customizes fields to align with proposed process flow, and undertakes testing in partnership with backbone team	IT manager	1/9	20/9	
2.	**Whole School Communications Session** Vice principal (VP)/ assistant principal briefs all colleagues on the centralized detention system and collects feedback on proposed process flow	VP	30/9	30/9	
3.	**Staff rota and room bookings** Staff rota set for term and detention room booked	Backbone team	20/9	29/9	
4.	**Monitoring and feedback walks** VP building walks for first month to ensure that no staff continue to administer decentralized detentions	VP	1/10	30/10	
5.	**Evaluation review** End of term "Lessons Learned" meeting with all staff to collect feedback and suggestions for improvement	VP	15/12	15/12	

So, you'll notice that the RE-ENGINEER tool does four things:

1. It defines the target area that is the focus for re-engineering.

2. It maps out the "as is" process—that is, what it is that people are currently doing—and how much time this expends.

3. It sets out the "to be" process—that is, what people will do in the future—and how much time will be saved.

4. It then lays out a more detailed list of actions, action owners, and dates.

In this case, the "to be" process that is mapped out is not the only way that the detention process *could* be re-engineered. One of the other possibilities—aside from a completely centralized system—would have been to institute a more efficient decentralized approach. This could involve teachers continuing to supervise their own detentions in their own classrooms directly but bundling the detentions together so that all children come on a single day of the week rather than spreading the detentions out over multiple days. However, while this is more efficient than decentralized ad hoc detentions, a centralized system saves even more time: only one or two colleagues need to be present in the school to man the detention room on behalf of all teachers.

You might also notice that the proposed "to be" process actually has more steps within it than the "as is" process—six versus four. What it highlights is that sometimes you need to RE-ENGINEER more complexity into your system to generate greater efficiency. Although, where possible, you should also be looking at ways to reduce the number of steps in a process chain. But what matters most is the overall number of minutes and hours that are saved by implementing your new and improved process.

Finally, you will also notice within the list of actions that there is an "Evaluation Review." This action has been explicitly inserted because during the Side Effects and Pre-Mortem analysis, the Backbone team identified the following areas of (potential) concern:

1. The risk that teachers continue to administer decentralized detentions, with this actually increasing the overall level of workload (i.e., local detentions plus having the scheduled staff in the centralized detention room)

2. Potential side effects for high-risk students who, during their decentralized detention, received much-needed one-to-one pastoral care and homework support from their teacher. Although, it might also be that they are "acting up" to gain access to that one-to-one tuition service!

Of course, there will be no way of knowing whether this risk and these side effects will materialize until the backbone team implements the re-engineered process and collects evaluation data to see and decide what to do next!

> **If you are Re-engineering, you also need to Stress Test** – using one or more of the approaches that we introduced during the **Remove** case study. These include, for example, pre-mortem, side effects analysis, variant analysis, bodystorming, and/or delivery chain mapping.

Preparing to REPLACE – Case Study

The final type of de-implementation strategy that you could progress is to REPLACE. However, before we get into illustrating this, we want to provide two health warnings:

1. **REPLACE is the second-hardest approach to progress after REDUCE.** The reason it's so hard is that you are attempting to do two things at once:

    a. *Thing One*: Remove an existing set of habits (i.e., stop or go cold turkey)

    b. *Thing Two*: Introduce a new set of practices instead (i.e., those agreed upon replacement actions)

    The reason that this is hard is that there is significant risk that you are not able to fully remove those old habits. And that, instead, everyone ends up merging two sets of behaviors together into something that is *less* than the sum of its parts. Something that takes more time, energy, and motion for the same outcomes. Or, even more dangerously, for *worse* outcomes.

2. **REPLACE is (arguably) the default mode of most school improvement activity.** This occurs with school leadership teams after they return from conferences enthused about the latest shiny program or widget to be inserted into the school day (i.e., the new and improved version of something already being done).

These two health warnings are why REPLACE is in quadrant four: we explicitly want you to think of it last—because you are probably doing too much replacing already. Your endless cycles of replacement may be one of the reasons that you are now so focused on de-implementation.

With those health warnings out of the way, you will remember that we previously introduced the Rohit, Samantha, and Eddie case study, which we have been following through some of the previous chapters. These intrepid three had identified that, in their school, a significant proportion of teacher time was being expended on developed detailed, bespoke, and localized teaching and learning materials. They realized that teachers were spending their evenings producing their lesson content from scratch but without any evidence that **this** "artisanal" activity was making a significant difference to student outcomes.

To recap, Rohit, Samantha, and Eddie had defined their target de-implementation as per Figure 7.11.

FIGURE 7.11 Recap of Rohit, Samantha, and Eddie's Analysis of Target De-Implementation Area

TARGET AREA FOR DE-IMPLEMENTATION			
Overarching Description of De-Implementation Target Area	Development of Bespoke and Localized Teaching, Learning, and Student Assessment Materials by Our Teaching Teams		
SUBCOMPONENTS	WHEN/WHERE DOES THIS OCCUR?	WHO DOES THIS?	HOW MUCH TIME IS SPENT?
1. Development of overarching scheme of work	Usually prior to the start of the academic year and it is reviewed and refined at the start of each term	Head of department, with input from all teachers	40 hours per term x 3 people
2. Development of detailed lesson plans	On a daily/weekly basis and mostly out of school during evenings and weekends	All teachers and mainly independently (i.e., without sharing materials with each other)	Average of 5 hours per week per teacher
3. Development of student activity and resource sheets	As above	As above	Average of 3 hours per week per teacher
4. Development of student assessment tools	As above	As above	Average of 2 hours per week per teacher

They had also postulated what it was that sustained these existing practices—in the form of a fishbone diagram, which is recapped in Figure 7.12.

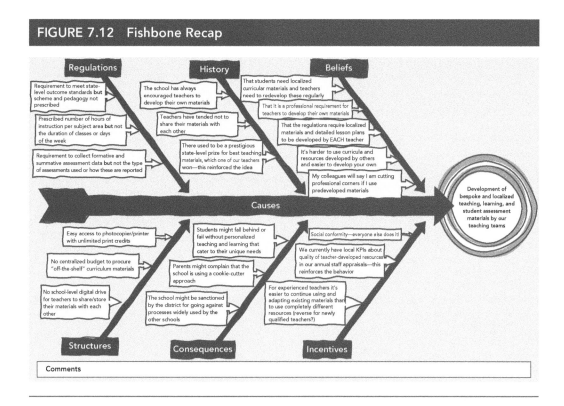

FIGURE 7.12   Fishbone Recap

The full landscape version can be found in Figure 5.3/Chapter 5 on page 113.

They then agreed on their "Antidote Actions" for the most crucial nodes on their Fishbone, which we recap in Figure 7.13.

FIGURE 7.13   Recap Antidote Actions Framework

FISHBONE NODE	ANTIDOTE OPTIONS i.e., WHAT *COULD* WE DO?	ANTIDOTE ACTIONS i.e., WHAT *WILL* WE DO?	WHY?
Habit	• Send WhatsApp reminders to staff in evening, when they usually do their curriculum development work • Formal behavioral change contract • Social sanctions	WhatsApp reminders	Other approaches seem too "Orwellian" to start with

(Continued)

(Continued)

FISHBONE NODE	ANTIDOTE OPTIONS i.e., WHAT *COULD* WE DO?	ANTIDOTE ACTIONS i.e., WHAT *WILL* WE DO?	WHY?
Belief that teachers should always develop their own materials	• Reframing group identity • Cueing incompatible beliefs	Both of the identified strategies – in particular we could cue/seed the incompatible belief that teaching materials need to have undergone rigorous evaluation to verify their effectiveness	It will be challenging for our teachers to "rigorously" evaluate their own materials. The new belief primes everyone to adopt third-party materials that have been carefully tested in a wide range of similar contexts to our own
Belief that locally developed materials are always better	• Information from a credible authority to debunk this belief • Information on consequences of maintaining status quo	Information from a credible authority to debunk this belief	The researcher team that developed the curriculum package has agreed to present their evaluation data to our teaching teams
Staff performance objectives reinforce the practice	• Amend local policies to *prohibit* self-developed materials • Amend local policies to *discourage* self-developed materials	Amend local policies to **discourage** self-developed materials	We don't want to dictate, as we don't know for sure that the new curriculum will be effective until we implement it and then evaluate
Physical environment enables status quo	• Move photocopier to distant location • Put sign above photocopier reinforcing use of the new curriculum • Prompts and cue posters in staffroom	All of these	They are all very easy to implement
Support required to implement replacement actions, i.e., use of new external curriculum	• Training in new use of new curriculum materials • Social incentives, e.g., scoreboard • Social support network, e.g., embedding review, and self-help cycles within team PLC meetings	• Training in new use of new curriculum materials • Social support network embedded in existing PLC meetings	We need to provide training in the new curriculum anyway. Embedding social support in existing PLCs will take less time than establishing new structures

What they are now going to do is develop a de-implementation plan with two key elements:

- **REMOVE** – These are actions/behaviors that are going to be stopped and the activities that are going to be undertaken to ensure that this stop happens.

- **REPLACE** – These are actions/behaviors that will be started in direct substitution of those being removed. Here, the purpose is predominantly about efficiency of impact (i.e., the replacement actions take less time, energy, and motion)—while generating *at least* the same level of student outcomes.

In Figure 7.14, we illustrate a REPLACE de-implementation plan, which outlines both the REMOVE and REPLACE actions that Rohit, Samantha, and Eddie have agreed on with their wider school.

FIGURE 7.14   A REPLACE De-Implementation Plan

TARGET AREA FOR DE-IMPLEMENTATION	
Overarching Description of De-Implementation Target Area	Development of Bespoke and Localized Teaching, Learning, and Student Assessment Materials by Our Teaching Teams

A. REMOVE PLAN					
Behaviors to be REMOVED:					
• Educators stop developing their own teaching and learning materials from scratch					
NO.	**TASK DESCRIPTION**	**OWNER**	**START DATE**	**END DATE**	**PROGRESS**
1.	**Whole School Communications Sessions** Training session delivered by the organization providing the professionally developed teaching and learning materials	External Org	1/5	1/7	
2.	**PLC Social Support Meetings** PLC meetings that focus on de-implementation of locally developed teaching materials. Head of department (HoD) colleagues will report on progress and collectively identify actions to address any backsliding	HoDs: - Arts - Science - Sports	1/9	Ongoing	

(Continued)

(Continued)

NO.	TASK DESCRIPTION	OWNER	START DATE	END DATE	PROGRESS
3.	**Incentives** School policy changed to discourage development of own materials Individual performance objectives to be tied to use of the third-party program	Principal	1/6	1/7	
4.	**Nudges and Friction** Daily WhatsApp reminders for first month Photocopier moved to annex building to make it difficult for teachers to print/copy their own individually developed materials Poster prompts placed above photocopier and in the staff room	VP	1/9	Ongoing	
5.	**Monitoring and Feedback** Weekly auditing of teaching and learning materials by VP to check whether any locally developed materials are "creeping back in"	VP	1/9	Ongoing	

B. REPLACE PLAN					
Replacement Actions: • **Teachers use high-quality teaching and learning materials that have been professionally developed and evaluated by a third-party organization**					
NO.	TASK DESCRIPTION	OWNER	START DATE	END DATE	PROGRESS
1.	**Third-Party Curriculum Offerings Identified** Backbone team undertakes landscape analysis of potential curriculum programs, including review of evaluation data and visits to other schools. Wider school body consulted with decision on preferred program reached.	Backbone team	8/1	28/2	

NO.	TASK DESCRIPTION	OWNER	START DATE	END DATE	PROGRESS
2.	**Selected Third-Party Curriculum Offer Procured** Competitive procurement with vendor presentations and review of contract terms, support provided, and impact data	Backbone team	1/3	15/4	
3.	**Teaching Teams Trained in Use of New Curriculum Model** Initial training in new program delivered on whole school basis	External org.	1/5	1/7	
4.	**Ongoing Support Via PLCs** Linked to Action 2 on REMOVE plan – the PLCs will simultaneously review progress on the REPLACEMENT actions	Head of department (HoD)	1/9	Ongoing	
5.	**Monitoring and Evaluation Activity** Vice principal/assistant principal to undertake weekly sampling audits to ensure teachers are using the new materials Monthly evaluation feedback sessions via data collected from PLCs	VP	1/9	Ongoing	

As you review the plan in Figure 7.9, you might notice that many of the dates for the REPLACEMENT actions precede the REMOVE actions by several months. In this instance, educators cannot stop lesson planning until a suitable replacement practice has been identified and is ready to be substituted.

The final point we want to reiterate is that REPLACEMENT actions are exceedingly hard to implement. In this particular example, there is a major risk that the teaching teams "sorta" adopt the new third-party materials but that they continue to spend their evenings and weekends making tweaks and adjustments—so that the materials are more suitable for the individual needs of their specific learners. Hence the need for meticulous stress testing. Otherwise, the danger is that this REPLACEMENT strategy becomes the worst of all possible worlds: the additional costs of procuring the third-party program, local adaptions that may actually reduce the fidelity and impact, and no time saved, as teachers continue to tinker!

Hence, where possible, we suggest you start your planning for actions that sit in the REMOVE or RE-ENGINEER Quadrants as these are likely to be far easier to implement than either a REDUCE or REPLACE action.

> **If you are REPLACING, you also need to Stress Test** – using one or more of the approaches that we introduced during the **Remove** case study. These include, for example, pre-mortem, side effects analysis, variant analysis, bodystorming, and/or delivery chain mapping.

Summary

During the **(2.2)** *Prepare*-**step** you have:

- **Key Action 1:** Developed detailed de-implementation plan (i.e., to Remove vs. Reduce vs. Re-Engineer vs. Replace)

- **Key Action 2:** Stress tested your plan (using, for example, pre-mortem, bodystorming, and/or side effects analysis to further improve your approach).

With this completed, you are now ready to select and set evaluative criteria for your agreed on de-implementation plan, which takes you to *(2.3) Picture*!

(2.2) Prepare: Convergent Cross-Checking and Agreeing

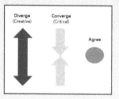

Before you get to (2.3) *Picture*, here are some of the critical cross-checking questions for you to consider:

1. Have we developed a sufficiently detailed de-implementation plan?

2. As part of this planning have we reconfirmed that our chosen high-level strategy (i.e. Remove vs. Reduce vs. Re-Engineer vs. Replace) is the most suitable?

3. Does our detailed plan also incorporate our identified Chesterton's Fence Antidotes?

4. Have we stress tested our detailed plan (e.g., by using one or more of pre-mortem, bodystorming, and/or side effects analysis)?

5. Have we refined our detailed de-implementation plan, based on the outcomes of our stress testing?

If so, we are now ready to progress to (2.3) *Picture*!

Picture (2.3)

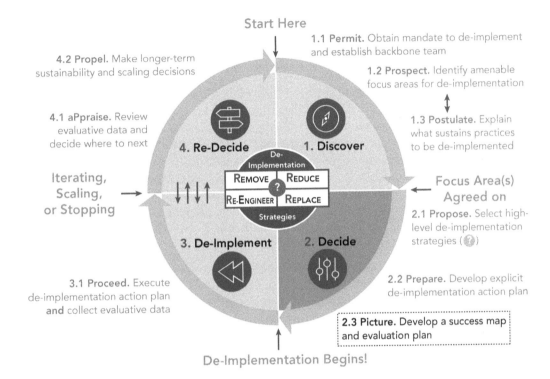

Start Here

1.1 Permit. Obtain mandate to de-implement and establish backbone team

1.2 Prospect. Identify amenable focus areas for de-implementation

1.3 Postulate. Explain what sustains practices to be de-implemented

4.2 Propel. Make longer-term sustainability and scaling decisions

4.1 aPpraise. Review evaluative data and decide where to next

4. Re-Decide

1. Discover

De-Implementation

| REMOVE | ? | REDUCE |
| RE-ENGINEER | | REPLACE |

Strategies

Iterating, Scaling, or Stopping

Focus Area(s) Agreed on

2.1 Propose. Select high-level de-implementation strategies ( )

3. De-Implement

2. Decide

3.1 Proceed. Execute de-implementation action plan **and** collect evaluative data

2.2 Prepare. Develop explicit de-implementation action plan

2.3 Picture. Develop a success map and evaluation plan

De-Implementation Begins!

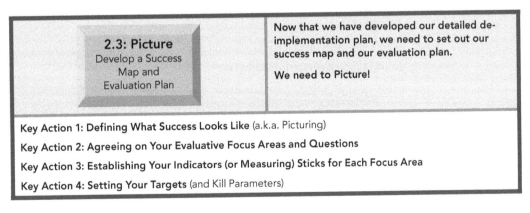

| **2.3: Picture** Develop a Success Map and Evaluation Plan | Now that we have developed our detailed de-implementation plan, we need to set out our success map and our evaluation plan. We need to Picture! |

Key Action 1: Defining What Success Looks Like (a.k.a. Picturing)

Key Action 2: Agreeing on Your Evaluative Focus Areas and Questions

Key Action 3: Establishing Your Indicators (or Measuring) Sticks for Each Focus Area

Key Action 4: Setting Your Targets (and Kill Parameters)

Introduction

As you read these words, an estimated 42 percent of adults across the globe are currently trying to lose weight; and a further 23 percent are thought to be consciously working *not* to increase their current size (Santos et al., 2017). One of the reasons we need to watch our weight is buried in our evolutionary past. Our ancestors operated in a world of great uncertainty and scarcity. They evolved to eat as much as they could, whenever they could, because the next meal was a great unknown. We, by contrast, live in an era of far greater certainty and abundance. The availability of delicious and affordable foodstuffs, coupled with our evolutionary engrained tendencies to "make hay while the sun shines," is (unfortunately) resulting in many of us eating too much. Hence, for many, the perennial need to diet.

Dieting is, of course, a form of de-implementation. Not by Removing—because without food we cannot live. But by Reducing our calorific intake; and, sometimes by Re-engineering how, what, and when we eat; and, also sometimes by Replacing "bad" foods with "better" alternatives. Many strategies to weight loss have been invented over the years, including the Keto diet, the Hollywood diet, the Master Cleanse, the Cabbage Soup diet, Weight Watchers, the Sleeping Beauty diet, the Paleo diet, the 5/2 diet, the 16/8 diet, Intermittent Fasting, Slim Fast, the Atkins diet, the Zone diet, the Dukan diet, the South Beach diet, Whole30, the Low Carb diet, the HGC diet, and even the Cigarette Diet!

When you peel away at the surface structure of all these diets, they are each a rules-based means to the end of consuming fewer calories. But here comes the rub: When dieters are tracked over the long term, most regain their weight within two to five years (Engber, 2019). No matter the dieting strategy, many even end up heavier than when they started. De-implementing food is exceedingly hard—because you can't just *Remove* it from your life! And, as we discussed in the previous chapter, *Remove* is by far the easiest of the four de-implementation strategies to progress.

When we look, however, at those dieters who are successful, they seem to be better at doing four things:

1. **Picturing what success looks like**. This is about having a clearly articulated and realistic goal—for example, "by the end of the calendar year I will have lost 14 kg. I will do so at a rate of half a kilogram per week, and *I will maintain this new weight* into the long-term future."

2. **Having a strategy for weight loss**. This is often a rules-based approach with clear criteria about what, when, where, how, and how much to eat. It generally also involves "Chesterton's Fence" analysis to understand when and why overeating occurs

and the development of countermeasures such as reshaping the environment (changing what you keep in your refrigerators, using smaller plates, eating with a teaspoon), or adding social support systems (a weekly group weigh-in, or a public declaration of the goal, so that dieters co-opt others into policing their progress).

3. **Monitoring implementation** – which simply means checking (by documenting) whether you did what you set out to do. Did you, indeed, fast for sixteen hours a day, or cut out carbs or eat only cabbage soup? Monitoring is more successful if it happens daily before any backsliding can set in. This helps to ensure that implementation intentions are converted into actions and that new (long-term) habits are formed and maintained.

4. **Evaluating the impact.** This is about checking whether there is actual impact after you followed the regimen. And there are a host of direct and indirect evaluative tools that *could* be used including regularly getting on the scales, measuring waist circumference, body-fat composition analysis, blood-sugar level, blood pressure, body-mass-index, and so on. Each of these comes with different opportunity costs of measurement.

These critical four elements take you from setting a goal (A); establishing a plan of action (B); checking that you implemented said plan (C); and determining whether successful implementation actually got you to your goal (D). It's this feedback loop that is crucial because if your cabbage soup diet is not resulting in any actual weight loss, you then need to decide whether to:

- **STOP** – and abandon the plan, going back to the drawing board to identify and implement an entirely new strategy;

- **ITERATE** – and make some incremental changes to your diet plan, like adding exercise or reducing calories yet further; or

- **CONTINUE** as is and check again later on to see if things improve over time.

These exact same principles apply to educational de-implementation. In the previous P-steps, you have already agreed on your focus area and plan of action (covering points A and B in our discussion above). Therefore, what you are going to focus on during **(2.3) *Picture*** is to address points C and D. And you will do this by:

- **Key Action 1: Defining what success looks like** (a.k.a. picturing)

- **Key Action 2: Agreeing on your evaluative focus areas and questions**

- **Key Action 3: Establishing your indicators or measuring sticks for each focus area**

- **Key Action 4: Setting your targets** (and kill parameters)

You are doing this because you have no certainty that what you are about to de-implement will work. And even if it does, you can often make it work even better with some iterative tweaks and enhancements as you go.

In the sections that follow, we will unpack each of these four Key Actions, in turn. Note, also, that while (2.3) has more Key Actions than any of the other P-steps, many of these can be worked through quickly. What you are developing during (2.3) *Picture* is the evaluation plan that you will collect data against as you de-implement (3.1) and that you will then aPpraise (4.1) your success against. So, right now, during Picture, you are just selecting the evaluative questions, tools, indicators, and targets that you will be measuring and judging against, later.

Key Action 1: Defining What Success Looks Like (a.k.a. Picturing)

Your first key action is to picture what success looks like. You are likely to have already begun thinking about this and you may already have informally set out your success criteria during some of the previous P-steps. However, we suggest the following four criteria to enable you to lay this out even more systematically:

- **Criterion 1: What will we have done?** This a summary of the high-level actions in your de-implementation plan—for example, removing wall display or reducing homework or re-engineering student detention, or replacing teacher-developed teaching and learning materials with a high-quality external package of materials, and so forth.

- **Criterion 2: What is the impact on students?** This is about whether you expect the de-implementation to have positive, neutral, or negative impact on student outcomes. Of course, it's highly unlikely that you would proceed with any initiative that has a significantly negative impact, but in your context you might conclude that de-implementation that saves considerable time/resources and without harming student outcomes is absolutely fine; that is, a neutral "do no harm" type of outcome.

- **Criterion 3: What is the impact on staff?** This might be expressed in terms of the amount of time saved, increased well-being, and/or the opportunity to reinvest energies in higher leverage activities and so forth. **Criterion 3 is the motherlode—the whole point of a *Room for Impact* inquiry is to save time, energy, resources, and motion.** Doing less to achieve the same, or more.

- **Criterion 4: What are we doing with the savings?** Given our core focus on efficiency of impact, this raises the central question of what it is you are going to do with those savings. A perfectly reasonable answer is "nothing, we are going to go home earlier and generate more work-life balance." But if you intend to reuse the saved time/resource for higher-impact activities, you need to make sure these genuinely are higher impact—otherwise you may just be substituting one ineffective practice with another!

In Figure 8.1 we illustrate how you can lay out your success criteria using the example of re-engineering decentralized detentions into a centralized system that requires far fewer teachers to supervise the same number of after-school detentions. You may remember this case study from the previous chapter.

FIGURE 8.1   De-Implementation Success Criteria (a.k.a. Picturing) – Centralized Detention System Worked Example

DE-IMPLEMENTATION SUCCESS CRITERIA	
Overarching Description of De-Implementation Target Area	Establishing a Centralized Student Detention System With Teachers No Longer Supervising Their Own Detentions (i.e., Re-Engineer)
Criterion 1 – What will we have done?	• *All* teaching staff will have **completely stopped** administering decentralized detentions • A new centralized detention system is in place and **is being used by** *all* **staff**
Criterion 2 – What is the impact on students?	• **Neutral** – our focus is on reducing staff workload without harming student outcomes. This initiative is not specifically designed to increase student outcomes
Criterion 3 – What is the impact on staff?	• Staff save **an average of three hours per person per week** in supervising decentralized detentions • Improved staff well-being – staff report being happier and less stressed
Criterion 4 – What are we doing with the savings?	• **Nothing** – this initiative is designed to improve staff well-being. We want staff to enjoy the extra time and *not* to fill it with other school-related activity

Note that these four criteria are not exhaustive. There may be other success criteria in addition to or instead of these that are more relevant to your chosen de-implementation initiative. But the idea is that you use this type of thinking (and recording) to formally and systematically articulate your picture of success. By picturing, everyone remains clear about the *purpose* of your *Room for Impact* initiative.

Key Action 2: Agreeing on Your Evaluative Focus Areas and Questions

Now that you have laid out your success criteria, the next key action is to identify the type of evaluative questions that would be helpful to ask, as you proceed to de-implementation. In Figure 8.2 we list six focus areas that you *might* consider and a range of questions within each.

FIGURE 8.2   Focus Areas and Questions

FOCUS AREAS	KEY QUESTION(S)
Monitoring	• Did we de-implement exactly as intended? • Did we follow *all* the agreed upon actions/activities/steps in our plan?
Time	• By de-implementing, did we save time? • If so, how much time was saved? • Is this in line with our expectations?
Resources Funding, infrastructure, equipment, and so forth	• By de-implementing, did we save resources? • If so, what type and how much was saved? • Is this in line with our expectations?
Use of Savings	• What did we do with the saved time and/or resources? • Is this a better use? • Are we sure? **N.B.** it might be that there is no intended re-investment agenda and that the focus is on pure efficiency of impact.
Side Effects	• Were there any noticeable side effects that emerged from our de-implementation activity? • Are these serious enough that we need to address them? • And, if so, how should they be addressed?
Student Outcomes	• What was the impact on student outcomes of this de-implementation activity? • Was the impact positive, negative, or neutral? • Do we need to make any adjustments as a result of this? **N.B.** Neutral impact might be perfectly fine if your intention is to reduce teacher workload without harming student achievement, i.e., a status quo student outcome.

Not all of these will necessarily be relevant to your de-implementation initiative—for example, you might be focused on saving time rather than material or financial resources. And, if your focus area is, say, removing (pretty rather than pretty useful) wall display, you might already be confident that this will have negligible impact on student achievement and therefore just opt to get on and do it—without creating overengineered evaluative processes that actually increase your workload!

However, we strongly recommend that—at the very least—you include monitoring questions and processes. **This is because the global research on effective implementation identifies ONE common factor that seems to matter more than all the others: whether you regularly checked in to confirm that you are indeed doing the things you intended to** (Daniels et al., 2021; DuBois et al., 2002; Smith et al., 2004; Tobler, 1986; Wilson et al., 2003). By including this simple monitoring step, you significantly increase the probability that you will turn intentions into action, which generates impact.

Key Action 3: Establishing Your Indicators (or Measuring Sticks) for Each Focus Area

Once you have agreed on the Focus Areas and Questions that are most worth collecting evaluative data against, your next step is to select the most appropriate indicators or measuring sticks that you can use for each. Back at the start of this chapter, we gave the (noneducational) example of weight loss. Returning to this example, let's say that one of the key outcomes you wanted to evaluate against was whether you actually lost weight. There are several different indicators that you *could* use, including changes in:

- Weight on a set of weighing scales

- Waist circumference on a tape measure

- Belt buckle notch

- Clothing fit, that is, whether your clothes have become baggy

- Comments from friends and family about your changing appearance

Most people stick to using weighing scales. Here, the opportunity cost is low because most of us have them in our bathrooms already, and it only takes a couple of seconds to take a reading and jot it down. But, if for some reason, you didn't have access to weighing scales, one of those other measuring tools *could* be used to give you a broad indication of your changing weight. None of the measures is perfect. For example, if you combine dieting with a regimen of strength training, your weight might not decrease, or may even increase (since muscle weighs more than fat), but your waist circumference would decrease. Also, some indicators give you data quicker than others (for example, the weighing scales are likely to report incremental success several weeks before your trousers fall down).

The exact same principle applies to measuring your *Room for Impact* progress. Again, there are many different types of indicators that you *could* use. Some will be more accurate but also potentially more costly to measure because they are not things you are already collecting data against in your school. Indeed, one of your *Room for Impact* initiatives might even be to reduce your overall level of data collection!

In Figure 8.3, we provide you with high-level ideas about indicators that *might* be appropriate to help you answer those key evaluative questions across the six Focus Areas.

FIGURE 8.3   Six Domains—Potential Indicators

FOCUS AREAS	KEY QUESTIONS	POTENTIAL INDICATORS
Monitoring	• Did we de-implement as intended? • Did we follow *all* of the agreed upon actions in our plan?	• Observation • Interviews • Document audit • Progress checking against the implementation plan
Time	• By de-implementing, did we save time? • If so, how much time was saved? • Is this in line with our expectations?	• Time journaling • Time and motion studies • Perceptions via focus groups, interviews, or surveys
Resources e.g., funding, infrastructure, etc.	• By de-implementing, did we save resources? • If so, what type and how much was saved? • Is this in line with our expectations?	• Budget tracking • Asset tracking, i.e., before vs. after analysis
Use of Savings	• What did we do with the saved time and/or resources? • Is this a better use? • Are we sure? **N.B.** It might be that there is no intended reinvestment agenda and that the focus is on pure efficiency of impact.	• Interviews • Focus groups • Observation • Time logging • Meta-analyses and systematic reviews on the effectiveness of any newly inserted practices

FOCUS AREAS	KEY QUESTIONS	POTENTIAL INDICATORS
Side Effects	• Were there any noticeable side effects that emerged from our de-implementation activity? • Are these serious enough that we need to address them? • And, if so, how should they be addressed?	• Interviews • Focus groups (staff, students, and/or parents) • Observation
Student Outcomes	• What was the impact on student outcomes of this de-implementation activity? • Was the impact positive, negative, or neutral? • Do we need to make any adjustments as a result of this? **N.B.** Neutral impact might be perfectly fine if your intention is to reduce teacher workload without harming student achievement, i.e., a status quo student outcome.	• Student voice • Student attendance • Student achievement • Student detentions and exclusions • Student self-efficacy surveys

Some of these indicators—particularly those related to **time** and **resources**—are closely related to the questions and tools you may already have used in the (1.2) *Prospect*-step. You will remember that in chapter 4 we included suggested tools and approaches for **time logging**, **expenditure tracking**, and a **staff workload perception survey**. If you took baseline readings with these tools at the beginning of your inquiry, you have already "stepped on the scales" and now have your starting values. You can then continue to use the same tools to collect data during de-implementation to check your impact.

Evaluative Look-Fors

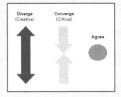

As you explore all the possible evaluative measuring sticks that *might* give you useful insights into whether your *Room for Impact* initiative has been successful, you are likely to identify many more indicators than you can feasibly leverage. So, it would be best if you focus on those that will give you the biggest bang for your buck. Some of the things you will want to consider as you do this are as follows:

(Continued)

(Continued)

1. **Opportunity cost.** Every action comes with a cost, even evaluation. Collecting data takes time, adding to the workload your *Room for Impact* inquiry is designed to reduce! So, where possible, you want to identify efficient measuring sticks that give you the insights that you need but without significant additional effort. You might, for example, opt to leverage preexisting data-systems that are already widely used within your school—including student outcomes data, timetabling and staff utilization data, and resource/expenditure management systems—rather than wastefully reinvent the wheel. And, where you do need to collect new types of data, you will want to identify ways of doing this efficiently. For example, the monitoring of wall displays could be embedded into your leadership team's existing daily building walks. There is no need to walk just to look at the walls!

2. **Perverse incentives.** As Bank of England economist Charles Goodhart remarked in 1983, "Once a measure becomes a target, it ceases to be a good measure" (Strathern, 1997). This is now known as Goodhart's Law (generally known as Campbell's law in the United States). Sometimes, when people become fixated on a specific metric and their numerical performance against this, they can become incentivized to move the needle at all costs. A recent example from England is that hospitals were evaluated on how long patients brought into the Emergency Room (usually called "Casualty" in England) had to wait to be seen by medical personnel. The result? Hospitals were keeping patients in ambulances because as soon as the patient came out of the ambulance, the clock started ticking. For an educational example, system-level school accountability tools are often implemented to improve teacher performance, but these measures have often resulted in unintended (but predictable) consequences, such as teaching only the material that is likely to be included in the test or to suggest to parents that it might be helpful to keep weaker students at home on the day of the exam—so that they didn't drag the school averages down. The educational equivalent of keeping patients in ambulances!

   To be fair, your *Room for Impact* measurements will likely encourage educators to become more efficient and achieve the same or more but in less time. But you still need to think about any potential for perverse incentives as you select your evaluative indicators.

3. **Covering the bases.** Our discussion above about opportunity cost and perverse incentives may leave you with the impression that perhaps it's better not to evaluate at all. But you really do need to cover your evaluative bases. For example, you cannot assume that what is written in your plan will actually get done and that, even if it does, this results in successful de-implementation. Instead, you increase your probability of success by assuming that things will not work out (quite) as intended and that you really do need to monitor and evaluate to check and then decide where to next.

Continuing with the wall display case study that we have been following across some of the previous chapters, you might narrow in on the domains and indicators illustrated in Figure 8.4. Remember that the goal of this de-implementation initiative is to stop teachers generating fresh wall displays.

FIGURE 8.4	Selecting Evaluative Indicators–De-Implementing Wall Display Worked Example	
NO.	**EVALUATIVE DOMAIN**	**INDICATOR**
1.	Monitoring	**Wall Display Counting** Via daily building walk from vice principal
2.	Time	**Time expended on wall display per teacher per term** Estimated via informal teacher discussions
3.	Side Effects	**Student voice group** Checking whether students raise questions or concerns about the removal of wall display

In this case, the backbone team has decided that they are most interested in measuring three things: first, whether new wall displays are being generated; second, how much time is being saved by not developing wall displays; and, third, whether the absence of new wall displays are resulting in any negative side effects for students. They've kept it relatively simple because wall displays are one of many de-implementation strategies they are pursuing and because it's also one of the more straightforward.

Key Action 4: Setting Your Targets (and Kill Parameters)

Now that you have agreed on your evaluative question focus areas and indicators, your next step is to set targets against this. You are also deciding how frequently you will sit down and review the collected data and to what end (including pre-agreeing on the circumstances under which you would "kill" your project).

Setting Target Values

For each of your selected evaluative instruments, you are now going to record your baseline or starting value and also set out how you expect that value to change over time.

Going back to our dieting example at the very start of the chapter, this is like:

- agreeing that you will measure success through the use of weighing scales;

- getting on said scales on January first and recording a baseline weight of one hundred kilograms; and then

- setting yourself the target of getting it down to eighty kilograms by October thirty-first – at a rate of two kilograms weight loss per month.

In our sister volume, *Building to Impact*, we outlined several approaches to target setting. These included theoretical best, international best, national best, regional/local best, (apples with apples) comparator best, and plain old incremental gradient. The last one is a little like licking your finger, sticking it in the air, and then just plotting out straight line growth—at a narrow gradient.

Of course, when you are implementing, there are lots of comparative data points to give you insights about what is possible. These come from a range of places including effect size data, PISA rankings, and program evaluations in similar schools to your own. From these, you can plot out what is theoretically possible for your school to achieve—with a fair wind.

But you are not implementing. You are de-implementing! And alas, there really isn't much data from other contexts that you can leverage to help you answer the question "how low can we go?" As we highlighted in the introductory chapters, there are only a handful of education sector publications on de-implementation. And although the vein is slightly richer in the healthcare literature, the lion's share of the research is still focused on socializing the idea of de-implementation rather than providing metric data on prior successes.

So, until the data gap is plugged, we suggest that (for now) it is perfectly fine to use common sense to set your targets and think deeply about what is feasible vs. practical vs. possible and by when. This means that you set yourselves (sufficiently) stretching but achievable targets and that during de-implementation you review often to see whether you are under or overshooting.

You might use a tracking tool like the one in Figure 8.5 to lay out your agreed upon indicators, baseline values, and target values across time.

FIGURE 8.5   Indicator Tracking—Wall Display Worked Example

NO.	EVALUATIVE DOMAIN	INDICATOR	BASELINE VALUE	T1 TARGET	T2 TARGET	T3 TARGET
1.	Monitoring	Wall Display Counting Via daily building walk from VP	Lots	None	None	None
2.	Time	Time expended on wall displays per teacher per term Estimated via informal teacher discussions	28 hours	0 hours	0 hours	0 hours
3.	Side Effects	Student voice group Checking whether students raise questions or concerns about the removal of wall displays	No questions	Some concerns	Acceptance	Acceptance

You will notice that this worked example—which, again, illustrates the removal of wall displays—seeks to keep the evaluative processes as simple as possible. The monitoring of wall displays is basically a binary calculation; that is, there are currently "lots" of wall displays to a target of there being "none" and for this being maintained across time. There is no value in going around the school and counting the individual display items and then recounting each month to come to an exact figure (i.e., "last month there were seventy-eight new items of display put up but this month only eleven"). For wall displays, eyeballing and estimating is likely to be completely fine. But the backbone team still needs to monitor and ensure that no new wall display has sneaked up.

Measuring expenditure of time is a more critical activity as the whole point of wall display de-implementation is to save time. Through time-logging, the twenty-eight-hour-per-term figure was established. But the opportunity cost of continuing to time-log into the future is quite high, so there is agreement by the backbone team that informal teacher discussions will be used to estimate the future time savings. Obviously, if the wall displays stop getting changed (as measured through the monitoring activity), the teachers are no longer spending twenty-eight hours a term generating it!

Finally, we have side effects, which are about checking that the removal of wall displays are not making the school uninviting and that the students accept the change. Rather than directly asking students how they feel about the removal of wall display, the backbone team has instead simply opted to tell the children what is happening and the rationale. And then to qualitatively gauge the reaction of voice groups and to qualitatively plot how this changes over time. There are pros as well as cons to this strategy.

On the one hand, by not overtly asking students "how they feel" or whether the removal of wall displays "makes them sad," the children are not being pre-primed to think and respond negatively about the change. But, on the other hand, simply assuming that when questions about wall displays from voice groups stop emerging, this means that the students now welcome the change, is not necessarily a sound assumption either. The children may say nothing but feel aggrieved or, more optimistically, say nothing because they have gotten used to the new "wallpaper" of bare walls.

This draws attention to the fact that there is always ambiguity. Firstly, there is fuzziness about whether your de-implementation initiative will actually be successful. And, secondly, it compounds the haziness about whether you have selected the most appropriate evaluative questions and measuring sticks to properly check on progress and then decide what to do next. As you undertake divergent and convergent thinking during this P-step, you are beginning to preempt these questions. And, of course, you will come back to this all again during the **(4.1) aPpraise-step** because part of appraising is also about reviewing (and reconsidering) your evaluative approach!

Setting Frequency Intervals (and Kill Parameters)

The second thing you will do during Key Action 4 is set your evaluative frequency intervals. For, while you are likely collecting data on both a daily and weekly basis, it is likely not very helpful to look at this constantly and in real time. The danger is that you might not be able to see the signal in the noise.

Therefore, we recommend that your Backbone Organization commits to a formal and fixed review cycle—in advance. Although we offer no hard and fast rules, we suggest that you:

- **Monitor:** on a weekly basis

- **Evaluate:** on a three- to six-week cycle

Let's unpack this. Monitoring is about tracking progress on your agreed upon actions. Back in (2.2) *Prepare*, you developed your de-implementation action plan. This laid out your *what, who, when,* and *how* parameters. So, the idea is that you commit to going back to this activity plan every week to reconfirm that your agreed upon de-implementation actions have, indeed, been acted upon.

Evaluation, by contrast, is about checking that these de-implementation actions have saved sufficient time/resources and (most importantly) without harming student outcomes. You will want to commit to reviewing this data every three to six weeks and to getting these review dates/ checkpoints formally inserted in your project plan/calendar. In the earlier weeks and months of your de-implementation initiative, we suggest that you hold these reviews at three-week intervals (enough time for you to have done something but not so much that interest and momentum start to fizzle). You can then space these evaluative checkpoints further out as your de-implementation initiative beds in and you have greater confidence in the impact.

Kill Parameters

A cognitive bias that sometimes afflicts the implementation of new initiatives is the Plan Continuation Bias. This is where we continue with something that isn't working even though we know it isn't working. There are several reasons we might do this:

- Because we have invested heavily in the new initiative (e.g., time, resources, goodwill, political capital) and because it's hard to admit defeat (a.k.a. the sunk cost fallacy)

- Because we think that if we wait long enough, we might pull up from the initial nosedive (a.k.a. the optimism bias)

- Because we *like* doing it. People are having fun de-implementing and don't want to look at data suggesting that they are busy fools.

This means ineffective actions can get carried forward because no one has the heart (or the guts) to kill them. In the business world, companies often use formal protocols such as the Stage-Gate process to change the default from "We carry on unless we have good reason to stop" to "We stop unless we have good reason to carry on."

In a similar vein, the *Room for Impact* protocols provide a formal check on progress so that you can take stock of all those energy-zapping happy projects that make not one iota of difference and get rid of them.

(Continued)

(Continued)

However, it is also possible that you inadvertently de-implement the wrong things, use the wrong de-implementation strategy for your context, and cause harm. This is the principal reason that you are evaluating as you go—because while you want to save time/resources and be more efficient, you do not want to do this at the cost of declining student outcomes.

But the counter risk is that the Plan Continuation Bias afflicts your de-implementation initiatives, too. That you ignore dips in student outcome data, that you become enthralled with following the P-steps, and that you are reluctant to change course because of all the political capital you have attended to when setting up the backbone team in the first place.

Of course, generating failure with one de-implementation initiative does not mean you need to give up the whole notion of de-implementation. It just means you need to go back to the drawing board and identify a different thing to de-implement and/or a different strategy to get there for the existing one.

But by setting your **Kill Parameters** in advance—in writing—you have established a rules-based system for stopping. You are saying "if X, Y, or Z happens, we kill this thing immediately. There is no debate. There are no get-out clauses. We just stop. Immediately. The end."

Setting Kill Parameters are a highly suggested (but optional) component of this P-step. Two of the kill-signs you might consider include:

1. **Where the time/resources required to successfully de-implement have turned out to be greater than what you are supposed to be saving via your *Room for Impact* inquiry,** particularly where this is not a short-term objection and where there is no obvious end in sight—that is, the cure is worse than the disease.

2. **Where there is clear evidence of harm to student impact—that is, the side effects are excessive.**

Once you have laid out your Kill Parameters, you ask, as part of your three- to six-week evaluation checkpoints, "Yes or no; have we breached the Kill Parameters?" And if yes, you stop immediately.

Summary

During **(2.3)** *Picture* you have undertaken four key actions:

- **Key Action 1:** Defined what success looks like (i.e., pictured it)
- **Key Action 2:** Agreed on your evaluative focus areas and questions
- **Key Action 3:** Established your indicators (or measuring) sticks for each focus area
- **Key Action 4:** Set your targets (and kill parameters).

You have done this because of outcomes ambiguity. While, in advance of de-implementation, we can make educated guesses about how things will play out and even talk in terms of probabilities, we can never be certain. And this is why we need an evaluative plan set out in advance, so that we can check as we go.

With this now in place, we are ready to activate our de-implementation plans. We are ready for (3.1) Proceed!

(2.3) Picture: Convergent Cross-Checking and Agreeing

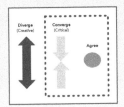

Before you get to (3.1) *Proceed*, here are some of the critical cross-checking questions for you to consider:

1. Have we fully pictured/defined what success looks like? Are there any additional criteria that we could/should include?

2. Have we selected the most appropriate evaluative focus areas/questions?

3. Have we considered the opportunity cost of collecting data against each of these?

4. Have we explored and selected the most appropriate measuring sticks/indicators? Why did we select the ones we did?

5. Have we set reasonable targets that meet the Goldilocks criteria of being not too hard, not too easy, but just right? And are we sure we are genuinely aiming for the Goldilocks zone?

6. Have we agreed on the frequency that we will review data and (optionally) our kill parameters?

If so, we are now really ready to progress to the De-Implement Stage and to (3.1) *Proceed!*

Part 4

De-Implement Stage

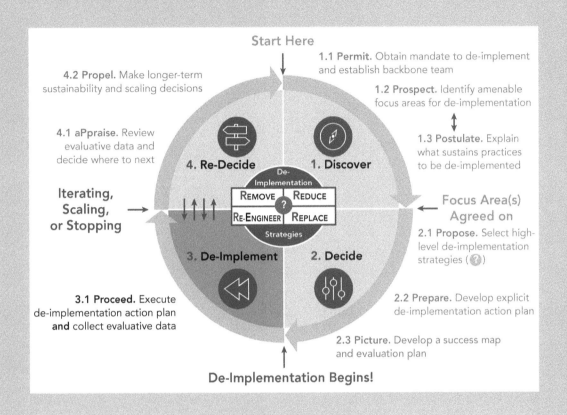

Start Here

1.1 Permit. Obtain mandate to de-implement and establish backbone team

1.2 Prospect. Identify amenable focus areas for de-implementation

4.2 Propel. Make longer-term sustainability and scaling decisions

1.3 Postulate. Explain what sustains practices to be de-implemented

4.1 aPpraise. Review evaluative data and decide where to next

4. Re-Decide

1. Discover

De-Implementation
| REMOVE | REDUCE |
| RE-ENGINEER | REPLACE |
Strategies

Iterating, Scaling, or Stopping

Focus Area(s) Agreed on

2.1 Propose. Select high-level de-implementation strategies ( )

3. De-Implement

2. Decide

3.1 Proceed. Execute de-implementation action plan **and** collect evaluative data

2.2 Prepare. Develop explicit de-implementation action plan

2.3 Picture. Develop a success map and evaluation plan

De-Implementation Begins!

3.1: Proceed
Execute
De-Implementation
Action Plan

Proceed (3.1)

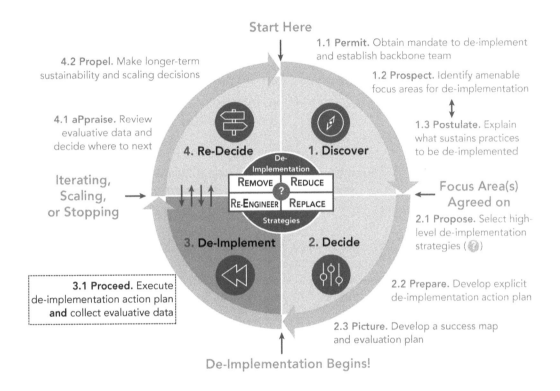

Start Here

1.1 **Permit.** Obtain mandate to de-implement and establish backbone team

1.2 **Prospect.** Identify amenable focus areas for de-implementation

1.3 **Postulate.** Explain what sustains practices to be de-implemented

4.2 **Propel.** Make longer-term sustainability and scaling decisions

4.1 **aPpraise.** Review evaluative data and decide where to next

4. Re-Decide

1. Discover

De-Implementation

| REMOVE | ? | REDUCE |
| RE-ENGINEER | | REPLACE |

Strategies

Iterating, Scaling, or Stopping

Focus Area(s) Agreed on

2.1 **Propose.** Select high-level de-implementation strategies ( )

3. De-Implement

2. Decide

3.1 Proceed. Execute de-implementation action plan **and** collect evaluative data

2.2 **Prepare.** Develop explicit de-implementation action plan

2.3 **Picture.** Develop a success map and evaluation plan

De-Implementation Begins!

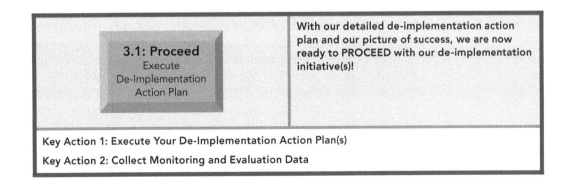

3.1: Proceed Execute De-Implementation Action Plan	With our detailed de-implementation action plan and our picture of success, we are now ready to PROCEED with our de-implementation initiative(s)!

Key Action 1: Execute Your De-Implementation Action Plan(s)

Key Action 2: Collect Monitoring and Evaluation Data

Introduction

If you are an avid reader and have devoured many books by different authors in different styles, no doubt you will have noticed their various literary devices. One common trick is to start chapter introductions with a smattering of quotes from the great and the good (or at least attributed to them) on the theme that is to be discussed. So here goes:

"By failing to prepare, you are preparing to fail."

Benjamin Franklin

"You were born to win, but to be a winner, you must plan to win, prepare to win, and expect to win."

Zig Ziglar

"Luck is what happens when preparation meets opportunity."

Seneca the Younger

"Give me six hours to chop down a tree and I will spend the first four sharpening the axe."

Attributed to Abraham Lincoln

In their respective ways, these quotations express the notion that prior to (most) success, a significant quantum of time, energy, and thinking have been (necessarily) spilled on planning and preparation. And that it is this foundational work that primes for success.

It is exactly for this reason that we have ended up two-thirds through this book—and our P-steps—without any de-implementation yet occurring. All the prior P-steps have been designed to take you by the hand and support you in thinking and working through the optimal parameters for de-implementation success. They've helped you sharpen the axe: because it's all in the planning.

You started by establishing a de-implementation backbone team and by getting your permit and mandate to proceed (1.1). You then prospected your current terrain, looking at all the things you currently do within your school or system that are inefficient, selecting the one(s) that are ripe for de-implementation (1.2). After this, you then explained or postulated what it was that sustained those existing practices (a.k.a. Chesterton's Fence) to help you select the most appropriate de-implementation strategies (1.3). You then proposed those high-level strategies—that is, whether to Remove, Reduce, Re-Engineer, or to Replace (2.1). With this agreed, you prepared further by fleshing this out into a more detailed plan (2.2). Then, you Pictured what success looks like and established your success criteria and evaluation plan (2.2).

All this prior thinking and planning now brings you to **(3.1) *Proceed***. This is the moment where the pedal hits the metal or where Abraham

Lincoln takes the axe to the tree. However, unlike the other P-steps, we have no specific protocols or processes that you must work through as you bring your plans to action as you Proceed. All the heavy lifting in this regard has largely been completed during the previous P-steps.

During (2.2) *Prepare*, you fleshed out a detailed action plan for each of your agreed upon de-implementation initiatives. This plan set out your *what*, *where*, *when*, *who*, and *how* parameters. You also stress tested this via, for example, pre-mortem to reduce the probability that things go off the rails during de-implementation. And, during (2.3) *Picture*, you also laid out your evaluative questions and indicators in some detail, including who, when, and how readings would be taken. And what would be done with all the delicious data.

For want of a better expression, (3.1) *Proceed* is largely a black box—to us. Your prior workings and thinking mean that you have already undertaken significant planning. You know what is inside your specific black box, so by definition it isn't a black box to you. But, literally, "all" you are doing during this P-step is:

- **Key Action 1: Execute Your De-implementation Action Plan(s)** – here, you are following the agreed upon steps, to the agreed upon timelines, with the agreed upon action owners. You are executing to de-implement!

- **Key Action 2: Collect Monitoring and Evaluation Data** – this is your equivalent of getting on the weighing scales each day, taking the reading, and writing it down so that you can review it later and consider the data in light of the bigger picture.

In this chapter, we work through these Key Actions, which do not take long to unpack. Then we provide a recap of all the key thinking and decisions that have led you to (3.1) Proceed. You can think of this as a form of spaced repetition—a means for us to consolidate and reinforce some of the main look-fors of de-implementation.

Key Action 1: Execute Your De-implementation Action Plan(s)

Back in (2.2) *Prepare*, you laid out your step-by-step de-implementation plan(s). You might have just one plan that progresses a big, meaty, and challenging de-implementation agenda. Or you might have several plans, which could be a concurrent mixture of easier "low-hanging fruit" initiatives and harder-to-achieve goals.

Within your detailed de-implementation plan(s), you have already described each key task, the action owner, start date, and end date. You will remember that there was also a final column called "Progress"; this is to help you track and record the degree to which you have achieved each task.

As you (3.1) *Proceed* to de-implementation, we recommend that one member of your backbone team or Professional Learning Community

BE explicitly tasked as the **project manager**. The core part of this role is to keep track of progress, to check in with action owners for each task, to chivvy them, and to report to the backbone leader/organizational sponsor on progress and slippages.

Figures 9.1, 9.2, and 9.3 illustrate what such reporting could look like. You will recognize the REMOVE Wall Display, RE-ENGINEER Student Detentions, and REPLACE Bespoke Curriculum Materials case studies from Chapter 7. In these worked examples, however, you will see that the Progress column has now also been completed. This contains a RAG (red, amber, green) dashboard, followed by a written commentary for each task.

As you review these three worked examples, we want you to understand that these are intended to be living documents. The idea is that the project manager reviews progress against each task—**ideally on a weekly basis**—and updates the RAG indicator and the narrative for any still open tasks.

You might notice, too, that in some instances the narrative text goes beyond merely reporting on whether the agreed upon things have been done. On occasion, it also gets into whether what is being done is working. This thinking is critical because we cannot know for sure whether seemingly good ideas turn out to be good, in reality, until we collect monitoring and evaluation data to know the impact. This brings us to the second key action of (3.1) *Proceed*—collecting your agreed upon monitoring and evaluation data.

FIGURE 9.1   Implementing Your Explicit Action Plan – Example 1 "REMOVE"

TARGET AREA FOR DE-IMPLEMENTATION	
Overarching Description of De-Implementation Target Area	De-Implementation of Wall Displays for Classrooms, Corridors, and Public Areas of the School

NO.	TASK DESCRIPTION	OWNER	START DATE	END DATE	PROGRESS
1.	**Whole School Communications Session** Vice principal (VP)/assistant principal briefs all colleagues on the (lack of) research evidence on benefits of wall displays and primes behavior change. This also includes information on material incentives, i.e., the team lunch from stationary budget savings.	VP	1/10	1/10	Red Amber Green **Complete**. Briefing took place and was well received by teams.

NO.	TASK DESCRIPTION	OWNER	START DATE	END DATE	PROGRESS
2.	**Subject Team Communications** Each head of department (HoD) reinforces VP messages at weekly team meeting.	HoDs: - Arts - Science - Sports	2/10	10/10	Red Amber Green **Partially Complete.** Arts team still to complete. But does not seem to be dampening whole-school enthusiasm.
3.	**Removal of Display Wall Stationary** This will be locked away in the principal's private storage closet.	VP	2/10	2/10	Red Amber Green **Complete.** All locked away!
4.	**Monitoring Walks** Weekly monitoring walk to review all wall space and ensure no new materials have been pinned. VP feedback discussion with colleagues from any areas of the school where new wall display is pinned.	VP	15/10	Ongoing	Red Amber Green **Inconsistent.** VP is struggling to find time to progress.

FIGURE 9.2   Implementing Your Explicit Action Plan – Example 2 "RE-ENGINEER"

1. TARGET AREA FOR DE-IMPLEMENTATION

Overarching Description of De-Implementation Target Area	**Decentralized Student Detention System With Teachers Supervising Their Own Detentions**

2. "AS IS" PROCESS: DECENTRALIZED DETENTIONS	TIME EXPENDED

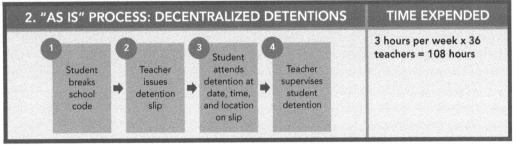

3 hours per week x 36 teachers = 108 hours

1. Student breaks school code
2. Teacher issues detention slip
3. Student attends detention at date, time, and location on slip
4. Teacher supervises student detention

(Continued)

(Continued)

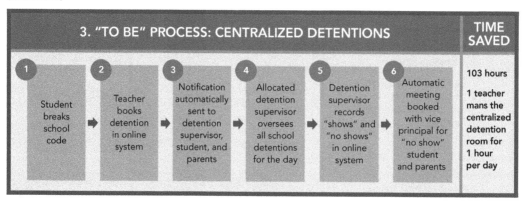

3. "TO BE" PROCESS: CENTRALIZED DETENTIONS	TIME SAVED
1 Student breaks school code ⇒ **2** Teacher books detention in online system ⇒ **3** Notification automatically sent to detention supervisor, student, and parents ⇒ **4** Allocated detention supervisor oversees all school detentions for the day ⇒ **5** Detention supervisor records "shows" and "no shows" in online system ⇒ **6** Automatic meeting booked with vice principal for "no show" student and parents	103 hours 1 teacher mans the centralized detention room for 1 hour per day

4. DETAILED TASK LIST

NO.	TASK DESCRIPTION	OWNER	START DATE	END DATE	PROGRESS
1.	**Activation and Testing of Behavior Management Module in School Online Management System** School IT Manager activates system module, customizes fields to align with proposed process flow, and undertakes testing in partnership with backbone team	IT manager	1/9	20/9	Red **Amber** Green **Incomplete.** System customization has proven more difficult than expected. IT manager is currently working directly with the vendor. In the meantime, we are using an online spreadsheet to log detentions. This creates slightly more friction/admin work for staff.
2.	**Whole School Communications Session** Vice principal (VP)/ assistant principal briefs all colleagues on the revised plan	VP	30/9	30/9	Red Amber **Green** **Complete.** Well received. Feedback from staff was that this initiative made a great deal of sense.
3.	**Staff Rotation and Room Bookings** Staff rotation set for term and detention room booked	Backbone team	20/9	29/9	Red Amber **Green** **Complete.** Some staff are informally swapping but this is not currently creating any issues.
4.	**Monitoring and Feedback Walks** VP building walks for first month to ensure that no staff continue to administer decentralized detentions	VP	1/10	30/10	Red **Amber** Green **Ongoing.** VP is consistently undertaking monitoring walks but has not had feedback conversations with the three staff members who are still persisting with decentralized detentions.

4. DETAILED TASK LIST					
NO.	**TASK DESCRIPTION**	**OWNER**	**START DATE**	**END DATE**	**PROGRESS**
5.	**Evaluation Review** End of term "Lessons Learned" meeting with all staff to collect feedback and suggestions for improvement	VP	15/12	15/12	Red Amber Green **Ongoing.** We are collecting the agreed upon monitoring and evaluation data, but we have not yet properly reviewed it to decide "where to next?"

FIGURE 9.3   Implementing Your Explicit Action Plan – Example 3 "REPLACE"

TARGET AREA FOR DE-IMPLEMENTATION	
Overarching Description of De-Implementation Target Area	Development of Bespoke and Localized Teaching, Learning, and Student Assessment Materials by Our Teaching Teams

A. REMOVE PLAN					
Behaviors to be REMOVED:					
• Educators stop developing their own teaching and learning materials from scratch					
NO.	**TASK DESCRIPTION**	**OWNER**	**START DATE**	**END DATE**	**PROGRESS**
1.	**Whole School Communications Sessions** Training session delivered by the organization providing the professionally developed teaching and learning materials	External Org	1/5	1/7	Red Amber Green **Complete.** The session was a partial success. Not all staff bought into the idea that off-the-shelf materials can be as effective as their locally developed resources.[1]

(Continued)

---

[1]But this is OK, because even if the off-the-shelf materials are not as good as the materials the teacher would have produced, the time freed up could be used to improve student learning in other ways. This is at the heart of Pareto analysis. It's not whether the off-the-shelf materials are as good as those the teacher would produce. It's whether the extra time that teacher-produced materials would require is a use of that time that has the greatest benefit for students.

(Continued)

NO.	TASK DESCRIPTION	OWNER	START DATE	END DATE	PROGRESS
2.	**PLC Social Support Meetings** PLC meetings that focus on de-implementation of locally developed teaching materials. Head of department (HoD) colleagues will report on progress and collectively identify actions to address any backsliding	HoDs: - Arts - Science - Sports	1/9	Ongoing	Red Amber Green **Ongoing.** Social support framing is proving effective except for one specific PLC group.
3.	**Incentives** School policy changed to discourage development of own materials Individual performance objectives to be tied to use of the third-party program	Principal	1/6	1/7	Red Amber Green **Work in Progress.** Some challenges with members of the school board that are still to be unpicked. Principal is on the case!
4.	**Nudges and Friction** Daily WhatsApp reminders for first month Photocopier moved to annex building to make it difficult for teachers to print/copy their own individually developed materials Poster prompts placed above photocopier and in the staff room	VP	1/9	Ongoing	Red Amber Green WhatsApp messages **ongoing.** Photocopier moved to annex and posters in position!
5.	**Monitoring and Feedback** Weekly auditing of teaching and learning materials by VP to check whether any locally developed materials are "creeping back in"	VP	1/9	Ongoing	Red Amber Green **Ongoing.** Monitoring and feedback data being collected in line with the plan. We are not yet using the data for improvement conversations.

B. REPLACE PLAN					
Replacement Actions:					
• Teachers use high-quality teaching and learning materials that have been professionally developed and evaluated by a third-party organization					
NO.	**TASK DESCRIPTION**	**OWNER**	**START DATE**	**END DATE**	**PROGRESS**
1.	**Third-Party Curriculum Offerings Identified** Backbone team undertakes landscape analysis of potential curriculum programs, including review of evaluation data and visits to other schools. Wider school body consulted with decision on preferred program reached.	Backbone team	8/1	28/2	Red Amber Green **Complete.** We identified four potentially viable programs and undertook study visits to schools to further evaluate.
2.	**Selected Third-Party Curriculum Offer Procured** Competitive procurement with vendor presentations and review of contract terms, support provided, and impact data	Backbone team	1/3	15/4	Red Amber Green **Complete.** Process included representation from all affected subject departments to help increase buy-in and adoption.
3.	**Teaching Teams Trained in Use of New Curriculum Model** Initial training in new program delivered on whole school basis	External org.	1/5	1/7	Red Amber Green **Complete.** Several workshops held, with follow-up modeling and coaching. Not all staff completely bought in, however. Some evidence of teachers expending time customizing new materials/blending with existing offerings.
4.	**Ongoing Support Via PLCs** Linked to Action 2 on REMOVE plan – the PLCs will simultaneously review progress on the REPLACEMENT actions	Head of department (HoD)	1/9	Ongoing	Red Amber Green **Ongoing.** Same issue with one PLC group – as per item 2 in the "REMOVE" plan.
5.	**Monitoring and Evaluation Activity** Vice principal/assistant principal to undertake weekly sampling audits to ensure teachers are using the new materials Monthly evaluation feedback sessions via data collected from PLCs	VP	1/9	Ongoing	Red Amber Green **On track.** Data is being collected to the Monitoring and Evaluation plan indicators but is not yet being consistently used for performance improvement conversations – as per item 5 in "REMOVE" plan.

Key Action 2: Collect Your Monitoring and Evaluation Data

Back in **(2.3)** *Picture*, you identified your evaluative questions, your indicators (or measuring sticks) for each of these, and then set your targets across time. The reason you did this is because of *outcomes ambiguity*. We cannot assume that there will genuinely be impact just by successfully progressing an initiative and keeping all your RAG tracking indicators firmly in the green. Too often we mistake activity for impact. We assume that if we implement the agreed upon actions on time, on budget, and with high fidelity, this will always and automatically convert to successful outcomes. Instead, we need to firmly keep the distinction between inputs, outputs, and outcomes in our minds. And we delineate each of these in Figure 9.4.

FIGURE 9.4	Inputs, Outputs, Outcomes
CATEGORY	**DEFINITION**
Inputs	The time, resources, materials, action, and energy that we invest
Outputs	The products or deliverables that we create with these inputs, e.g., workshops, online platforms, coaching programs, and tasks ticked off on our de-implementation action plan
Outcomes	The impact generated, e.g., time saved, resources rekindled, educator well-being enhanced, student learning outcomes maintained or enhanced

The activity tracking described in the previous section (Key Step 1) can help you keep on top of inputs and outputs. It can tell you whether your teams are investing the *intended* time and energy on the key tasks in your de-implementation action plan, i.e., the inputs. And it can also tell you whether this energy is being converted into the intended artifacts, i.e., ticking off the outputs on your task list. But this does not tell you whether there will be strong outcomes. To know about outcomes, you need to collect the evaluative data in line with the tracking system you established in (2.3) *Picture*.

In Figure 9.5 we recap the Wall Display evaluative tracking grid unpacked in the last chapter. You will remember that this was deliberately kept simple because removing wall displays is *sort of* straightforward, so why overthink the evaluation systems. We simply need to eyeball that no new wall displays have gone up, confirm that teachers have saved time by not creating it, and check that the students are OK with it.

For smaller initiatives like this, it's perfectly acceptable for the backbone team to informally track whether the data is being collected simply by having weekly and then monthly conversations with those tasked with collecting it. Why boil the ocean in the generation of tracking paperwork when a two-minute conversation will do? But for more complex endeavors, you might want to use a tracking sheet for each indicator, like the one illustrated in Figure 9.6.

FIGURE 9.5 Indicator Tracking – Wall Display Worked Example

NO.	EVALUATIVE DOMAIN	INDICATOR	WHO	WHEN	BASELINE VALUE	T1 TARGET	T2 TARGET	T3 TARGET
1.	Monitoring	**Wall Display Counting** **Via daily building walk from VP**	VP	Daily	Lots	None	None	None
2.	Time	**Time expended on wall display per teacher per term** Estimated via informal teacher discussions	PM	Termly	28 hours	0 hours	0 hours	0 hours
3.	Side Effects	**Student voice group** Checking whether students raise questions or concerns about the removal of wall displays	PM	Termly	No questions	Some concerns	Acceptance	Acceptance

FIGURE 9.6 Indicator Tracking Sheet

INDICATOR | WALL DISPLAY COUNTING

NO.	EVALUATIVE DOMAIN	INDICATOR	WHO	WHEN	BASELINE VALUE	TERM 1 TARGET	TERM 2 TARGET	TERM 3 TARGET
1.	Monitoring	Wall Display Counting Via daily learning walk from VP	VP	Daily	Lots	None	None	None

TRACKING

Week 1 Daily Checks Y/N	Findings	Week 2 Daily Checks Y/N	Findings	Week 3 Daily Checks Y/N	Findings	Week 4 Daily Checks Y/N	Findings	Week 5 Daily Checks Y/N	Findings
Y	No New Display	Y	No New Display	Y	New Display in Science Corridor	N	N/A	Y	No New Display

There is no rocket science to this. You have an evaluative plan with agreed upon action owners, indicators, actions, and baseline values. You are now just tracking to make sure that you are indeed collecting the data you agreed to, enabling you to know your impact. That's all there is to it. The complexity comes from what's inside the black box—the specific actions and indicators that you are progressing and tracking—which, in turn, is down to the decisions that you have taken during the preceding P-steps.

—

To summarize, during the **(3.1) *Proceed*-step**, you have undertaken the following:

- **Key Action 1:** Executed Your De-implementation Action Plan(s) – you are following the agreed upon steps, to the agreed upon timelines, with the agreed upon action owners. You are executing to de-implement!

- **Key Action 2:** Collected Monitoring and Evaluation Data – this is your equivalent of getting on the weighing scales each day, taking the reading, and writing it down, so that you can review it later and consider the data in light of the bigger picture.

Recap of Your Building to Impact Journey

Now that you have launched and are monitoring your de-implementation initiatives, we want to pause for a moment and take stock by recapping *Eight Things* that you need to keep in view. You can think of this section as a sort of spaced-repetition memory consolidation device—the sort of thing that TV shows provide in the form of a three-minute season one recap before you start watching season two.

Thing 1: Your System-level Will Affect
How You Leverage the P-Steps

There are many ways that you can utilize the *Room for Impact* protocols. For example, you might be reading this book from the perspective of an **individual practitioner**—looking for ideas to help you to reduce your personal workload. Or you might be leveraging the P-steps within your **Professional Learning Community**—working in partnership with other educators to permit, prospect, postulate, propose, and all the rest.

Alternatively, you might be working at school level having established a formal backbone organization or well-being committee, for example. And be searching for de-implementation opportunities that can be progressed at **whole-school level**. Or you might even be working at **system level**, whether that be a collection of schools in the same locality (a.k.a. a district, community of learning, local authority, or multi-academy trust, etc.) or at a regional or even national level.

We think you will find the *Room for Impact* protocols useful in all these contexts. If you are exploring the P-steps as an individual practitioner, you will likely draw on them more for inspiration and ideas rather than following them step-by-step. Where our suggested processes come into their own is when you work collaboratively with other practitioners to collectively explore the possibilities and collectively traverse from divergent thinking to convergent thinking, and then to agreement on what will be done.

Obviously, at different levels of the system, you will have different levels of permission. At the regional or national level, you can rewrite the rules and regulations to promote efficiency of impact, but you have less control over how local agents interpret those rules. At the local level, you are rule takers more than rule makers, but as you explore the existing regulations, we suspect you might find more wiggle room to progress your *Room for Impact* initiatives than you ever felt possible. And you may be surprised to find that some things you thought were "against the rules" are not. And that the rulebook in your head differs from what is written on paper!

Thing 2: Your Rationale for De-Implementation

You might be interested in de-implementation for a host of reasons, including:

- **Efficiency of Impact**—that is, generating the *same outcomes* but with less time, energy, and resources (**a.k.a. achieving the same for less and getting Lean**)

- **Choosing Wisely**—that is, generating *stronger outcomes* by substituting or swapping out existing "good" practices with "better" approaches that drive up student outcomes (**a.k.a. achieving more with the same**)

- **Resource Conservation**—that is, you might be facing budgetary constraints that force you to make difficult choices about what to invest in and what to cut (**a.k.a. getting more bang for your buck**)

- **Educator Well-being**—that is, reducing practitioner workload and stress (**a.k.a. getting your lives back**).

Most of these reasons are compatible with one another. Efficiency of impact, resource conservation, and educator well-being all pull in the same direction and can be pursued simultaneously as part of a strategy to do less to achieve *at least* the same student outcomes.

However, few educators are comfortable thinking and acting from this perspective of Lean efficiency. Instead, there's often the tendency to seek new shiny things to fill the void generated by de-commissioning and de-implementing—the desire to keep the plate equally full but to choose more wisely.

This is, of course, what schools already do all the time: cycling through different fads and fancies. The only difference is that here you would be using *Room for Impact* to ensure you properly excavated the roots and branches of those existing initiatives. Indeed, as Dylan often says, *The difficulty isn't in getting new ideas into teachers' heads, it's in getting the old ones out.* The difficulty is in unlearning and deliberately forgetting, so you don't end up recombining bits of incompatible ideas and programs into disastrous mutations.

While we accept that you may be approaching *Room for Impact* from this Choosing Wisely perspective, we want you to be open-minded to the idea that it's also perfectly acceptable to de-implement without filling the saved time with something else. But if you really must fill it up again, make sure you choose wisely rather than replacing average with average. And our sister publication *Building to Impact* can help you with that.

Thing 3: Your Rate of Travel

In life we can do things fast, slow, or somewhere in between. And the same applies to your *Room for Impact* initiatives. At one extreme you might have formed a backbone team, cleared your collective calendars for a three-to-four-day window and used this time to traverse steps 1.1 *Permit* to 2.3 *Picture* in succession. If you did this, you would have managed your agenda tightly and had clear milestones for which P-step you would be at on respective times and days, so that you didn't rush through your decisions at the end of the final day. You would also, likely, already have Permission (1.1) sorted before you started and the ability to pull in other colleagues—as needed—for second and third opinions as you go.

At the other extreme, you might spend several days in workshops and on data analysis per P-step. This would be followed by yet more workshops to converge and then agree on the most appropriate de-implementation actions. This could see you taking several months to get to the moment where you press play and bring your de-implementation intentions to life.

We think you are more likely to take it slow if: (A) you are working at the system level or planning on de-implementing something that will be very difficult to reverse later; or (B) if you simply do not have the time to pull yourself out of the day-to-day and come together for a multiday sprint. You are more likely to be able to take it fast if you are working at Professional Learning Community level or on de-implementation initiatives that are no-brainers and where you face no entrenched resistance.

Thing 4: How Many De-Implementation Balls to Juggle?

We can do multiple things at once if those things are easy, if we have overlearned them, and if they require little time and mental energy to make them happen. When driving a car, for example, we can talk to our passenger, swig our coffee, put the indicator on, and also make decisions to get to the destination. Conversely, progressing big things—like walking a tightrope between two towers—requires gargantuan levels of concentration to avoid deadly slippage. So, one thing at a time. The same ball-juggling principle applies to *Room for Impact*.

You can either do **one big thing** like getting teachers to uniformly pivot away from developing their own bespoke curriculum materials and instead use a (high-quality) third-party program, with fidelity; or you can implement **ten little things** that are each the equivalent of removing wall displays or introducing stand-up meetings, or setting up a cloud-drive for teachers to share their resources. There is still a lot of habit-based follow-up and reinforcement required to get people to consistently repeat the new behaviors without backsliding. Hence, all that Chesterton's Fence analysis. When we understand what sustains the status quo, we can better guard against relapse.

Thing 5: The Ball-Juggling Technique

There are also (at least) four ways to progress each of our agreed upon de-implementation initiative areas. These are the 4Rs: Remove vs. Reduce vs. Re-Engineer vs. Replace.

REMOVE	REDUCE
i.e., just **stop doing it** completely	i.e., **do it less** frequently or apply it to fewer people
RE-ENGINEER	**REPLACE**
i.e., do it **more efficiently** with fewer steps/actions	i.e., **substitute it** with a more efficient and/or effective alternative

The default course of action, in many schools, is **Replace**. The leadership attends a conference or is introduced to a shiny new idea, program, or widget through some other means. And said leadership team then decides to introduce the new "X-Program" at their school as a replacement for the "Y-Program." Although, in reality, this often ends up with practitioners blending elements of X and Y in a pick-n-mix because they have mentally automated those prior practices and perhaps also like doing them. This can end up being the worst of all possible worlds: a world of disastrous combinations and mutations. So, if you are going to continue with the default position and replace, replace, replace, you need to confirm that the X-Program is worth the trouble and have a clear (and parallel) Remove strategy alongside for the Y-Program. Not a bit of X and a dash of Y.

By far the easiest strategy to progress is **Remove**. It's far easier to stop something completely than it is to **Reduce**—back to that distinction between the rates of success with giving up smoking (removing) and eating less (reducing) that we have discussed in previous chapters. After Remove, we think **Re-Engineer** is likely to be the second easiest strategy to progress. It's about making process efficiencies to existing ways of doing things, chiseling here and optimizing there, resulting in fewer battles about beliefs. Blended phonics implementation in six steps rather than eight. No beliefs-oriented reading wars.

So, pick your high-level de-implementation strategy with great care.

Thing 6: The Psychology of De-Implementation

As we explored in, Chapter 1, there are many reasons for thinking that de-implementation might actually be harder than implementing a new habit or learning a new skill. To recap, some of the reasons for this include:

- **Cognitive bias** – where the literature (tentatively) suggests we may be primed for addition, although we can also be trained out of it—the whole point of the *Room for Impact* protocols!

- **Unlearning is (probably) impossible** – we have no obvious mental trash can. At best we can quarantine unwanted behaviors, but it seems they remain ready to be reactivated and can never be totally purged—unless we sustain a brain injury. And because the unwanted behaviors never go away, we need to be aware they can reemerge, and remember why we decided we did not want them.

- **De-implementation will likely increase your workload in the short term**, while you simultaneously decide what and how you will de-implement *and* carry on implementing as you are deciding and planning.

- **The lack of "oven-ready" processes for successful de-implementation.** Hence, the three of us collaborated on this volume, which is certainly not the last word on the subject. But we hope it will pry the door open to a new way of thinking and acting that others can build atop of and improve yet further–a sort of KonMari for education.

- **What works *here* might not work *there*** – hence we give you processes to help you identify your own locally appropriate actions rather than a list of "sure-fire" de-implementation prescriptions. As Dylan often says, "In education, 'What works?' is not the right question because everything works somewhere and nothing works everywhere." The right question is "Under what circumstances will this work?" which is why your expertise and your knowledge of your local context is essential.

- **You need to attend to de-implementation continually.** As Parkinson's Law attests, the work gradually creeps up to fill the time available unless you consciously work to keep it down!

Inevitably, you may also find that there is resistance among your colleagues to de-implementation. This might be because of a mixture of those guilt- and shame-based drivers. It might be because folks do not believe de-implementation will result in better outcomes (possibly a reasonable belief that needs careful testing). Or it might be because they just *like* doing things the overengineered way and that the superfluous steps are the aspects of their role that give them the most joy and that make them feel the most alive—or at least virtuous! Hence, the whole focus of (1.3) *Postulate* is exploring what sustains existing practices (a.k.a. Chesterton's Fence analysis), so that you can respond to this.

Thing 7: Outcomes Ambiguity

As with much in life, we only know when we know. When our de-implementation plan is put into action, we can see with our eyes whether it "worked" or not. So many things seem like a good idea at the time but subsequently turn out not to be.

In our work we are consistently finding that impact is more likely when everyone:

- treats the endeavor as an experiment,

- is committed to gathering the data to see how it went, and

- uses this collected data for continuous improvement rather than for cherry-picking success stories.

This is the difference between evaluation to test a hypothesis and evaluation to "prove" something worked, even if it didn't.

Our prior research and planning can only give us a sense of the probabilities. If we assume that by planning properly the outcome will always be "and they all lived happily ever after," we are not going to double-check that they did. We need to be gleeful evaluators of our impact and not bury our heads in the sand if we don't like what we see when we look at the data (which in the cognitive bias literature is known as the Ostrich Effect). We will come back to this in (4.1) *aPpraise*. Yes, a whole P-step devoted to checking and deciding what to do next!

Thing 8: There Are Many Roads to *Room for Impact*

Throughout the book, we have provided a range of worked examples of things that you *could* de-implement and different ways for bringing this about. Back to that decision about whether to Remove, Reduce, Re-Engineer, or to Replace (i.e., the 4Rs). In **Appendix 1** we also provide a detailed **shopping list of over eighty *potential* de-implementation areas**. This is by no means exhaustive. For a start, many of those listed strategies only address one of the 4Rs, so you can expand that list out (yet) further as you consider it in relation to the other three Rs. This means that there are literally hundreds of de-implementation strategies that are *theoretically* possible. But the question is whether they will be suitable for your local context. The whole point of *Room for Impact* is to give you a stepwise process to figure this out. To take the right road, for you.

Conclusion

The **(3.1) Proceed-step** is where the magic happens. It's where you Proceed, where you bring your initiative to life and de-implement with rigor. What happens here is (to us) a black box. It all depends on the initiatives that you decided on. Your key actions are to Proceed according the Prepared plan—following the what, where, when, how, and whom of your task list and tracking all this to ensure your inputs and outputs are on track. And to collect evaluative data as you go, so that you can check that there is an impact.

With that data to hand, it's now time to *(4.1) aPpraise* your de-implementation impact!

Part 5

Re-Decide Stage

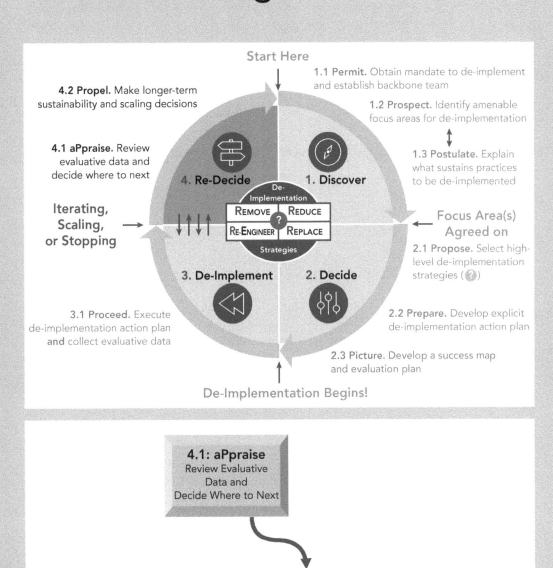

Start Here

4.2 Propel. Make longer-term sustainability and scaling decisions

4.1 aPpraise. Review evaluative data and decide where to next

4. Re-Decide

Iterating, Scaling, or Stopping

3. De-Implement

3.1 Proceed. Execute de-implementation action plan **and** collect evaluative data

De-Implementation
REMOVE | REDUCE
RE-ENGINEER | REPLACE
Strategies

1. Discover

1.1 Permit. Obtain mandate to de-implement and establish backbone team

1.2 Prospect. Identify amenable focus areas for de-implementation

1.3 Postulate. Explain what sustains practices to be de-implemented

Focus Area(s) Agreed on

2.1 Propose. Select high-level de-implementation strategies ( )

2. Decide

2.2 Prepare. Develop explicit de-implementation action plan

2.3 Picture. Develop a success map and evaluation plan

De-Implementation Begins!

4.1: aPpraise
Review Evaluative Data and Decide Where to Next

4.2: Propel
Sustain and Scale

aPpraise (4.1)

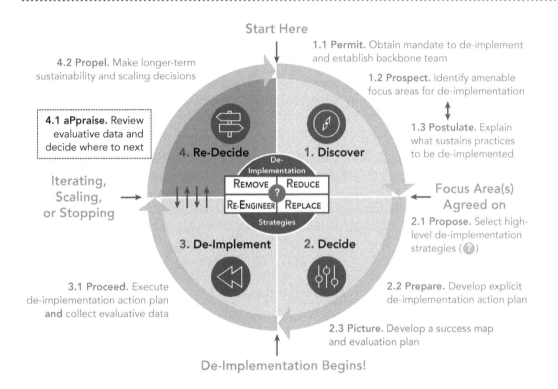

Start Here

1.1 Permit. Obtain mandate to de-implement and establish backbone team

1.2 Prospect. Identify amenable focus areas for de-implementation

1.3 Postulate. Explain what sustains practices to be de-implemented

4.2 Propel. Make longer-term sustainability and scaling decisions

4.1 aPpraise. Review evaluative data and decide where to next

4. Re-Decide

1. Discover

De-Implementation
REMOVE | REDUCE
RE-ENGINEER | REPLACE
Strategies

Iterating, Scaling, or Stopping

3. De-Implement

2. Decide

Focus Area(s) Agreed on

2.1 Propose. Select high-level de-implementation strategies

3.1 Proceed. Execute de-implementation action plan **and** collect evaluative data

2.2 Prepare. Develop explicit de-implementation action plan

2.3 Picture. Develop a success map and evaluation plan

De-Implementation Begins!

4.1: aPpraise
Review Evaluative Data and Decide Where to Next

Now that we have Proceeded to de-implement, we need to check that our carefully designed actions have generated the intended impact.

We aPpraise to know and grow our impact!

Key Action 1: Confirm You Are Using Your Agreed Upon Monitoring and Evaluation Systems

Key Action 2: Review Your Monitoring and Evaluation Data and Decide Where to Next

Key Action 3: Review Your Evaluative Systems (optional)

Introduction

In life, many things seem like a good idea at the time (i.e., the ISLAGIATT problem). Filling the *Hindenburg* with hydrogen rather than helium seemed like a good idea at the time.[1] Carrying fewer lifeboats on the *Titanic*, because an abundance might scare the passengers, seemed like a good idea at the time. Patchwork repairs to the Minneapolis Bridge, rather than a wholesale upgrade, seemed like a good idea at the time. And covering Grenfell Tower in London with pretty (but flammable) external cladding also seemed like a good idea at the time. Yet all ended in tragedy.

In the case of these manufactured disasters, the cause is often a mix of underappreciated risk, a desire not to waste money, along with—seemingly—fluke circumstances that create an unstoppable doom loop. But the same ISLAGIATT principle applies equally to the world of program design, to both implementation and de-implementation. Sometimes seemingly minor contextual features can be make or break.

In India during the 1990s, for example, there was a concerted effort to reduce the child mortality rate. One identified reason for the high infant mortality was that expectant mothers were deliberately starving themselves during pregnancy (Cartwright & Hardie, 2012). They were doing this to keep their baby's head small for easier delivery at home—because they didn't trust hospitals. Of course, significantly lower birth weight also is correlated with higher infant mortality, developmental delays, and lifelong learning difficulties. What's good for not dying in labor comes with an extremely high back-end cost.

One of the regional governments in India addressed this issue through a maternal feeding program that comprised four relatively simple mechanisms: (1) visit pregnant mothers and explain the risks of not eating; (2) tell them that the hospitals have improved significantly and that they should deliver at a hospital; (3) give them a bag of rice and tell them to eat it; (4) come back regularly to reinforce the message and provide more rice.

The program, it turned out, was highly effective. The mothers ate the food. As a result, the (bigger) babies were born in hospital and far fewer died during their infant years. Given the success, neighboring Bangladesh decided to adopt the program. However, after several years of implementation, the impact was scant. This left the evaluators scratching their heads. Was it because under-eating during pregnancy was not a major cause of high infant mortality in Bangladesh? *No.* Was it because the health visitors had failed to visit all the expectant mothers? *No.* Was it because the mothers did not believe the message? *No.* So what was it?

---

[1]At the time, helium was far too expensive, so it was either hydrogen or nothing . . .

It turns out that family structure is different in Bangladesh. After women marry, they often move into their in-laws' house, and the mother-in-law is usually "chief controller" of the food. Ergo, after receiving rice from the health worker, the pregnant women dutifully handed the bag to their mothers-in-law, who then redistributed it to the working men.

To be clear, it wasn't that the mothers-in-law were "wicked." They just didn't understand. They didn't get the memo. In the program design—cut and pasted from India—no step explicitly involved the health worker sitting down with the mother-in-law to have that all-important conversation on "why maternal eating during pregnancy is super important . . . for *your* future grandchild." **Small thing. Big difference.**

Closer to home, in our world of education improvement, there have been projects across the United States to reduce class size. The theory of improvement is that if educators can keep track of, support, and engage with *fewer* students each lesson, learning outcomes will go up. The Tennessee STAR Project attempted this in the 1980s and the evaluation reports suggested it "worked" (Finn & Achilles, 1990; Mosteller, 1995).

However, when other states attempted to replicate the approach, they did not see anywhere near the same level of impact. For example, the California Class Size Reduction (CSR) program reported mixed results (Stecher et al., 2003). Part of the reason is that the context was very different. In California, there was a shortage of teachers and a shortage of classrooms, and many untrained teachers were hired. Ergo, the cost of "fixing" the background context in California to make it similar to Tennessee—where there was a surplus of qualified teachers and a surplus of classrooms—was extremely high. **Big thing. Big difference.**

These case studies illustrate that seemingly "trivial" micro-details can have significant consequences. In Bangladesh (i.e., **Small Thing – Big Difference**), this would have been easily fixable if the program had been evaluated much earlier: Quickly brief the mother-in-law. But in the case of California (**Big Thing – Big Difference**), it suggested it was perhaps a bad idea to proceed with speedy large-scale class size reductions at all because the opportunity cost was too high. There was a need to build more classrooms and to quickly hire (minimally qualified) teachers.[2] The cost and side effects of the treatment, arguably, outweighed the benefits. Instead, it would likely have been better to pivot to an entirely different theory of improvement. An easier route to educational success. In Figure 10.1, we unpack this notion of Big and Small a little further.

In cases of Bangladesh maternal feeding and California class-size reduction, we have a clearer picture because of 20:20 hindsight—coupled with the fact that someone decided that these programs needed to be carefully

---

[2]To be fair, most people at the time did not understand the magnitude of teacher quality effects, so even if new teachers were not quite as good as existing teachers, it was assumed that the class-size effect would overpower the teacher quality effect. It didn't.

FIGURE 10.1   The Big and Small Four-Quadrant Matrix

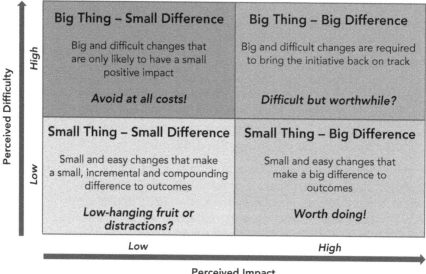

evaluated at some point. Imagine if there had been no evaluation at all. The projects might still be going strong in their original form, with everyone clapping at their apparent success, but with no actual impact.

Our key message—repeated several times in this book—is that we don't know until we know. That in everything we do there is always outcomes ambiguity. What worked *there* may not work *here*. And that might turn out to be because of a small, piddly, seemingly inconsequential reason that can easily be remedied—like briefing the mother-in-law (**Small Thing-Big Difference**). Or it might be because of a major difference in context, like lacking additional classrooms and more trained teachers, which is super hard to get right without generating unintended side effects or expending significant additional resources (**Big Thing—Big Difference**). Small-Big can be remedied, but with Big-Big you should probably pack up and stop. But you can only address these if you know.

And because you don't know until you know, our other oft-repeated message is that you should assume that what you are about to do won't work right the first time and that it won't (immediately) result in an "and they all lived happily ever after" outcome. Instead, you should consider and treat all your work as a grand experiment. You are implementing (or rather de-implementing) something because you hypothesize it will work. And you are going to collect the data to see and then—having looked carefully at that data—you are then going to decide what to do next.

This way of thinking especially applies to de-implementation, because this is a whole new field. We don't have reams of meta-analysis on what happened previously when others stopped doing things. Often, we can only infer by flipping the research—for example, if the OECD finds that student literacy outcomes flatten out after three hours of instruction per week (Hamilton & Hattie, 2022), then we might ask whether the current five hours of instruction *could* be reduced to three hours. But, of course, asking requires evaluation and long-term follow-up. Even if three hours of instruction is as effective as five hours of instruction in the short term, this might be due to Hawthorne effects, which tend to diminish over time. It requires deep *aPpraisal* as we go.

Ergo, during **(4.1) *aPpraise***, you are going to undertake the following key actions in relation to the de-implementation initiatives that you currently have underway:

- **Key Action 1: Confirm You Are Using Your Agreed Upon Monitoring and Evaluation Systems**

- **Key Action 2: Review Your Monitoring and Evaluation Data and Decide Where to Next**

- **Key Action 3: Review Your Evaluative Systems** (Optional)

In the subsections that follow, we will walk you through each of these in turn.

Key Action 1: Confirm You Are Using Your Agreed Upon Monitoring and Evaluation Systems

Back in the (2.3) *Picture*-step, you established your monitoring and evaluation plan. Then, during the (3.1) *Proceed*-step, alongside executing your de-implementation action plan, you should also have collected:

- **Monitoring Data** – which is about tracking whether you actually did the things you set out to do. And whether you did them on time and to the required quality standards. And this involved RAG (red, amber, green) tracking of each activity within your de-implementation plan:

Red   Amber   Green

- **Evaluation Data** – which is about determining whether your de-implementation activity saved time/resources, checking what was done with the savings, checking on the side effects, and making sure that student outcomes were not harmed as per Figure 10.2.

FIGURE 10.2   Recapping the Key Evaluative Questions

DOMAIN	KEY EVALUATIVE QUESTION(S)
Time	• By de-implementing, did we save time? • If so, how much time was saved? • Is this in line with our expectations?
Resources e.g., funding, infrastructure, etc.	• By de-implementing, did we save resources? • If so, what type and how much was saved? • Is this in line with our expectations?
Use of Savings	• What did we do with the saved time and/or resources? • Is this a better use? • Are we sure? **N.B.** It might be that there is no intended reinvestment agenda and that the focus is on pure efficiency of impact.
Side Effects	• Were there any noticeable side effects that emerged from our de-implementation activity? • Are these serious enough that we need to address them? • And, if so, how should they be addressed?
Student Outcomes	• What was the impact on student outcomes of this de-implementation activity? • Was the impact positive, negative, or neutral? • Do we need to make any adjustments as a result of this? **N.B.** Neutral impact might be perfectly fine if your intention is to reduce teacher workload without harming student achievement, i.e., a status quo student outcome.

You might not have collected data in each of these areas—there's an opportunity cost to evaluation, after all. For easier to implement "low-hanging fruit" like de-implementing wall displays, you might (reasonably) have decided to only collect data for a few areas, using a narrow range of indicators. For slightly more complex initiatives like Re-engineering your student detention system, or even more complex like Replacing your curriculum, the range of indicators is likely to go up and up.

However, before you go any further, we want you to check and confirm that you are indeed collecting the monitoring and evaluation data that you committed to. We want you to do this because, too often, we find that such plans get stuck in the proverbial drawer—never to be put into action. So, as per Figure 10.3, are you engaged in Fake evaluation or Real evaluation?

FIGURE 10.3   Fake Evaluation vs. Real Evaluation

FAKE EVALUATION HALLMARKS	REAL EVALUATION HALLMARKS
• We skipped (2.3) *Picture* and didn't set any systems up OR • We only paid cursory attention to (2.3) *Picture* and picked some random indicators and targets AND/OR • We put the plan in the drawer and have not looked at it since, let alone implemented it! AND/OR • We are not really clear about why we need to evaluate (and we might also have forgotten to collect baseline data) AND/OR • We are evaluating, but the data isn't looking good, so we are cherry-picking the positives, *so* that we don't demoralize the team AND/OR • We see the purpose of evaluation as *proving* that we've had impact—because we always knew it was going to work	• We paid close attention to (2.3) *Picture*—after all, this is a separate P-step because so many forget to evaluate. But not us! • We are collecting the agreed upon monitoring and evaluation data at the agreed upon intervals • We are reviewing the collected data at the agreed upon intervals • We are reviewing it to carefully decide where to next • We are clear that we need to do this, because of outcomes ambiguity • If the data isn't looking good, we systematically decide whether to continue, iterate, or stop the de-implementation initiative • We see the purpose of evaluation as *testing* whether we have had impact – because we've no firm idea whether we've generated impact until we check and then we decide what to do next!

What we want you to do now is to go back to the monitoring and evaluation plan that you developed during (2.3) *Picture* and also the tracking tools that you should have been using during (3.1) *Proceed*. And we want you to ask yourselves:

> *Are we engaged in real monitoring and evaluation or are we fakers? Or even forgetters?*

> *And, what are we going to do about it?*

That's *all* there is to it. We *just* want you to hold the mirror up to your faces and check that you did develop a monitoring and evaluation plan. That it was a considered plan. That you are actually implementing it. That you are collecting the data. And that you are looking at it.

If you conclude that you are in the Real Evaluation camp—all good! It's now time to move to Key Action 2 and start reviewing and interpreting all that delicious data to decide where to next. However, if you conclude you are in the Fake Evaluation camp, do not pass go, do not collect $200. Instead, you must ask yourself why you are faking or even forgetting it.

If your answer is that:

1. **We would like to evaluate but the systems we set up during (2.3) Picture have turned out to be too time-consuming to implement**, then proceed immediately to Key Action 3 in this P-step. This is about reviewing the opportunity cost of your evaluation plan and making efficiencies, so that you can gather useful and useable data without climbing evaluative Everest.

2. **We *know* it's working, so there's no real need to evaluate** – then you are engaging in magical thinking. To repeat our repeated message, there is outcomes ambiguity even in the most well-designed initiatives. We don't know until we know. Often, it's the act of evaluating that turns out to be the most critical ingredient in any educational intervention. Sometimes things that shouldn't work *plus* evaluation end up having more impact than things that should work *minus* evaluation. The evaluation (and evaluative mindset) is key.

   If you are not prepared to evaluate your impact, we think you should *stop* and down tools. After all, how can you be sure that your de-implementation initiatives are actually saving time/resources and that they are doing this with *acceptable* side effects? How can you be sure that you have done no harm to student outcomes unless you check?

3. **We know it's not working but everyone is committed to the cause, enjoys the work, and will become demoralized if we pull the rug out now**, then you need to recognize that you are falling into a nest of cognitive biases, as illustrated in Figure 10.4. The whole point of your *Room for Impact* initiative is to save time/resources and without harming student outcomes. If your workload is actually going up, it's not working, and you need to go back to the drawing board. Equally, if student outcomes are diminishing, you are achieving the time/resources savings at an unacceptable cost. Again, you need to go back to the drawing board.

Key Action 2: Review Your Monitoring and Evaluation Data and Decide Where to Next

Now that you have confirmed that you are collecting the monitoring and evaluation data you need to use these to review your progress and measure your impact. Key Action 2 is exactly about that. The idea is to look at that data and then use it to make decisions about where to next.

FIGURE 10.4 The Nest of Cognitive Biases

COGNITIVE BIAS	DEFINITION
Sunk Cost Fallacy Arkes et al. (1985)	The tendency to continue with underperforming initiatives because so much time/money/goodwill has already been invested in them, which can never be recovered
Ostrich Effect Karlsson et al. (2009)	The tendency to bury your head in the sand and not look at the evaluative data at all, because you know you won't like what you see
Confirmation Bias Nickerson (1998)	The tendency to only look at or accept data that confirms what you want to see and believe, for example by being more critical of research findings and data that contradict your beliefs than you are of findings that support them
Cherry-Picking Bias Hansson (2017)	The tendency to zoom in on a small string of positive data in a wider negative chain, so that you can sugar-coat and remain positive
Plan Continuation Bias Winter et al. (2020)	The tendency to continue with the status quo and to assume that things will come right in the end

The basic process involves your backbone team coming together to:

1. **Account**: To both report back on the commitments/activities that were supposed to be undertaken by this time period (a.k.a. monitoring) *plus* the impact data (a.k.a. evaluation). How frequently (and for how long) you account is a local judgment call; and you should already have decided on this during (2.3) *Picture*. For complex initiatives, you might, for example, decide to account weekly and for many months. For low-hanging fruit you might opt to account monthly over a single term or trimester. But as you account, you will be considering the following questions:

    a. **Did we do what we set out to?** Did we perform all our key tasks on time, to the required quality standards, and within the prescribed resource constraints?

    b. **Is it working?** Are we saving the intended time/resources?

    c. **Is it worth it?** Are there any side effects, particularly those related to student outcomes? If yes, are these side effects an acceptable cost? Can we live with them?

2. **Clear the Path** – This where you deliberate and agree on tactics and strategies to overcome any identified de-implementation issues. If you have not identified any issues, there is nothing to clear!

3. **Commit** – This is where you make fresh commitments to report on in the next period. Then, what gets written and reported on is more likely to get done.

Figure 10.5 re-illustrates this process diagrammatically. In the diagram, the reporting frequency is weekly. Yours might be anything from daily to termly—a local call for you to make depending on the importance and complexity of what you are de-implementing.

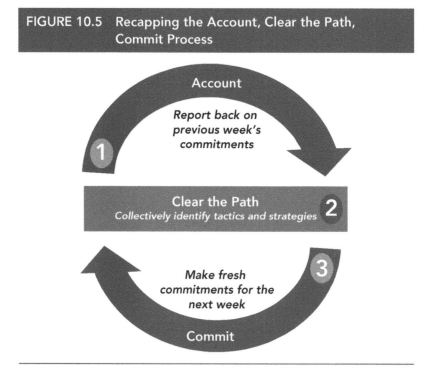

FIGURE 10.5   Recapping the Account, Clear the Path, Commit Process

Now, you might be thinking that "Clearing the Path" feels like a bit of a black box. For example, an open-ended meeting can go in any direction depending on who is in the room. To some extent, this is always going to be true. But in Figure 10.6, we provide you with a three-pronged algorithm to help with this process:

- **PRONG 1: CONTINUE** – If you are doing what you set out to do and it is achieving the intended impact, just keep going until the next review gate. Equally, if you are at an early stage of de-implementation and don't yet have much in the way of impact data, you should also continue and review again, as the data starts to come in.

- **PRONG 2: STOP** – If you are doing things that result in unacceptable side effects and/or directly harms student outcomes, then you need to *stop* immediately. A decision to stop can be emotionally difficult to take because of that nest of cognitive biases that can prime us to continue and hope for the best. But you will remember that in (2.3) *Picture*, one of the recommended actions was for you to set out your **Kill Parameters;** that is, to clearly state that if X, Y, or Z occurs, we will stop immediately—no matter what anyone thinks or feels about it. Having Kill Parameters automates this process and means you can make a more rules-based and dispassionate decision. To reiterate, you don't need to establish Kill Parameters for everything, but they are highly recommended for big complex de-implementation initiatives that are difficult to row back. You are more likely to kill something in the Big-Big zone; that is, a big issue with big consequences, like reducing class size in California.

- **PRONG 3: ITERATE** – This is what you do if your initiative is in the Small-Big zone; that is, you have identified a small (and fixable) issue that's having big consequences for impact. Like that realization that the health workers need to have a chat with the mother-in-law, as well as the expectant mother. This is easy to fix, they both live in the same house, and can be spoken to together with some simple changes to the health worker protocols. You can also incrementally iterate on the "Small-Small" dimension—tiny changes to your activity design, each resulting in a micro-improvement in your impact.

The basic idea is that you pivot back and forth between a stretch of (3.1) *Proceed* (i.e., bringing your de-implementation plans to life) and (4.1) *aPpraise* (i.e., checking whether you did what you set out to and whether by doing it you achieved your intended goals). It's as simple as this. Do. Check. And repeat, until you are either happy with the outcome and can move on to the next thing, or you are unhappy and either have the option of iterating or "wiggling" your tactics a little or of killing the initiative and going back to the drawing board.

This might seem quite abstract, so let's now apply this approach to the three case studies that we have been dipping in and out of during the preceding chapters.

Sizewell High: De-Implementing Wall Displays

If you have been following closely, you will remember that when Sizewell High set up their *Room for Impact* Backbone Organization, they decided to pursue the "low-hanging-fruit." Some, but by no means all, of these initiatives included standup staff meetings; switching off the email servers at the weekend; reducing the number of lesson observations; setting up a cloud-based system for staff to share their curriculum

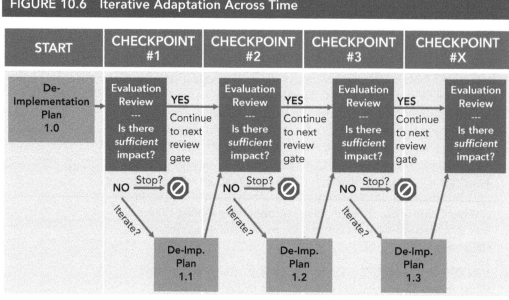

FIGURE 10.6   Iterative Adaptation Across Time

Adapted from Hamilton et al. (2022).

resources; removing the need to write lesson plans of any kind; and removing displays from classrooms and corridors.

Not all of these initiatives turned out to be successful. Turning off the email servers at 4 p.m. on Friday, for example, had the unintended side effect of increasing stress as staff feared the pile of emails that would await them on Monday morning. So, it was subsequently reversed. But let's focus in on the de-implementing wall display initiative and that process of accounting, clearing the path, and committing across a series of checkpoints:

- **Checkpoint 1.** After a successful staff briefing where (almost) everyone seemed supportive of de-implementing wall displays, the vice principal began weekly monitoring walks to check that no new display had been created. But she found it difficult to track whether what she was looking at was "old" display or whether "new" display was slowly creeping in. So, during the first evaluation checkpoint meeting, it was agreed that the caretaker would be tasked with taking all the existing wall displays down, so that it would be easier to monitor whether new displays were being generated.

- **Checkpoint 2.** Two pieces of good news. Firstly, the caretaker removed all of the old displays and very quickly, too. Second, the vice principal could see that the walls remained bare. There were no new wall displays going up, and this meant that it was likely that twenty-eight hours per teacher per term were being saved!

However, there was also one piece of less good news. The student voice groups—without being prompted—all reported that the school now felt cold and uninviting. The backbone team deliberated and identified three ways forward:

1. **Ignore the feedback** and hope that things quiet down by the time of the next consultation,

2. **Put the old wall display back up,** or

3. **Buy some third-party art** and display this in the classrooms and corridors.

The team was split between option A and option C. But, in the end, they decided not only to buy some art but also to enlist the student voice groups to select it, so that the children felt greater ownership of the school. The backbone team reasoned that this would only have to happen once—the existing students were unhappy about a change they had no control over. Once it was done and new students came in, they would be more likely to accept the artwork and treat it as "part of the furniture." But this meant, of course, the strategy had pivoted from Remove to Replace—that is, they were no longer just removing the wall displays; they were now Replacing them with something else. Something external.

- **Checkpoint 3.** The backbone team reviewed the revised action plan. The voice groups had selected the artwork for the corridors, and individual classes had also been allowed to do the same for their homerooms. The qualitative feedback was that this was really well received. Of course, pivoting to Replace meant that not as much time had been saved as originally intended. Many teachers had been roped into the student consultations—with voting exercises and online spreadsheets created and tallied. The time-cost looked about the same as what the teachers had invested in wall display creation in previous years. But the good news was that this was to be a one-time project. There would be no need to return and repeat the exercise until the new artwork fell off the walls, hopefully in several years!

- **Checkpoint 4.** The backbone team came together for what would be a final review. The vice principal confirmed that no new teacher- or student-created wall displays had gone up during the last term and everyone agreed that the new artwork was holding up well. It was decided that wall display de-implementation no longer needed to be actively monitored but that the teacher handbook would be updated to explicitly state that no teacher/student wall displays were to be created, to explain why, and to explain the time that had been saved, so that the decision could be codified and maintained.

Re-Engineering Student Detention Systems

Let's now go back to our Re-Engineer case study, which was about reformulating student detentions, so that these could be administered centrally—by fewer staff—enabling those not staffing the detention room on a particular day to go home earlier. In Figure 10.7, we provide a "niggles table" that lists the backbone team's key challenges and what they did. In this case study, the approach was more fluid with backbone team members coming together on a daily/weekly basis to account, clear the path, and commit.

FIGURE 10.7   Student Detentions Niggle Table

NO.	DESCRIPTION	RESPONSE	OUTCOME
1.	**The cloud-based centralized detention management module does not work** – this means that teachers cannot centrally book detentions, send scheduling confirmations to students and the detention teacher, or receive confirmation that the students attended	Pivoting to an online spreadsheet that all teachers can input into and cross-check against	An acceptable stop-gap until the platform module is ready. Although teachers cannot access the spreadsheet on their phones, this creates administrative niggles/frictions
2.	**Monitoring and feedback walks have identified that some staff are still undertaking decentralized detentions** – vice principal (VP)/assistant principal has not discussed with the staff in question	VP needs to engage with the staff to understand why they are continuing with the old system	Engagement has occurred and it seems that the staff are using the sessions to provide informal 1:1 tutoring to selected students – this raises wider questions for team to consider whether we also need a centralized Response to Intervention/Multitiered Systems of Support model in the school
3.	**Some students have been skipping their detentions** – because they believed the detention supervisors did not know who should be in detention	Issue raised at school assemblies – to reinforce that the school is tracking and that parents will be looped in if students miss their detentions	Issue resolved

What this "niggles table" highlights is that most of the niggles were administrative and procedural. During (1.2) *Prospect*, the backbone team had already undertaken in-depth consultations with educators, and centralized detentions was one of the most popular and widely endorsed suggestions to emerge from the process. This meant that there was already a high-degree of buy-in.

When the vice principal finally confronts (or should we say engages) with the small number of teachers who appear to be working outside the new system, he discovers that they are not delivering detentions but instead undertaking out of hours one-to-one tutoring. This gives the backbone team another potential area for de-implementation in their next inquiry cycle. This is especially relevant given that the teachers appear to have just started offering students this new service—in the hour they have saved from not undertaking detentions. This case is a prime example of Parkinson's Law: work expanding to fill the time available, although this is a step forward in Pareto optimization, since using the time for one-to-one tutoring is a better use of the time.

Rohit, Samantha, and Eddie: Replacing Bespoke Locally Developed Curriculum Materials With a Third-Party Curriculum Package

Finally, we rejoin Rohit, Samantha, and Eddie, who have been working to Replace bespoke locally developed teaching and learning materials with a high-quality external package of materials. To some extent, the initiative has been a success. In the early months, the key challenge was buy-in. It was about convincing teaching teams that an externally developed package could be equally (if not more) effective than their individually designed materials. Initially, quite a bit of time was wasted on buy-in sessions, which seemed to backfire with people hunkering down yet further into their preexisting beliefs. Then, it was decided to avoid this altogether—to, instead, give staff the protocols, ask them to implement them while being supervised by a coach, and then reflect on the impact. This, it turned out, was more effective. Rohit, Samantha, and Eddie realized that for their school and their teachers, seeing the impact was believing that it worked. Educators were more likely to implement the new program by being required to adopt it under supervision for a day, seeing that it worked, and wanting to try it again the next day.

The trouble, however, was that the **Replacement activity did not seem to have reduced teacher preparation time**. We now join Rohit, Samantha, and Eddie as they discuss this and as they decide what to do next:

Rohit:	So, to recap the saga so far. We introduced the third-party curriculum package, and everyone resisted. We then tried reasoning and explaining why it was better, but going down the "buy-in" path didn't work. We then "forced" everyone to implement it for a few days under the supervision and guidance of coaches from the program developer. And we got an "aha!" as people started to see with their eyes that it worked.

(Continued)

(Continued)

Eddie:	Yeah, so we should be really pleased. Because, looking at the monitoring and evaluation data, people have adopted it now. The kicking and screaming have pretty much stopped. Boy, was it hard though!
Samantha:	Guys, I think we are congratulating ourselves a bit too prematurely. Yes, the teams are indeed using the program—we can see it when we do lesson observations and review student work. And, yes, it's also true that student achievement has increased slightly—we can see this at the end of topic tests. But I think we are missing why we introduced the new curriculum in the first place.
Eddie:	OK, go on.
Samantha:	To reduce workload! So, what's the impact been on workload?
Rohit:	Well, theoretically it should have gone down because no one needs to develop their own lesson plans, resources, or homework anymore.
Samantha:	Well . . . you remember we decided to do a termly pulse survey for workload? Anyways, we did the survey last week and for about half of our people, they spend the same amount of time on lesson preparation as before we introduced the new program.
Eddie:	OK, that's weird. Maybe it's because they still need to localize the materials for their specific learners?
Samantha:	The whole point was to stop that! Anyway, I took a quick look at who was and wasn't spending additional time on lesson preparation and I cross-referenced it with the student achievement data. And the thing is, our colleagues who are *not* localizing the materials are getting better outcomes than the ones who are.
Rohit:	So, you're basically saying that while everyone has *adopted* the new program, half of our people have adopted and *adapted* it. And that the ones who are adapting are spending much more time and getting worse outcomes?
Samantha:	Yes!

Eddie:	If people are putting more in but getting less out, that doesn't sound like de-implementation to me! We need to double-check those numbers. But assuming they're correct, we need a strategy to get people to stop adapting and localizing.
Rohit:	We need to understand why the "localizers" are localizing before deciding what to do. Maybe they think they are supposed to be doing it and have misunderstood. Maybe they don't think the materials will work without localization. Maybe they think the materials will work fine either way but just "like" spending their evenings creating new case studies and examples from scratch.
Samantha:	You're right. We can't decide the right strategy until we know why they are doing it.
Eddie:	Yeah, depending on the *why*, it might be enough just to tell and show them that everyone else is getting the same level of success without the additional evening work. Or we might need to mandate use of the materials without adaptation and enforce it. Or just that we need to send nudges to people in the evening to tell them not to localize the material—to break the habit.
Samantha:	Or it might be that their students are unique and need the investment in materials localization.
Eddie:	I guess that's possible, too. We need to investigate to know!
Rohit:	OK, so to summarize our key actions. First, we are going to double-check the data. And, second, if there is a clear pattern, we will *gently* speak to the "localizers" and understand why they are doing it. And then we are going to decide what to do next.

And this takes the team back to those Chesterton's Fence tools and to discussions with their teams, so that they can better understand *why* and then use this to select the most appropriate antidote to continue to grow their success!

Key Action 3: Review Your Evaluative Systems (Optional)

Finally, you might also want to take the time to review your evaluative systems. This action is optional but recommended unless you are not evaluating your impact, in which case it's compulsory. This is because you need to check, check, and check to know your impact!

There are two key look-fors as you undertake this review.

Look-For 1: Efficiency of Evaluation

Here you are simply asking whether your systems, tools, and indicators give you the most insight for the least obtrusive level of input. Some of the key questions that you might want to ask include the following:

- Are we measuring too many or too few things?

- Are we measuring too frequently or not frequently enough?

- Are we coming together too frequently or not frequently enough to review the data and decide where to next?

- How are we recording and reporting our evaluative findings? How long is this taking us? What's the opportunity cost?

- Is our evaluative activity helping us decide whether to continue, iterate, or *stop*?

Depending on what you uncover, these questions and answers might take you back to (2.3) *Picture*—to review your success map and your monitoring and evaluation indicators.

Look-For 2: Perverse Incentives

Here you are double-checking that no obvious perverse incentives are being generated as a result of your evaluative activities. This is back to the Goodhart Law adage that once a measure becomes a target, it ceases to be an effective measure. One danger is that you fixate so much on time savings that you lose sight of side effects and the potential for harm to student learning outcomes. Ergo, you really need to make sure that you are collecting insights that enable you to answer the following questions:

1. Are we saving time/resources? How much, and is this in line with our expectations?

2. Are there any side effects? What are these? Are they an acceptable "cost of doing business"?

3. What is the impact on student outcomes? At the very least this is about enforcing the "do no harm" principle. Although "doing less to achieve more" is the far bigger prize!

Conclusion

During **(4.1)** *aPpraise* you have undertaken three key actions:

- **Key Action 1:** Confirmed you are using your Agreed Upon Monitoring and Evaluation Systems

- **Key Action 2:** Reviewed your Monitoring and Evaluation Data and Decided where to next

- **Key Action 3:** Reviewed your evaluative systems (optional)

You have done this because of outcomes ambiguity. We literally don't and can't know for sure whether our *Room for Impact* initiatives have been successful until we check. Although, for avoidance of all doubt, checking is *not* a postmortem-type activity that happens at the end to diagnose the causes of death in things that have failed. Nor is it a sugar-coating exercise designed to hunt for and celebrate success stories within the noise selectively.

Instead, it's about treating your *Room for Impact* initiative as an experiment or a hypothesis. It's about gathering data in real-time and interpreting it—to know and grow your impact. This means that it is *not* a linear step but a dance. As you de-implement, you need to continuously dance back and forth between Proceeding (3.1) and aPpraising (4.1) to turn outcomes ambiguity into certainty. See Figure 10.8.

FIGURE 10.8 Recapping the Dance of *Proceed* and *aPpraise*

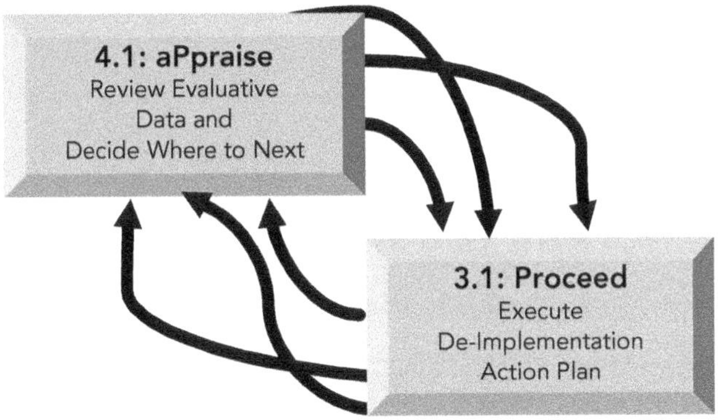

Propel (4.2)

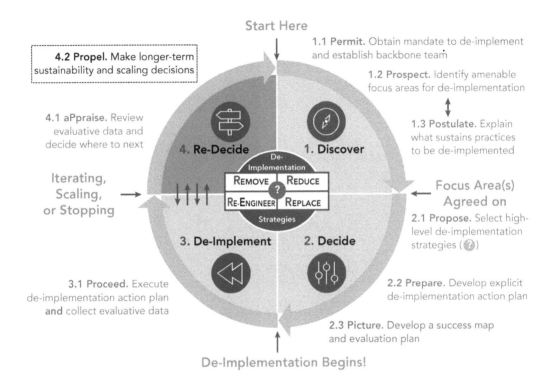

Start Here

1.1 Permit. Obtain mandate to de-implement and establish backbone team

1.2 Prospect. Identify amenable focus areas for de-implementation

1.3 Postulate. Explain what sustains practices to be de-implemented

4.2 Propel. Make longer-term sustainability and scaling decisions

4.1 aPpraise. Review evaluative data and decide where to next

4. Re-Decide

1. Discover

De-Implementation

REMOVE	REDUCE
RE-ENGINEER	REPLACE

Strategies

Iterating, Scaling, or Stopping

3. De-Implement

2. Decide

Focus Area(s) Agreed on

2.1 Propose. Select high-level de-implementation strategies ( )

3.1 Proceed. Execute de-implementation action plan **and** collect evaluative data

2.2 Prepare. Develop explicit de-implementation action plan

2.3 Picture. Develop a success map and evaluation plan

De-Implementation Begins!

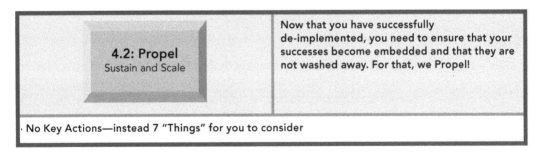

4.2: Propel
Sustain and Scale

Now that you have successfully de-implemented, you need to ensure that your successes become embedded and that they are not washed away. For that, we Propel!

· No Key Actions—instead 7 "Things" for you to consider

Let's start with the good news. By the time you get to (4.2) *Propel*, all the hard work and heavy lifting have (largely) all been done. You may have gone around in circles a little (or a lot) to get to this point. Perhaps you have Proposed (2.1) and Prepared (2.2) your de-implementation approaches; Proceeded (3.1) to de-implement; and aPpraised (4.1), only to discover niggles, teething problems, or (perhaps) even more significant issues, and then revised or iterated your de-implementation plan, aPpraising yet again. As Figure 11.1 re-attests, the road is (almost) never straight and it often involves doubling back to previous decisions to recheck, to test assumptions, to tweak, and then to press play once more.

FIGURE 11.1   Around and Round We Go

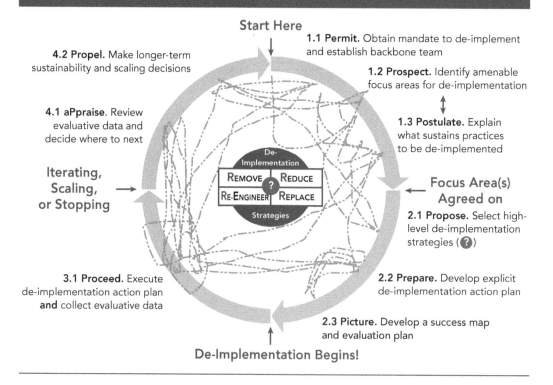

But the continued good news is that by the time you have arrived here, you have already made major inroads with de-implementation. You have saved significant amounts of time and resources without harming student outcomes.

This means that you can think of (4.2) *Propel* as an after-show party or as some bonus material for you to think about and reflect on before you say "cool beans, we've 'done' *Room for Impact*—we can forget about de-implementation now and move onto the next thing, never to return." In this chapter and P-step, we present some considerations and look-fors to help ensure that in the longer term all your hard work does not end up becoming washed away. So, rather than being explicit actions, they are instead "things" for you to consider. Things related to **sustaining** and **scaling** your endeavors.

Thing 1: Chalk Up the Wins

By the time you have gotten here, you will have been implementing (or should we say de-implementing) for some time. The risk is, however, that your wider organization may have begun to lose sight of the original goal or that people are not sure whether "good enough" progress has been made.

One way to address this is to chalk up the wins on a publicly displayed leaderboard. Maybe this is a physical whiteboard in your staff room or an online dashboard. That's something for you to decide. But the idea is that you use this to remind people of the original goal and the progress that has already been achieved. It could look something like the dashboard we present in Figure 11.2. You can regularly update it and regularly get folks to huddle around the board to see and celebrate progress.

FIGURE 11.2   Chalking Up the Wins

Goal	To reduce teacher workload significantly, without harming student outcomes

NO.	INITIATIVE	INTENDED SAVING (PER TEACHER PER ANNUM)	ACTUAL SAVING (PER TEACHER PER ANNUM)
1.	Removing Wall Displays	60 hours	47 hours
2.	Centralized Detention System	120 hours	97 hours
3.	Standardized Teaching and Learning Materials	400 hours	220 hours
4.	Stand-Up Staff Meetings	20 hours	12 hours
5.	Removal of Individual Subject Reports for Parents	50 hours	35 hours
		Total Intended Savings	Total Actual Savings
		650 hours	411 hours

STUDENT ATTENDANCE RATE 2022	STUDENT ATTENDANCE RATE 2023		STUDENT GRADUATION RATE 2022	STUDENT GRADUATION RATE 2023
96%	94%		65%	66%

For certain, this process is not foolproof. The opportunity cost of under-taking a time and motion study to get accurate data down to the hour or minute might not be worth the trouble. So, you might be relying on teacher estimates and perceptions of the time they have saved. The figures might also vary widely between educators with the averages hiding consider-able variation, with some staff having successfully de-implemented, while others have not. And your high-level student impact indicators might not give you the full picture. The positives (and negatives) might vary by year, socioeconomic status, and a host of other variables. They might also be lagging indicators that take time to change. It's also quite possible that you have inadvertently de-implemented something that in fact, over the longer term, improves student outcomes but the problem takes a few years to become apparent. But it still gives you a public leaderboard of sorts on which to focus. To rally the team. To keep your eyes on the prize.

You can also ask your educators to maintain a personal copy of this track-ing sheet, listing their individual pre- and post-data and then aggregat-ing this into a dashboard for the whole school, like the one presented. Tracking your personal progress, although it can seem silly, is surpris-ingly motivational. That's why step counters, sleep trackers, water intake logs, heart rate monitors, and stress trackers have also caught on. Indeed, as management guru Peter Drucker (apparently) once lamented: what gets measured gets done.

If your teams struggle to conceptualize what a savings of forty or eighty or 120 hours translates into, Figure 11.3 helps to put this into context. Assuming a "standard" forty-hour working week—which is what most educators are supposed to be working but rarely, if ever, manage to keep to—each block of forty hours saved is the equivalent of an "official" work-ing week. But for avoidance of doubt, these are not going to be weeks off work; instead, they are weeks of unpaid overtime that used to be under-taken in the evenings and on the weekends that have been reclaimed!

FIGURE 11.3   From Hours to Weeks

Hours Saved	40	80	120	160	200	240	280	320	360
Working Weeks Saved	1	2	3	4	5	6	7	8	9

Thing 2: Nothing Lasts Forever

Did you hear the one about the bodybuilder who, after attaining his ideal physique, never needed to go to the gym again? No, nor did we. Ditto the warm cup of coffee that never gets cold or the carpet that never needs to be vacuumed. No such thing. With the possible exception of diamonds, everything in life requires maintenance.

Decay is literally hard baked into the fabric of the universe. The technical term is *entropy*, which refers to the tendency for energy to dissipate gradually—for hot things to cool down and for everything to decay. To not do so is a violation of the Second Law of Thermodynamics.

We are equally sorry that the same principles apply to your *Room for Impact* initiatives. So, while, yes, for a time, you might succeed in removing wall displays, stopping or reducing homework, or banishing decentralized detentions, once you take your eye off the prize, decay gradually creeps in.

In the case of wall displays, perhaps it happens very slowly. Maybe all the current teaching team and leadership are on board and with the program. But with a staff churn rate of 20 percent per annum, the entire team *could* be gone in five years. Or at the very least you will have several new joiners who did wall displays at their previous school and who decide to import it here as an "improvement." Maybe they do this to make a positive impression or just because they think it's what a good teacher does. Maybe the type of wall displays they are using actually are "pretty useful" rather than "pretty" (Sharratt, 2019), something that is closely interlinked with their classroom pedagogy to making learning visible. But little do they know that there are no wall displays because they were consciously taken down to make room to focus on other things. And by now, the backbone has also been dismantled or has moved on to new things and there is only a hazy memory of said wall display removal initiative. So, when the new joiners plaster their walls in lovely (but time-consuming) wall displays, no one thinks to mention that there is a method in the (apparent) madness of no wall displays. Indeed, maybe the leadership has also changed once, twice, or three times. And maybe the new leader loves wall displays. Maybe, too, "pretty useful" wall displays now get consciously adopted, schoolwide, as an additive improvement to enhance student outcomes. This was something the original backbone team had even considered.

Things can also decay at an even faster rate. Think about Rohit, Samantha, and Eddie's Replacement initiative. They were expecting teachers to simultaneously Remove (i.e., *stop*) producing their own bespoke teaching and learning content. And to, instead, Replace these with a third-party program—with pre-built lesson plans and teaching materials. Maybe these were even scripted, with the expectation that the role of the teacher is to be like an actor, to learn their lines and bring the script to life. And then go home and spend time with their families rather than spending their evening printing, cutting up, and laminating card-sort activities for the next day.

With a Replacement initiative, like a new externally developed curriculum, the risk is that it doesn't get out of the starting blocks at all. That everyone quietly (or loudly) resists. Or, perhaps even worse, that they implement while also adapting it so much that it's no longer the original intervention. This is potentially the worst of all possible worlds. Time spent on implementing plus time spent on adapting equals more time than status quo (and possibly reduced returns for students). You will remember that we worked through this conundrum and some potential countermeasures in the previous chapter. But the key is to monitor, keep your eye on the prize, and decide what to do if you don't like what you see. The moment you stop doing that, decay sets in.

Of course, you can't monitor everything all the time. It's both impossible and a tad Orwellian. But you need to keep your eye on the big things likely to decay quickly—the ones where you need to keep spinning the plates to keep them aloft. While only occasionally checking back in on wall display, detentions, parental reporting, timetabling, homework, and all that jazz— once you've got the systems set up, working, and (largely) on autopilot.

Thing 3: Parkinson's Law (Nothing Is Impossible)

A central goal of *Room for Impact* initiatives is almost always about clearing the decks. About doing things more efficiently to generate more out for less in. A key outcome of all this Lean efficiency is that you and your teams will have much more free time on your hands.

But with time comes a dilemma: what to do with it. You've probably heard the phrase "nothing is impossible." Usually, it is uttered as a positive affirmation. A suggestion that even the most difficult obstacles can be overcome. But there is also a second meaning: It is physically impossible to do nothing. When you free up time, by implication, you are always going to fill this up with something else. Even if you spend the saved time looking out the window, or doing yoga, or dog walking, or even sleeping, you are doing *something*. You are using that saved time for an alternative purpose.

If the purpose of your *Room for Impact* initiative is to clear out your evening and weekend working so that you can do other joyous things and return to school rejuvenated, then what you fill that regained time with is a matter for you. Whether that be gardening, amateur dramatics, paragliding, or just watching Netflix. But if the purpose is to clear the deck to make room for more impactful things during your working hours, you need to take great care in selecting your Replacement activities. Otherwise, the danger is that you end up Replacing actions that generate an average-level of impact with other things that do the same or maybe even less.

Many years ago, John worked with a school in New Zealand that had concluded that its thirty-eight after-school co-curricular programs were a waste of time and resources. That they led to no discernible impact. The school embarked on a successful initiative to remove these programs. But when John re-visited the school a year later, what did he find? That they had simply replaced the thirty-eight with another thirty-eight. There was no clear analysis to determine whether the co-curricular offering was necessary at all. And even if it was, to determine whether thirty-eight was the right number vs. twelve or three. Or, indeed, what those three should be. Their argument was "We have always had co-curricular programs so bring them on!"

If you are not careful, the danger is that you will replace average programs with other average programs. This can occur via osmosis, without thinking about it. Like Parkinson's Law, the volume of work will creep up and up to fill (and sometimes exceed) the time available. And then you will be back where you started. If you are simply going to replace crud with more crud or average with more average, you may as well not even begin. Leave as it is.

You will find further thoughts on this in Thing 5. And we suggest that you leverage our *Building to Impact* protocols to help you identify things that really are worth adding.

Thing 4: Culture

One of the things that will determine whether you can keep your *Room for Impact* initiatives going into the long-term is your organizational culture, specifically your collective beliefs about work. If your local values are akin to the Protestant or Puritan Work Ethic, you might see hard work as an end in itself. You might believe that to be a good teacher you need to be working long hours, be seen to be doing so, and to even brag about your commitment. And you might even see it as a badge of honor to be marking essays and taking calls from parents, while waiting to be stretchered in for your nonelective op and during recovery on the other side.

A busy teacher is not necessarily a good teacher. Being effective is not in competition with being efficient. In one open-class school that we have seen, three teachers taught ninety students in open plan classrooms. By all measures, the student learning and outcomes of this school were exemplary. There are three terms/semesters in the year, and the school model was for one teacher to undertake all the planning for the team for one semester and the other two teachers were told not to plan but spend all their time delivering the teaching. The motto was direct: For two terms, nights and weekends are your own. But there was a condition—they were not to tell teachers in other schools who argued that these two teachers were lazy and clearly incompetent. Efficiency was punished.

In East Asian societies, it is not uncommon for these values of public hard graft to pervade entire organizations. Here, the corporate culture involves sitting at work for long hours and not going home until after the boss has left. But sometimes that work ethic is more about shame-based drivers encouraging people to be *seen* working. To be witnessed, still, at their desks and to be sending emails at 3 a.m. Sometimes, this can be more about the theatrics of *appearing* to excel rather than actually excelling.

By focusing more on inputs– the hours worked—rather than outputs (i.e., whether the work had a profound impact), we can end up privileging the wrong things.

Some other organizational cultures work hard to stamp out this fake work. Here, the leadership does not see working long hours as a badge of honor or something to be celebrated. Instead, they see it as a sign that something has (badly) gone wrong. Arran got this wakeup call early in his career when his then boss suggested that all his late-night emails were not a sign of hard work, but, instead, a sign that he wasn't on top of his work. That is, he was being a busy fool and filling his days with unproductive busywork that required him to do his "real" work in the evenings.

To support a focus on developing a culture of Real Work within your organization, we propose the following ten *Room for Impact* mind frames:

1. I am focused on my *efficiency of impact* above all else.

2. I see that working long hours is only a badge of honor if each hour *truly* contributes to student outcomes (otherwise it's a badge of shame).

3. *I use each hour wisely* and focus only on the things that significantly improve student learning.

4. I am an evaluator of my impact *and* my efficiency of impact.

5. I am not a busy fool: Being busy is not the same thing as having real impact.

6. I strive to do less to achieve far more.

7. I know how and when to Replace, Remove, Reduce, or Re-engineer.

8. I celebrate and share the efficiencies I have generated.

9. I de-implement with great care, checking that my actions generate no harm.

10. I accept that there is outcomes ambiguity in everything I do; this is why I chose my de-implementation priorities with care and why I evaluate to know and grow my impact.

You may see some of these as a little too strident and want to adopt only some of them: all good. The main thing is that you signal to your team (and yourself) that you need to make every minute count, choose wisely and efficiently, and aPpraise your impact!

Thing 5: Yin and Yang

The philosophy behind *Room for Impact* is strongly influenced by Japanese efficiency systems like Lean, Kaizen, and Six Sigma. These are extremely good at chiseling away at existing processes to reduce *muda* (the Japanese word for waste). They do this to find ways to generate *at least* the same outcomes but with less time, motion, resources, and processing. Less in, same out. Or even better, less in for more out.

What these methodologies (and *Room for Impact*) are good at is asking *Is there an easier way of achieving the same goal?* That's great if your goals have not changed or if your goal is to be explicitly more efficient. But, if you have identified new goals like increasing student attendance, closing the equity gap, increasing your literacy rates, or something else, then *Making Room for Impact* is likely less useful to you. This is because you may need to design and implement new actions or programs to push the needle on new goals.

That's where our sister publication (and methodology) *Building to Impact* comes in. This is about identifying new goals worth progressing and the highest probability approaches to sustained impact. It's about creating, adding, and implementing, while *Room for Impact* is about reducing, subtracting, and de-implementing. We see these as being two sides of the same coin. The yin and yang are about creative destruction to rekindle resources for more fruitful endeavors (see Figure 11.4).

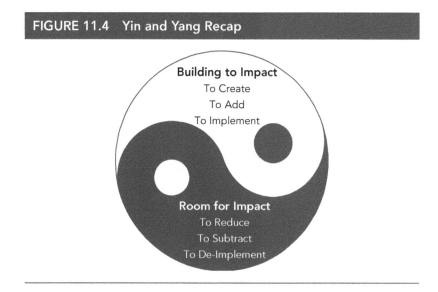

FIGURE 11.4   Yin and Yang Recap

That said, we are skeptical that it is easy to think from both perspectives simultaneously (Hamilton & Hattie, 2022). Suppose you have established a backbone team to focus exclusively on de-implementation. In that case, we think it's more likely that they will identify actions in the Remove, Reduce, or Re-Engineer quadrants. Whereas, if your backbone is thinking about both de-implementation *and* new goals simultaneously, we suspect that more (or most) of your initiatives will end up in the (more difficult) Replace quadrant—the place that also happens to be business-as-usual for all school improvement activity, i.e., de-commission program X and replace with program Y.

Indeed, many times as we three authors collaborated on the *Room for Impact* protocols, we kept inadvertently sleepwalking into this additive thinking. We kept coming at it from the perspective of removing or reducing X as a means of doing Y. We kept having to mentally jog ourselves out of this thinking to say instead, "No, *Room for Impact* is primarily about efficiency for its own sake!" That, depending on what X is, it might be perfectly fine to Remove, Reduce, or Re-engineer it and *not* to be seduced by shiny Replacement activities. And in many instances, this might even be preferable.

It's a bit like that scene in *Wayne's World*, where Wayne alternates between closing his left and right eye. And as he does so, he says, "camera one" and "camera two." *Room for Impact* and *Building to Impact* are different "cameras" that give us different perspectives. But activating both cameras simultaneously—and combining these two perspectives—might not be such a good idea. We might even want to establish two different Backbone Organizations—one for implementation and the other for de-implementation, although, of course, they both need to talk to each other. Otherwise, one might find the other is de-implementing something that the other was planning to use to progress a new and important goal.

Thing 6: To Disband or Not Disband

To progress your *Room for Impact* initiative, we recommended establishing a formal organization structure. This could be a Backbone Team that exists exclusively to progress your de-implementation projects, or the borrowing of a preexisting structure like your Professional Learning Communities or your well-being committee. The reason we want you to set up a specific de-implementation team is for two reasons:

(1) **It signals to the wider organization that this is important work that is taken seriously by the leadership.** That permission has been granted and progress expected. And that there is nothing to feel guilty or shameful about during de-implementation.

(2) **It focuses the team on thinking exclusively about de-implementation, as they work together.** This, in turn, reduces the probability that your de-implementation initiatives accidentally become implementation focused, that they end up being about finding things to Replace, rather than Remove, Re-Engineer, or Reduce.

But the question is, how long should you keep such a team together with a formal license and mandate to operate? Should you treat this as a short-term endeavor that you undertake for a term/semester or two (at most) before pivoting all your energies back to additive implementation? Or, at the other extreme, should you keep your *Room for Impact* team in place permanently to monitor existing de-implementation actions for backsliding and continuously prospect and propose new efficiencies?

We need to 'fess up that we don't have clearcut answers to this question. The notion of de-implementation is new to education, and there's little data and few case studies. So, instead, we present you with a range of options for your consideration.

Model 1: The Safety Valve (a.k.a. Do It and Move On)

Here, you establish *Room for Impact* teams as a direct response to specific local workload or resource challenges. You do it when people complain about workload—when it's already obvious that everything is not right. And you do this as a Safety Valve to lower the pressure, to let off some steam.

This means that after you have taken your agreed de-implementation initiatives through all the P-steps and come out the other end, you disband the team and you also do very little long-term monitoring of whether people are maintaining their commitments.

Then, when the pressure builds again, you re-establish the team and you embark on another wave of de-implementation. This could be a while—maybe even two or three years later.

The advantage of the Safety Value Model is that once you have seen your initiatives through, you can rekindle resources and set your team to work on other priorities. However, the obvious disadvantage is that you can—and should—expect much backsliding without clear ongoing monitoring. And there may be a whole host of other de-implementation initiatives that you could also progress but that you never quite get to.

Model 2: Monitoring and Evaluation Transfer

This is as per the Safety Value, where you disband your *Room for Impact* Team. But the key difference is that you do not stop the monitoring and evaluation of live initiatives. Instead, you seek to transfer these to another area within your organization. Maybe that's the "Data Team" or the "School Improvement Steering Group" or somewhere else. But whatever it is called, there is likely to be a preexisting function within your school that tracks and reports on live initiatives. That provides a dashboard to the leadership. We are suggesting under Model 2 that the ongoing monitoring and evaluation of your live de-implementation initiatives gets transferred to this team rather than going in the deep freeze.

The advantages of this approach are that it reduces the probability that all your hard work ends up in the dustbin because things that continue to get measured (and reported on) are more likely to continue to get done.

Model 3: Perpetual *Room for Impact*

Here, you decide not to disband your de-implementation-oriented Backbone Team at all. Instead, you keep them and their mandate intact on an ongoing basis. This means that the team is constantly cycling through the P-steps to identify new de-implementation areas and to Proceed, aPpraise, and Propel—over and over.

We suspect that, at the very start, you may not have had this option in mind. Instead, you may think that *"Room for Impact* responds to a need we have in our school, so let's try it and see how it goes." And, in all fairness, to us this seems to be a very sensible basis from which to proceed. But once you have got going, you might be surprised and impressed with the level of progress. Once you look and clap at the celebratory scoreboard at the end of a *Room for Impact* cycle, you might find the Backbone team saying, "Next year we want to move on to homework/timetabling/staff meetings/data management."

If these suggestions seem good, then why not keep the backbone team in place—at least for one more cycle? And then review things again. You might even find that it becomes a perpetual activity. Outside education, many other successful organizations do just this. They have ongoing in-house Lean teams or Six Sigma squads that spend their energies on ways to enable others to conserve theirs. So, if you are seeing success with *Room for Impact*, why not extend it a little more?

Obviously, the advantages and disadvantages of doing this are the diametric opposite to the Safety Value Model. The clear downside is that while your people focus on chiseling and Re-engineering existing processes, they are not progressing big new goals or meaty education challenges. They are not adding. The upside is that there are always things that can be chiseled: this is why those efficiency-oriented teams in the private sector can exist perpetually. So, why not perpetual *Room for Impact*? You decide.

Model 4: Dual Swim Teams

Here, two swim teams swim in different directions in the same pool. One is a *Room for Impact* Backbone, which lives, eats, and breathes de-implementation. And the second focuses on addition—perhaps using the *Building to Impact* protocols in our sister book of the same name.

While, yes, the membership and sponsorship of both "swim teams" is likely to overlap—particularly in smaller schools—we recommend that you treat them as separate entities, with separating meeting cycles. And that you don't mix up the language and terminology of the two approaches. Otherwise the risk (again) is that both groups become focused on addition: With your *Building to Impact* team looking (as they should) at new programs and initiatives to respond to important education challenges and your *Room for Impact* team also vectoring in on Replacement-type actions that are still very much about addition albeit with an efficient twist.

To reiterate, there are (as yet) no clearcut answers on which of these four models is likely to be "the best." We just want you to have them in mind, particularly as you come to the end of a *Room for Impact* cycle, so that you can explicitly decide where to next, and why.

Thing 7: Thoughts About Scale

As you leverage the *Room for Impact* protocols to de-implement things you have direct control over, you might also be having thoughts about how you could "spread the love;" that is, how you can scale. We have already written extensively on scaling (Hamilton & Hattie, 2021; 2022; Hamilton et al., 2022; Wiliam, 2007), and we don't want to pad this book by repeating our prior messages in detail—especially given that de-implementation is a relatively new idea that needs to be more carefully tested and iterated before it is explicitly scaled.

That said, there are a range of contexts/perspectives that you could scale up. You might be:

1. **An individual teacher** – who has been inspired by the book. You may have used some of our ideas and suggestions to streamline your personal workload and now you want to spread the love more widely within your school. One the best routes for doing this is to advocate for the establishment of a schoolwide of Backbone Organization or for your existing well-being committee to adopt the P-steps in their work.

2. **At teaching team level** – here, you might have used the *Room for Impact* protocols and run a de-implementation inquiry cycle within your Professional Learning Community. Your best routes for scaling are similar to those for individual teachers. You want to catalog your case studies and the data on time/resources saved and present these to decision makers in your wider school. Again, the idea is to advocate for a school-wide Backbone Organization (and to volunteer to be a part of it)

3. **At whole school level** – where you might already have successfully established an organization-level backbone team but where you have identified things that you would like to de-implement but cannot because existing rules are too rigid; *or* where you, again, want to spread the love and encourage your neighboring schools and the district to get with the program. In both cases you are likely to get most traction with show-and-tell

advocacy by virally spreading the word about what you have done and the impact it has had and what can be done next.

4. **At system-level** – where you might be concerned about teacher workload or resource allocations across *all* your schools and want to unlock efficiency of impact. There are two ways you can do this:

    a. **Establish a system-level backbone** – to identify and action regulatory changes that reduce the burden of individual schools, in their dancing to your tune

    b. **Encourage (or even mandate) the establishment of school-level backbone teams** – so that individual schools—with your support and training—can leverage the P-Steps as a local path to success.

What we provide in this book is the research, ideas, and protocols. The rest is up to you!

Conclusion

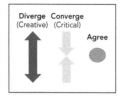

In this chapter, we considered some of the decisions you may need to take once you get to the end of a *Room for Impact* inquiry cycle. Decisions about how (and whether) to sustain, and also about opportunities for scaling up. These are local considerations for you to deliberate on. Our only suggestion is that you take these decisions carefully. That you diverge and converge before you then agree. And, also, that you take the opportunity to chalk up and celebrate your wins!

Part 6

Finito

Conclusion 12

The three of us collaborated on this book for one simple reason: across the predominantly English-speaking countries, there is a growing sense—and substantial evidence—that teachers and leaders are overworked. There is also remarkably little evidence that any of this additional energy and effort is necessarily translating into improved student outcomes at scale.

When we look at the comparative international student achievement data, the needle has hardly budged in many countries since the 1970s, and there is little evidence that any improvements are due to raising the workload of educators (Altinok et al., 2018). Further, as we illustrated in Chapter 1, some of the highest PISA performers achieve their feat with one thousand days *less* schooling than their lower performing counterparts (see Figures 1.2 and 1.3). It really does seem as if less could be more.

In some contexts, governments are already reshaping regulations to reduce educator workload—for example, by removing reporting requirements that make little difference to student impact. But the trouble is, this is not (yet) turning into significant, scalable, and sustained reductions in workload. It is not (yet) resulting in greater efficiency of impact.

There is many a slip between cup and lip. Much "devil in the detail" between thinking and agreeing that efficiency of impact should be a priority and then making it happen. Two reasons that it is so hard are that:

1. **we seem to be cognitively primed for addition rather than subtraction**; and

2. **there is not (yet) a set of concrete protocols that educators can follow in a stepwise fashion to successfully de-implement** (which is why we wrote this book!)

It's not enough to just say "work smarter" and expect this to happen. People need help along the way. Help to systematically unlock an efficiency of impact. Help to do less to achieve the same. Or even to do less and achieve more.

Arran and John first became interested in this area—and enthused about the possibilities—when they collaborated on *The Lean Education Manifesto: A Synthesis of 900+ Systematic Reviews for Visible Learning in Developing Countries*. As the title suggests, this was focused on low-income countries and how they could best use their extremely limited education budgets. The book examined how cash-strapped systems could get more out from less in, squeezing out every last drop of funding, teacher time, and expertise.

One of the case studies Arran and John happened upon was the BRAC Education Program in Bangladesh (S. Ahmed & Nath, 2003; Nath, 2005; Numan & Islam, 2021). This was (and still is) a voluntary sector education initiative that seeks to plug the gap in government provision by educating children the government cannot afford to reach. BRAC did this by focusing relentlessly on efficiency of impact. Rather than building schools, they rented individual rooms. Rather than providing schooling for the full day, they provided each child with only a couple of hours of instruction. Rather than having grade-based classes, they put children of different ages together, with the more advanced children peer-tutoring their less advanced peers. Tuition was guided by highly scripted curriculum materials suitable for teachers with minimal training (predominantly female middle-school graduates with around two weeks of preservice teacher training before they entered the classroom).

In many instances, the impact of the (efficient) BRAC program was significantly greater than that of government schools, where children spent the whole day in grade-based classes under the instruction of university-trained educators. Again, sometimes less really is more.

For avoidance of all doubt, we are *not* at all advocating for the establishment of BRAC-type schooling in the United States, Canada, UK, Australia, or New Zealand—the jurisdictions where most of the readers of this book are likely to reside. It just got us thinking (with Dylan now adding to the mix) that if BRAC could get reasonably good outcomes on two and a half hours a day of instruction—and without teachers having to undertake significant preparation outside classroom hours—there had to be things that high-income country school systems could easily dial back on, without harming student outcomes either.

It then got us further thinking that there were two paths to making this happen. The first path was to provide a *shopping list* of low-impact activities for schools to de-implement, whereas the second path was to provide schools (and systems) with a *process* for them to identify locally appropriate actions and for them to evaluate (or aPpraise) the impact.

For the full *shopping list* you can take a look at *The Lean Education Manifesto*. Some of the suggestions—like reducing the length of the school day/year; scripted/scaffolded instruction; multi-age/grade classrooms; and accelerated (but shorter) initial teacher training programs—may make you fall off the back of your chair (although there are many examples of these initiatives in more wealthy countries with good effect). For the (slightly) more palatable *shopping list*, see **Appendix 1**.

In *Making Room for Impact*, we have primarily sought to provide you with a *process* rather than that *shopping list,* although we have spelled out (less draconian) things that can be Removed, Reduced, Re-Engineered, or Replaced along the way. These include things like parental reporting, student behavioral management systems, data reporting, lesson planning, staff meetings, administration, co-curricular programs, homework, wall displays, and timetabling. We don't explicitly advocate for any of these areas, we just wanted to give you some ideas to consider as you undertake your local *Room for Impact* inquiry cycle in your school. Again, see Appendix 1 for our full list of provocations.

To be frank, we were also astounded that no one had already developed a set of stepwise de-implementation protocols for educators to use in their schools (i.e., a *process*). The few accounts we found were either hazy on the detail or sleepwalked into Replacement-oriented activity. They focused on de-implementation by identifying and clarifying the essential organizational goals and focusing everyone's attention on the critical actions to achieve these, while paying less attention to the help and support people required to quit existing, engrained, and automatic habits. This is the educational equivalent of telling people that smoking is no longer a priority, without helping them to actually stop.

Ergo, we mined all the leads we could find—across healthcare, business, and manufacturing—and the cognitive psychology literature on habit change, including successful strategies for giving up addictive substances. From this, *Room for Impact* was born.

Our intention is to give you tools to de-implement to achieve one or more of the following:

1. To save time and reduce your workload:
    a. **As an end-in-itself**—for example, to increase your individual and/or collective well-being
    b. **With the intention of positive organic washback**—that is, enabling you to be better and more impactful teachers, because you have time to quietly reflect, think, and improve organically
    c. **To explicitly reinvest your time and energy into the highest impact activities**—that is, you de-implement to create room for more effective impact, while carefully and systematically identifying those Replacement areas

2. **To save financial resources:**
   a. **As an end-in-itself** (more relevant during economic downturns when education budgets are sometimes reduced)
   b. **To reinvest** in higher probability initiatives, programs, technology, infrastructure, and/or training that you have carefully selected

Note that within the book, we have focused more on saving/rekindling time rather than financial resources. But the suggested protocols can also be used for budgetary efficiency, if required. And we provide some (simple) financial cost-benefit analysis tools.

As for the *Room for Impact* processes themselves, we recap these in Figure 12.1. These are:

1. Discover Stage
   - **1.1: Permit** – which is about receiving a permit/license to operate, to mitigate the guilt- and shame-based drivers that often result in people doubling down on efficient practices; and establishing a backbone team to undertake the *Room for Impact* inquiry cycle
   - **1.2: Prospect** – the act of identifying and provisionally selecting target areas that are ripe for de-implementation (i.e., targeting the Jenga blocks)
   - **1.3: Postulate** – explaining what sustains existing practices in those target areas (a.k.a. Chesterton's Fence) because in order to change the future, we need to have a good understanding of what causes the present

2. Decide Stage
   - **2.1: Propose** – which is about laying out a high-level de-implementation strategy, using one or more of the 4Rs (i.e., Remove, Reduce, Re-engineer, and/or Replace); that also addresses Chesterton's Fence
   - **2.2: Prepare** – where you flesh out that high-level proposition into a more detailed plan of attack (i.e., what, why, when, where, who, and how) and where you stress test it
   - **2.3: Picture** – the establishment of success criteria and an evaluative plan, to ensure you do no harm along the way

3. De-Implement Stage
   - **3.1: Proceed** – where (finally) you bring your de-implementation plans to life! And where you also collect monitoring and evaluation data

4. Re-Decide Stage

- **4.1: aPpraise** – which is about checking that you did what you intended and that there has been no harm; and decisions about whether to continue, to iterate, or to *stop*

- **4.2: Propel** – a hodgepodge of considerations about what you should do after you have successfully completed a *Room for Impact* inquiry cycle, including questions related to sustainability and scale

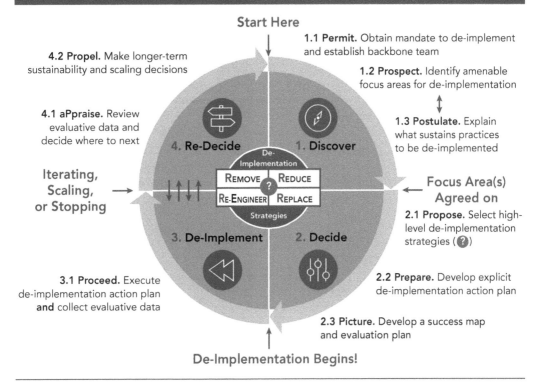

FIGURE 12.1   Recapping the *Room for Impact* Stages and P-Steps

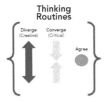 During each of these Stages and underlying P-steps, we provided you with a range of tools and approaches so that you could begin by thinking **divergently**, considering all the options and opportunities, then **converge** on the highest probability actions, and finally **agree** on what will be done.

When we unpack the *Room for Impact* inquiry cycle, the reception isn't always enthusiastic. The reaction from some is that the process *seems* overengineered. It is too difficult to put this into practice and, consequently, educators are likely to give up and get back on the implementation bus. To some extent, we understand their point. The truth is that de-implementation *is* hard. No one has (yet) cracked it. The complexity of the process is, we think, evidence of its authenticity. As H. L. Mencken said over a hundred years ago, "There is always an easy solution to every human problem—neat, plausible, and wrong" (Mencken, 1917/1949, p. 443).

It would have been tempting (and also less work) for us to have watered down the process—into a model that is easier to grasp and to remember. But you really do need to do what is in each of the four stages and their underlying P-Steps. We are not saying that if you miss one of the steps, then you are doomed to fail—schools are far too complex for such strong claims. But we do think that such omissions substantially reduce the likelihood of success.

Ergo, you do need to follow the P-steps—and in (broadly) the order we set out. But there is wiggle room in how much time and energy you invest at each stage—whether you engage in analysis-paralysis and boil the ocean before making decisions or whether you come together for a few short hours to dive deeply into the data and agree on what will be done. Back to that question of *optimal stopping*. Indeed, if you can pull yourself completely out of the day-to-day, getting from (1.1) Permit to (2.3) Picture in a three-day sprint is perfectly feasible. Although, if you are willing to space out your collaboration sessions for a few weeks, this helps with stress testing.

In addition, because de-implementation is such an under-researched area, we felt we needed to "go big" and produce as complete a process as we could—to provide the "Rolls Royce" model if you like—and outline many different ways you can gather data and make decisions. When you recognize that it is not a requirement that you use all the tools within each P-step, and that we have only included so many to give you options, the *Room for Impact* inquiry cycle looks a lot less daunting.

A second common criticism is that "most teachers don't think like this"—that an educator's mental model is geared toward addition and that we are going too much against the grain with all our de-implementation jibber-jabber. We don't disagree: the whole point of the book is to help reshape that mental model! Throughout history, many ideas were initially considered ludicrous before they caught on. The abolition of slavery, the rise of democracy, women's rights, and a whole host of other good ideas were considered utterly laughable. But gradually people stopped laughing and then, over time, everyone's mental models changed so that they would now automatically ridicule the prior (medieval) thinking. Out with the old. In with the new.

We are not suggesting that de-implementation is in anywhere near the same league as equal rights and democracy. Instead, we seek to illustrate that mental models can and do change. In fact, this change *should* be far easier because the vested interests are currently blowing in the direction of work-life balance. So, we think that we are pushing at an open door with efficiency of impact. And Joseph Overton's notion of the *window of discourse*—which is often called the Overton Window—nicely encapsulates this, as illustrated in Figure 12.2.

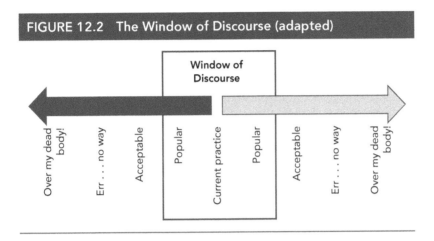

FIGURE 12.2   The Window of Discourse (adapted)

We think that in the post-COVID world, the idea of de-implementation has shifted from being "Over my dead body!" to being acceptable or even popular!

But it isn't just educators whose mental models have historically been geared toward addition. As we explained in Chapter 1, there may even be a cognitive bias that primes us to add and to forget completely about the possibility of subtracting. But that same research suggests that we can easily overcome this bias with training. We know, too, from work outside education that methodologies like Lean, Six Sigma, and Kaizen have proven highly effective in the business world at identifying and rooting out inefficiency. So, when people say, "Most teachers don't think like this," our response is, "Maybe it's about time they did." And in *Making Room for Impact*, we give much needed self-help tools.

Of course, there is then a counter risk that the pendulum swings too far the other way and that educators seek to de-implement "everything" and to vigorously avoid starting any new initiatives. That our message becomes misinterpreted as a license to "do the bare minimum." For avoidance of all doubt, we offer no such license and our key message— repeated often—is that you must evaluate (i.e., aPpraise) the impact of everything you are working to de-implement to ensure that you do no harm to student outcomes. And there are always going to be things worth adding in place of those you are subtracting. The key is to choose wisely, so that you are replacing "average" with "great."

A third criticism is that "efficiency-savings" is often a code word for redundancies, and we are asked if *Room for Impact* is about putting teachers out of jobs. We totally understand why this is asked. If someone turned up at your school with a stopwatch and a clipboard, and followed you around making copious notes, you would have every reason to call your union rep. But *Room for Impact* isn't about that. The person with the stopwatch and the clipboard should be *you*. The purpose of the inquiry is for you (and your colleagues) to identify efficiencies that you can either reinvest in work-life balance *or* in Replacement activities that have more impact on student outcomes. It's totally down to you and about what you decide locally in your *Room for Impact* backbone teams. And, where system-level authorities seek to leverage the process, we think the most mileage is likely to be in activating and scaling school-level backbones that make local decisions rather than an outside perspective. We also think there is major mileage for systems to use the process to review national regulations and, in each case, to ask "what's the worst that could happen if we Removed/Reduced/Re-engineered/Replaced this national requirement?"

A final question we often get asked is "Does it work?" The short answer is that it should but that there is a lot of devil-in-the-detail. To develop this toolkit, we reviewed all the available research on de-implementation (and implementation) that we could lay our hands on. For the interested, we've included appendices summarizing this trove (see **Appendices 2, 3, and 4**). But de-implementation is (surprisingly) a relatively new field of research and inquiry. Therefore, we think that what we have produced is probably the most comprehensive de-implementation field manual for education—to date. But it's certainly not the last word on the subject. Merely a useful stopgap to help you to stop!

In book conclusions, it's common to turn up the heat in the final few paragraphs—to say there is a crisis brewing, not a moment can be delayed. That if educators don't act fast, children will turn into bumpkins (or even pumpkins) and national GDP will plummet. The trouble, of course, with this little trick is that it primes you to act fast. It primes you to find shiny (additive) solutions to problems that might not even exist. It primes you to chase your tails.

Yes, every second counts and not a moment can be wasted. But let's focus on putting those seconds to use in the best possible way. By doing less to achieve more. Time to dig deep.

Time to de-implement with rigor.

Appendix 1

"Shopping List" of 80+ De-Implementation Opportunities

Preamble

To help you leverage the *Room for Impact* protocols effectively, this appendix contains a "shopping list" of de-implementation actions that you *could* consider. However, this list comes with the following health warnings:

1. **Some of these strategies might not comply with government regulations in your jurisdiction.** Make sure that you carefully cross-check your de-implementation plans against the local rules and regulations before you embark and seek advice from local experts! But equally, don't assume that "the rules in your mind" are necessarily the same as "the rules on paper"— you might find you have more wiggle room than you expected, but you still need to check.

2. **Some of these strategies are mutually exclusive**—you might choose one *or* an other approach within a category area, but it is sometimes incompatible to combine approaches. For example, you might decide to *Remove* all homework in primary/elementary school, but if you then introduce, say, quizzing homework, you have not actually removed all homework. Instead, you have *Replaced* your existing approach. However, many of the strategies are compatible and can be used together, so your key questions are likely to be:

   a. How many de-implementation balls can we juggle before we lose focus?

   b. Which initiatives are "easier" to implement in our local context?

   c. Which initiatives are *likely* to generate the most room, while not harming student outcomes?

3. **This list is not exhaustive.** For each strategy, we have indicated whether it is Remove, Reduce, Re-Engineer, or Replace – focused, as per the 4R Quadrants below.

   So, by implication, if the shopping list proposes a *Remove* strategy, you could also consider *Reduce, Re-Engineer,* and *Replace* alternatives to the same actions. And these could have a better fit with your local context.

FIGURE 13.1 Recapping the Four Rs of De-Implementation	
1. CAN WE REMOVE IT?	**2. CAN WE REDUCE IT?**
i.e., could we just **stop doing it** completely? — And HOW could we do this?	i.e., could **do it less** or could we apply it to fewer people (i.e., **Restrict**)? — And HOW could we do this?
3. CAN WE RE-ENGINEER IT?	**4. CAN WE REPLACE IT?**
i.e. could we do it **more efficiently**, with fewer steps/actions? -- And HOW could we do this?	i.e., **substitute it** with a more efficient alternative? -- And WHAT would this be?

Source: Adapted and extended from Hamilton and Hattie (2022); Northern Territory Government (Australia) (2020); Norton and Chambers (2020); Verkerk et al. (2018); V. Wang et al. (2018).

4. **There are always local judgment calls to be made about the opportunity cost of each strategy.** For example, some strategies like collaborative lesson planning are likely to go with the grain in your setting, but you might find that collaboration actually takes more time and results in curriculum "product" that wider stakeholders still do not feel confident using. Importing an external curriculum package might go heavily against the local grain and local beliefs about what good teachers are supposed to do. But it is likely to save more time *if* you select the "right" offer and *if* you can convince your colleagues to make the transition.

With these "health warnings" unpacked, let's now get to that shopping list!

The Shopping List

Domain 1: Teaching and Learning, Planning, and Curriculum Development

- Establishing a **cloud-based resource repository** that everyone uploads their existing teaching and learning materials into—to stop re-inventing the wheel, by providing a "base product" that can be localized and adapted (Reduce)

- Undertaking **collaborative lesson planning** rather than everyone planning the same lesson from scratch. Ideally this involves each team member taking complete responsibility for specific aspects; for example, lesson/scheme of work sequencing; producing full lesson plans and resources for allocated lessons that everyone can use/is required to use (Re-Engineer)

- **No longer creating differentiated learning objectives** and differentiated activity sheets (Remove)

- Buying **high-quality off-the-shelf curriculum and textbook packages** that provide all the teaching materials and learning resources so that there is no need to develop materials. This would include common, detailed lesson plans, unit plans, and assessments (Replace)

- **Using deep-learning AI algorithms** to automate the creation of bespoke homework assignments and then undertake minor adaptations/improvements (Replace and Re-engineer)

- **Removing the requirement to have a written lesson plan for each lesson** (Remove); and/or reduce the **amount of detail required** within lesson plans (Reduce/Re-engineer)

- **Stopping out-of-hours revision sessions** – focusing, instead, on high-quality learning during the regular school day (Remove and Replace)

- **Introducing creative timetabling,** so that teachers specialize in specific year groups and subjects, to reduce both planning time and attendance at parent meetings (Re-Engineer)

- **Lengthening school day and moving to four-day week** – allowing staff to have three-day weekend (Re-Engineer)

- **(Slightly) increasing class sizes** in return for teachers having a lower number of teaching hours/more planning time (Re-Engineer)

- **Part-time specialist teachers in primary**, for example, in science and math, to reduce planning and contact time for generalist teachers (Replace)

- **Combining classes** – across year levels; that is, multigrade classrooms to reduce teaching hours (Re-Engineer)

- **Streamlining curriculum offerings** or partnering with other schools to offer shared subjects (Reduce/Re-Engineer)

- Doing **more preparation and planning in nonterm time** (Re-Engineer)

- Covering lessons for absent teachers being undertaken by a **dedicated cover teacher** (Replace)

- **Introducing Multitiered Systems of Support** so that specialist staff offer tailored pull-out support to students with identified additional needs, reducing burden on classroom teachers (Re-Engineer/Replace)

- **Removing any "shiny" whole-school programs for which evaluation data is not being collected** and/or programs where evaluation data is being collected but which shows marginal impact vs. effort (Remove)

- **Beaming-in "guest" teachers from lower-cost international jurisdictions** to take pressure off your local teaching teams and give your students access to more global perspectives. This links to Sugata Mitra's concept of "the granny cloud" (Replace/Re-Engineer)

- **Using software for timetabling** that has been optimized for teacher workload efficiency, ensuring that there are **few/no very small classes** (Replace)

Domain 2: Extracurricular Activities

- **Removing all extracurricular activities and, instead, sign-post third-party programs** delivered offsite by trusted voluntary associations (Remove/Replace)

- **Outsourcing in-school delivery of co-curricular activities to vetted voluntary associations**—for example, sports coaching societies, Scouts and Guides, and so forth (Replace)

- Outsourcing extracurricular program delivery by **hiring part-time co-curricular facilitators**/deliverers or directly recruiting volunteers (Replace)

- **Removing requirement to run co-curricular activities after school hours**, instead embedding these in the official school day (Remove/Re-Engineer)

- **Reducing the number of teachers involved in extracurricular activities**, sports days, excursions, and so forth (Reduce)

- **Reducing the number of co-curricular activities offered** (Reduce)

- **Reducing the duration/time allocation of co-curricular** activities (Reduce)

- **Pooling co-curricular activities with neighboring school**s (Re-Engineer)

- **Delegating playground/yard and bus duties to nonteaching staff** and/or prefects (Replace)

- **Reducing the number of staff that attend assemblies** (Reduce)

- **Reducing the frequency of assemblies** from once per day to once per week (Reduce)

- Combining separate year group assemblies into a **single whole-school assembly** (Re-Engineer)

Domain 3: Professional Development, Meetings, Administration, and MISC

- **Reducing the number of staff meetings** and replacing them with (a short and snappy) staff update email (Reduce/Replace)

- **Stand-up staff meetings** to speed up progress and reduced number of meetings per month/year (Re-Engineer)

- Having **clear meeting protocols, agendas, and time limit per item** – no meetings for the sake of meetings! This might include meeting agendas being signed off by school leadership and meetings with no clear purpose and outcome being banned (Re-Engineer)

- **No out-of-hours email and no use of mobile phone to view/respond to emails**; for example, by disabling access to school communications network during evenings and weekends (Remove/Re-Engineer)

- **Using a *Priority Level* coding system in email headers** (e.g. red, amber, green) so that staff know which emails must be read and responded to urgently vs. those that are less urgent and those that are providing general updates (Re-Engineer)

- **After-school meetings rationalized** – time can be repurposed for departmental planning and subject specific PD (Re-Engineer)

- **Holding bite-sized PD during school hours** – no more attending workshops and conferences during school holidays (Reduce/Re-Engineer)

- **Removing all nonessential PD that does not have a clear and *demonstrable* impact** on improving student outcomes (Remove)

- **Staff not having to provide cover for absent colleagues** unless they are under their allocated number of lessons (Remove/Replace)

- **Staff not needing to do lunchtime or break time duties.** They get a break – just like the students! (Replace)

- **No more wall displays in classrooms and corridors** (Remove); or Wall displays not updated as frequently (Reduce); or only use of "pretty useful" wall displays, with "pretty" wall displays being removed (Re-Engineer)

- **Centralized admin** – so that teachers are not sucked into finance, data, safeguarding or reprographics—they focus on teaching! (Replace)

- **Software system to communicate with parents** and collect any payments for ancillaries (Replace)

- **Identification of pinch points during the academic year** – with explicit smoothing of workload across the yearly calendar (Re-Engineer)

- **Flattening school hierarchy to remove extra layers of staff meetings** at year-level/house management, or faculty-level (Re-Engineer)

- **Reducing the number of required peer-lesson observations** (Reduce)

Domain 4: Parental Engagement

- **Changing rules and norms so that parents are not permitted to email, use WhatsApp, or telephone teach staff directly.** All communication is to the "parent coordinator" who provides "Level 1 customer support" to reduce teachers' workloads (Replace)

- **Centralized parental engagement from school leaders on student behavioral issues.** Teachers do not have to phone parents or meet with them. Leaders do this, freeing teachers to teach (Replace)

- **Using automated systems to prepopulate parental reports/dashboards** with data on attendance, grades, and so forth that parents can access in real-time (Re-engineer)

- **Reducing the number of teachers that need to attend parent-teacher conferences/parents' evenings**, by having the form/homeroom teacher represent the wider teaching team (Re-engineer)

- **Reducing the number of teachers that need to contribute to parental report cards**—for example, by having a holistic report produced by the form/homeroom teacher, along with dashboard data, rather than individual subject teacher reports (Re-engineer)

- **Reducing the frequency of parental reporting and parent-teacher conferences** from, for example, termly to twice yearly (Reduce)

- **Adding a frequently asked questions/decision tree page to the school website** to reduce parental inquiries about common issues (Re-Engineer)

- **Having an automated WhatsApp inquiry line with numbered options and self-service** to reduce bespoke/manual parent handling—that is, use a chatbot (Replace)

Domain 5: Student Behavior Management

- **Using a clear behavior system and policy that is applied consistently.** Students are aware of the required behaviors and the accompanying sanctions. Staff undertake quick and simple logging (via an app) of sanctions applied to individual students (Replace)

- **Teachers pool their detentions into a single session per week**, so that they each only have to stay late one night (Re-Engineer)

- **Instituting a centralized after-school detention system for all behavioral issues**, with one or two teachers on rotation, to ease lunchtime and after-school burden on all other teachers (Re-Engineer)

- **Leveraging senior students as prefects**/hall monitors (Replace)

- **Adopting an automated behavior management system facilitated by an app** that is used by teachers to quickly flag student infractions in real time, which is then centrally managed; for example, automatically booking students into detention, counseling, and/or alerting parents, depending on agreed upon rules-based formulas (Replace)

- See also *parent engagement* strategies, above

Domain 6: Student Assessment and Feedback

- **Removing all homework in primary/elementary school settings** (Remove)

- **Reducing *frequency* of homework**—for example, from once a week per subject to once a fortnight (Reduce)

- **Reducing the *intensity* of homework assignments** – to decrease the teacher preparation time and marking time per student (Reduce)

- **Using standardized Self-Quizzing Homework for lower grades** to reduce planning, task setting, and marking requirements (Replace)

- **Using online self-marking tools that enable teachers to create online quizzes/questions and that provide automated feedback to students.** These tests can also be reused by teachers in subsequent years (Replace)

- **Using of deep learning algorithms** (e.g., chatbots) to create homework assignments and also to provide initial feedback to students, using the assessment rubrics (Replace)

- **Using standardized marking rubrics and shorthand feedback codes**, marking stamps and/or colored pens to reduce the time teachers spend recording written feedback (Re-Engineer)

- **Using voice note software to provide oral recorded feedback** that is tagged to specific parts of the students' work (Re-Engineer)

- **Using online intelligent tutoring systems** to further reduce homework planning, setting, marking, and feedback requirements (Replace)

- **Peer marking of homework for upper grades**, during class using self-assessment grids with teacher sampling checks (Re-Engineer)

- **No setting of homework the week before school holidays**, so that staff don't return to piles of marking (Re-Engineer)

- **Focusing on feedback rather than "marking"** (i.e., whole class feedback, verbal feedback, and daily quizzes). No more marking exercise books until 2 a.m. (Re-Engineer). Strategies include:
  - *Marking in the Moment* (i.e., direct real-time, verbal feedback during class);
  - *Marking Conferences* (where specific time is set aside in lessons for group and 1:1 feedback);
  - *Registering Feedback* (where students present small portions of their work to class and receive immediate feedback); and
  - *Strategic Sampling* (where teachers undertake a five-minute "flick review" of a random sample of student work to inform next steps).

- **Using third-party online platform for students to access their assignments, upload their responses, and enable them to access semiautomated feedback online**; some platforms can also scan for plagiarism. This saves time in printing, distributing, and collecting homework sheets (Replace)

- **Ensuring assessment cycles allow time to support identified student needs, before the next cycle begins**—that is, less formative assessment but more impact (Reduce)

- **Using externally developed tests/assessments to benchmark and measure student progress** – to save time in assessment development and also (potentially) to outsource marking to those external parties/artificial intelligence (Replace)

Domain 7: Data Management

- **Implementing whole school eMIS system**, so that data is only entered once and can be used many times across school and district (Re-Engineer)

- **Data auditing to review every data type being collected, what it's actually used for, and whether this meets (A) a regulatory requirement and/or (B) an educational requirement** – where the answer to A/B is "No," data collection is stopped/made proportionate to its usefulness (Remove or Re-Engineer)

- **Using automated systems for collecting and analyzing student attendance data**—for example, using AI deep-learning algorithms to flag patterns that potentially require intervention rather than having teachers manually scour the data. Many of these systems can also provide automatic notification to parents (Replace)

- **Implementing centralized data platform for student behavior management process flow**—That is, to book detentions; communicate with students and their parents (Replace)

- **Having school governing boards review the data they actually need for governance vs. the data they "like" to see** and strip out the latter to reduce reporting burden on school leadership team (Re-engineer)

- **Reviewing staff performance management system to ensure that evidence-collection requirements are proportionate with use/need** (Reduce/Re-Engineer)

- **Appointing a centralized data coordinator to take responsibility for all the above** (Replace)

Appendix 2

Overview of 50+ Cross-Disciplinary Research Studies on De-Implementation

AUTHOR, YEAR	CONTEXT	TREATMENT GROUP	DE-IMPLEMENTATION INTERVENTION	OUTCOME	STUDY DESIGN
Ashman and Stobart (2018)	Education	5 schools	Teacher workload reduction initiative focused on developing a common school-based summative assessment and data management system	**73% of teachers reported that the new systems reduced their workload**	**Action Research Project**
Augustsson et al. (2021)	Healthcare	N/A	Identified the following determinants for successful de-implementation of low-value practices: patient expectations; medical professional beliefs; professionals' knowledge; professionals' memory; policy and regulatory support; pressure from suppliers; organizational culture; and de-implementation process	N/A	**Scoping review** of 101 de-implementation citations
Augustsson et al. (2022)	Healthcare	N/A	Discussed the value of establishing national-level infrastructure to support and reinforce decentralized local de-implementation initiatives. Identified the following national barriers to successful de-implementation: unfavorable change incentives; unclear governance roles; and ambiguous evidence about practices to be de-implemented	N/A	**Qualitative case study** with 9 national institutions

(Continued)

(Continued)

AUTHOR, YEAR	CONTEXT	TREATMENT GROUP	DE-IMPLEMENTATION INTERVENTION	OUTCOME	STUDY DESIGN
C. R. Burton et al. (2021)	Healthcare	N/A	Identified five key variables that are likely to impact the success of de-implementation initiatives: (1) the selected target areas; (2) the reasons for de-implementation; (3) the de-implementation strategy; (4) whether de-implementation is planned or opportunistic; and (5) the opportunity cost of de-implementation	N/A	**Realist Synthesis** – focus groups and interviews with 31 healthcare stakeholders and review of 42 papers
Churches (2020)	Education	267 teachers from 14 teacher-led studies	Inquiry-cycle approach where schools in England used the Department for Education Teacher Workload Reduction Toolkit to identify, implement, and evaluate their own workload reduction initiatives	**Average time saving of 1 hour 20 mins per teacher, with a "small but positive" impact on student outcomes; teacher perception data on increased well-being**	**Randomized Controlled Trial**
Davidson et al. (2017)	Healthcare	N/A	Proposed a nine-step de-implementation process: (1) identify de-implementation practice; (2) document prevalence of current practice; (3) investigate what sustains current practices; (4) review viable extinction mechanisms; (5) choose extinction mechanism; (6) de-implement; (7) evaluate; (8) collect success stories; and (9) select next target area	N/A	**High-level de-implementation methodology**
Denvall et al. (2022)	Homelessness	N/A	Concluded that there is currently a lack of both practical frameworks and theoretical explanations of de-implementation. Key de-implementation variables: (1) identifying target area; (2) reviewing evidence of impact/importance of selected de-implementation areas; (3) demands from service users; and (4) financial incentives were identified	N/A	**Scoping article reviewing findings from 41 studies**

AUTHOR, YEAR	CONTEXT	TREATMENT GROUP	DE-IMPLEMENTATION INTERVENTION	OUTCOME	STUDY DESIGN
DeWitt (2022)	Education	N/A	Proposes 4-step de-implementation process: (1) Inquire, (2) Plan, (3) De-Implement, and (4) Evaluate	N/A	Process Manual
Ellis et al. (2017)	Education	1 school	Teacher workload education initiative focused on implementing shared teacher planning protocols	82% of teachers reported that the new systems reduced their workload	Action Research Project
Farmer et al. (2021)	Education	N/A	Identified the following de-implementation behavior change strategies: (1) extinction, (2) differential reinforcement, (3) response effort, and (4) punishment. Also identified need to select de-implementation target area with care and to undertake functional analysis of why low-value practices persist	N/A	Conceptual paper
Featherstone and Seleznyov (2017)	Education	4 schools	Moving from written to verbal student feedback in order to reduce teacher workload	Saved an average of 3.45 hours per week without an adverse effect on student outcomes	Randomized controlled trial
Gnjidic and Elshaug (2015)	Healthcare	N/A	Word-cloud of 43 terms for de-implementation – highest frequency terms: disinvest, decrease, discontinue, abandon, reassess, reverse	N/A	Terminology Review
Grimshaw et al. (2020)	Healthcare	N/A	Proposed four phases of de-implementation activity: (Phase Zero) identification of potentially low-value practices; (1) agreeing local priorities; (2) assessing potential local barriers and opportunities to de-implementation; (3) evaluating impact of de-implementation; (4) spreading de-implementation more widely	N/A	High-level de-implementation methodology

(Continued)

(Continued)

AUTHOR, YEAR	CONTEXT	TREATMENT GROUP	DE-IMPLEMENTATION INTERVENTION	OUTCOME	STUDY DESIGN
Gu et al. (2018)	Education	Multiple schools but unquantified	Teacher workload reduction via collaborative planning	Positive but qualitative data	Action Research Project
Handscomb et al. (2017)	Education	1 school	Teacher workload reduction trials across (1) marking, (2) planning, and (3) data management	82% of respondents reported a planning workload reduction	Action research project
Herbert et al. (2017)	Education	17 schools	Action research project to reduce teacher workload from student marking/assessment	Schools reported saving 50–70% in time previously spent on marking	Action research project
Ingvarsson et al. (2022)	Healthcare	N/A	Identified 71 unique de-implementation strategies grouped under nine categories: (1) education and training; (2) evaluative and iterative strategies; (3) stakeholder support; (4) developing stakeholder interrelationships; (5) change infrastructure; (6) financial strategies; (7) adapting and tailoring to context; (8) providing interactive assistance; and (9) engage consumers	N/A	Scoping Review of 310 studies
Ivers and Desveaux (2019)	Healthcare	N/A	Makes the case that successful de-implementation requires audit and feedback to ensure that the intended goals are achieved without harming stakeholder interests	N/A	Commentary Article
Kime et al. (2018)	Education	3 schools	Randomized controlled trial to reduce teacher workload from student marking/assessment	3.2 hours per week saving with no adverse impact on student achievement	Randomized Controlled Trial
King et al. (2018)	Education	1 school	Action research project focused on reducing teacher workload linked to "creation, input, analysis, sharing and communication of student assessment and progress data; evaluating the current workload	Inconclusive	Action Research Project

AUTHOR, YEAR	CONTEXT	TREATMENT GROUP	DE-IMPLEMENTATION INTERVENTION	OUTCOME	STUDY DESIGN
			demands linked to these activities; and exploring how workload can be reduced and better redeployed"		
Leigh et al. (2017, 2022)	Healthcare	N/A	Identified 29 distinct barriers and 24 distinct enablers to de-implementation. Barriers included entrenched norms and resistance; patient demands and preferences; and lack of credible evidence to justify de-implementation. Enablers included stakeholder collaboration; and availability of credible evidence	N/A	**Mixed methods study:** 172 articles & semi-structured interviews
Lovett and Harrison (2021)	Education	N/A	Suggests that low-value practices are maintained because of inaccurate background beliefs; immediate antecedents; and consequences. And that successful de-implementation requires staff training; providing alternative responses/ practices; and removing antecedents/behavioral primers	N/A	Commentary Article
McKay et al. (2018)	Health and Social Care	N/A	Identifies three criteria for identification of target de-implementation areas: (1) harmful practices; (2) inefficient or ineffective practices; (3) interventions that have become unnecessary. Catalogs a range of high-level de-implementation frameworks including (a) De-adoption Framework (Niven, 2015); (b) Framework for termination of public organization (Adam et al., 2007); and (c) The Reassessment Framework (Elshaug et al., 2009). Suggests that de-implementation needs to be thought of as an outcome *and* a process	N/A	Commentary Article

(Continued)

(Continued)

AUTHOR, YEAR	CONTEXT	TREATMENT GROUP	DE-IMPLEMENTATION INTERVENTION	OUTCOME	STUDY DESIGN
Montini and Graham (2015)	Healthcare	N/A	Suggested that a range of social, political, and economic factors beyond clinician and hospital preferences/control hindered the speed of de-implementation and that any de-implementation model needs to account for these wider meso/macro factors	N/A	**Case study:** de-implementation of radical mastectomy
Nilsen et al. (2020)	Healthcare	N/A	Inconclusive: suggested that more research needed to clearly delineate the difference between implementation and de-implementation	N/A	**Scoping review of 10 papers**
Niven et al. (2015)	Healthcare	N/A	Proposes high-level de-implementation methodology: (1) identify low-value practices; (2) assess prevalence of low-value practices; (3) assess barriers and enablers of de-adoption; (4) select de-adoption strategy; (5) evaluate outcomes; (6) sustain de-adoption	N/A	**Scoping review of 109 papers**
Northern Territory Government (Australia) (2020) – Evidence for Learning (2022)	Education	N/A	Proposes the following stages and process for de-implementation: 1. Explore: a. Identify the appropriate types of de-implementation b. Explore the outcomes of de-implementation c. Explore feasibility and fit of de-implementation 2. Prepare: a. Develop de-implementation plan b. Gauge readiness to implement plan c. Prepare/train staff	N/A	**High-level process manual**

AUTHOR, YEAR	CONTEXT	TREATMENT GROUP	DE-IMPLEMENTATION INTERVENTION	OUTCOME	STUDY DESIGN

			3. Deliver
			   a. Support staff to de-implement
			   b. Reinforce with training
			   c. Use data to drive intelligent adoption
			4. Scale
			   a. Plan for sustainability from the outset
			   b. Continuously acknowledge, reward and support good de-implementation practices		

Norton and Chambers (2020)	Healthcare	N/A	Identifies four types of de-implementation: (1) remove, (2) replace, (3) reduce, and (4) restrict. Suggests that the following variables may impact the success of de-implementation: (A) strength of evidence; (B) complexity; (C) beliefs/social norms; and (D) economic factors	N/A	Commentary Article
Norton et al. (2017)	Healthcare	N/A	Concluded that over the period 2000–17 very few research projects have been funded that focus on de-implementation of ineffective, harmful, inappropriate, overused, and/or low-value practices. And that promotional strategies are required to increase researcher and practitioner interest in de-implementation	N/A	Systematic review of U.S. research grants awarded to conduct de-implementation studies in healthcare
Parker et al. (2022)	Healthcare	N/A	Identified factors that encourage the maintenance of low-value practices (e.g. availability of data; lack of mandated de-implementation targets) and variables that support de-implementation	N/A	Qualitative review: Semi-structured interviews with individuals implementing Choosing Wisely Canada

(Continued)

(Continued)

AUTHOR, YEAR	CONTEXT	TREATMENT GROUP	DE-IMPLEMENTATION INTERVENTION	OUTCOME	STUDY DESIGN
			(e.g. hard-coded intervention strategies). The stakeholder interviews suggest unintentional/ unaccounted factors are highly significant and that de-implementation is an extremely complex process		recommendations in healthcare settings in four provinces.
Patey et al. (2021)	Healthcare	N/A	Proposes a typology of 30+ de-implementation behavior change strategies. The top five strategies (as measured by frequency of mention in the literature) are (1) instructions on how to perform the behavior; (2) feedback on the behavior; (3) monitoring by others without feedback; (4) behavior substitution; and (5) social comparison	N/A	**Systematic review** of intervention descriptions in 181 articles
Pinto and Park (2019)	Social Work	N/A	Suggests that more research is needed on de-implementation strategies and protocols and that these approaches should include consultation and collaboration with affected stakeholder groups	N/A	**Perspectives paper**
Pinto and Witte (2019)	Healthcare	N/A	Suggests that de-implementation theories and methodologies need to deeply account for system-level variables— e.g., governance, policy, politics, and economic considerations—that incentivize organizational level actions	N/A	**Commentary**
Prasad and Ioannidis (2014)	Healthcare	N/A	Postulates that the following drivers are likely to be significantly correlated with successful vs. unsuccessful de-implementation: (1) evidence base supporting de-implementation; (2) cost/ubiquity; (3) alternative options; (4) testing that de-implementation makes financial sense; and (5) proponents are open-minded about outcomes	N/A	Commentary

AUTHOR, YEAR	CONTEXT	TREATMENT GROUP	DE-IMPLEMENTATION INTERVENTION	OUTCOME	STUDY DESIGN
Prostiv et al. (2018)	Education	9 schools	Action research focused on opportunities to reduce teacher workload in assessment and marking (move from written to verbal feedback)	**Positive but qualitative data**	**Action Research** Project
Prusaczyk et al. (2020)	Healthcare	N/A	Provides a typology of de-implementation variables, including (1) acceptability, (2) appropriateness, (3) cost, (4) feasibility, (5) fidelity, (6) penetration, and (7) sustainability	N/A	**Commentary**
Pryor (2019)	Generic	N/A	Outlines a range of behavior change strategies that could be applied to de-implementation. These include (1) reinforcement, (2) shaping/priming, (3) stimulus control, (4) untraining, and (5) clicker training	N/A	**Self-help manual**
Raudasoja et al. (2022)	Healthcare	227 de-implementation Randomized Controlled Trials (RCTs)	Suggests that (1) education and training interventions have modest benefits; (2) intervention designs with fewer moving parts are more effective; and (3) intervention designs with an explicit theory of change/action are also more likely to be effective	**Not reported** – lists only frequency of intervention type	**Systematic scoping review** of 227 de-implementation RCTs
Richardson et al. (2017)	Education	16 schools	Action research into 6 approaches to reduce teacher workload: (1) Marking in the Moment; (2) Visible Learning into Action; (3) Minimal Marking; (4) Self-Assessment; (5) Symbols; and (6) Marking Conferences	**No negative impact on student achievement but some questions about whether sufficient teacher time was saved.**	**Action Research** Projects
Rietbergen et al. (2020)	Healthcare	27 RCTs	Concluded that the majority of studies with positive outcomes leveraged de-implementation strategies that had an "educational component." No wider conclusions due to both the low number of studies included in the systematic review and the high level of heterogeneity of de-implementation approach	**Mixed** – approximately half of the de-implementation RCTs generated their intended effect	**Systematic review** of 27 RCTs

(Continued)

(Continued)

AUTHOR, YEAR	CONTEXT	TREATMENT GROUP	DE-IMPLEMENTATION INTERVENTION	OUTCOME	STUDY DESIGN
Robert et al. (2014)	Healthcare	N/A	Delphi study of the factors and processes that facilitate successful de-commissioning. Variables that elicited strong consensus among expert practitioners, included (1) strength of executive leadership; (2) strength of local leadership and their involvement from an early stage; (3) quality of communications; (4) demonstrable benefits of de-implementation; and (5) establishing a clear rationale for change	N/A	**Delphi study** of 30 international experts
Selby and Barnes (2018)	Healthcare	N/A	Key observations: (1) a "science of de-adoption" is slowly emerging in healthcare; (2) it is currently hampered by a lack of standardized terminology and approaches; and (3) approaches that focus on "reeducation" alone are unlikely to be successful	N/A	**Commentary article**
Shaw (2021)	Education	N/A	Central points: (1) there are relatively few empirical papers that measure the impact of de-implementation initiatives and/or processes; (2) that even the de-implementation of practices that are widely acknowledged to be harmful has been "painful"; (3) successful de-implementation requires a structured methodology/consultancy approach to overcome the pitfalls and challenges	N/A	**Commentary article**
Verkerk et al. (2018)	Healthcare	N/A	Distinguishes between three types of low-value interventions: (1) ineffective activities, which should be limited; (2) inefficient processes; (3) unwanted interventions. Proposes three linked de-implementation strategies: (a) Limit, (b) Lean, and (c) Listen	N/A	**Literature review/ typology of de-implementation strategies**

AUTHOR, YEAR	CONTEXT	TREATMENT GROUP	DE-IMPLEMENTATION INTERVENTION	OUTCOME	STUDY DESIGN
Walsh-Bailey et al. (2021)	Healthcare	27 studies	Catalogs a range of healthcare implementation "field manuals" that have been applied to de-implementation initiatives but due to the heterogeneity of included studies were unable to offer firm conclusions about the high-probability processes and/or behavioral change techniques	Inconclusive	Systematic review of 27 de-implementation studies
T. Wang et al. (2021)	Healthcare	One hospital	Applies the Choosing Wisely Five-Phase De-implementation Framework to an Institutional Pilot to Reduce Rates of Sentinel Lymph Node Biopsy in Women >70 Years' Old With Hormone Receptor Positive Cancer – using provider education and training, feedback, and modeling interventions	Reduction in use of low-value procedure from 78% of patients to 46%	Case Study
V. Wang et al. (2018)	Healthcare	N/A	Proposes four types of de-implementation: (1) partial reduction, (2) complete reversal, (3) substitution with related replacement, and (4) substitution with unrelated replacement of existing practice. Also reviews the unlearning literature and its implications for "forgetting"	N/A	Conceptual article
Webb (2017)	Education	1 Multi-academy Trust	Investigation into the importance of clarity in teacher data collection, as a mechanism for teacher workload reduction	N/A	Action Research Project
White et al. (2018)	Education	6 schools	Investigation into mechanisms to streamline education data collection and use	N/A	Action Research Project

Appendix 3

Lean and Six Sigma Processes

Lean

The Lean methodology originated in the Japanese car industry and was anglicized, popularized, and extended through the work of Womack and Jones (1997, 2013). The core focus is on making existing processes as efficient as possible to reduce the time, motion, and processing required to complete core tasks.

The key components of Lean are the following:

1. **Define What Is Valued**—that is, the outcomes that customers/end users seek,

2. **Map the Value Stream**—that is, map the existing production process and identify efficiencies that reduce time, motion, and processing,

3. **Create Flow**—that is, map the interconnections and hinge points between different processes and handover points to reduce friction,

4. **Pull**—that is, reduce motion by only activating processes/ workflows as and when they are needed (a.k.a. just in time), and

5. **Pursue Perfection**—that is, repeat steps one to four over and over to continuously reduce the processing requirements.

The key sources of waste (or *muda*) in the production process are listed here:

1. **Defects** – finished products being scrapped or needing to be reworked due to failures in the production process

2. **Overproduction** – producing more of something than is actually needed

3. **Overprocessing** – producing something to a higher quality standard than is actually needed

4. **Waiting** – wasted time while waiting for the next step to proceed

5. **Transport** – unnecessary movement across space/geography

6. **Motion** – unnecessary movements/actions by people

7. **Unused potential** – not leveraging people skills and/or technology to their full potential

8. **Inventory** – having much more of a product or material on hand than is actually needed for downstream activity

Six Sigma

A quality management methodology to reduce variance and errors in production processes, which emerged in the U.S. telecommunications sector (Tennant, 2001). It employs the **DMAIC** process to improve existing processes:

- **D**efine the problem, need, or goal;
- **M**easure in detail the current process/activity flow ("as is" state);
- **A**nalyze data to identify root causes of inefficiency/error;
- **I**mprove the process ("to be" state); and
- **C**ontrol to ensure the improvements are implemented.

And the **DMADV** process is used to design new products/services:

- **D**efine the need or goal;
- **M**easure critical components of the process and the product capabilities;
- **A**nalyze the data, develop and stress test multiple designs, and pick the "best" one;
- **D**esign and prototype the new process; and
- **V**erify the design by running field tests, pilots, and simulations.

Some of the critical Six Sigma tools include:

- **Root Cause Analysis** – to identify the causes/source of defects, and
- **Critical-to-Quality Tree** – to identify mission critical processes and steps that need to be buttressed for better outcomes.

We have adapted relevant aspects of both Lean and Six Sigma for the "Re-Engineer" elements of de-implementation.

Appendix 4

50+ Methodologies for Implementation

IMPLEMENTATION MODEL	DESCRIPTION	DEPLOYMENT CONTEXTS
Agile Ashmore and Runyan (2014)	Iterative project management methodology that is principally used in software development. Key areas of focus include (1) iterative and incremental implementation, with short feedback loops; (2) efficient communication; and (3) quality focus.	Software development projects
Appreciative Inquiry (AI) Cooperrider and Whitney (2000)	Centers on identifying, celebrating, and leveraging existing strengths rather than searching for problems to fix and deficit theorizing. Proposes a 4D approach: (D1) Discover, (D2) Dream, (D3) Design, and (D4) Destiny.	Range of commercial and public sector deployments globally
Balanced Scorecard Lawrie and Cobbold (2004)	A strategy performance management tool that supports monitoring and evaluation of progress that assess data across four quadrants: (1) customer, (2) finance, (3) processes, and (4) learning and growth.	Various business and public sector contexts
Collective Impact Kania and Kramer (2011)	Proposes five key criteria for impact: (1) Common Agenda, (2) Shared Measurement, (3) Mutually Reinforcing Activities, (4) Continuous Communication, and (5) Backbone Organization.	Social impact programs in the United States
COM-B (Capability, Opportunity, Motivation and Behavior) Michie et al. (2011)	A framework devised in medical implementation science to support adoption decision-making. Posits that the success of implementation is strongly influenced by contextual fit linked to (1) local capability to implement the agreed intervention, (2) motivation to implement, and (3) opportunity/capacity to implement.	Health care explanatory model

(Continued)

(Continued)

IMPLEMENTATION MODEL	DESCRIPTION	DEPLOYMENT CONTEXTS
Communities That Care (CTC) Hawkins and Weis (1985)	A community-collaboration model that involves grass-roots stakeholders: (1) Get Started, (2) Get Organized, (3) Develop a Community Profile/Identify a Need, (4) Create a Plan, and (5) Implement and Evaluate.	Youth problem behaviors
Concerns-Based Adoption Model (C-BAM) G. Hall and Hord (2011)	Focuses on the cognitive concerns/barriers to implementation among educators for programs that are being implemented/scaled. Also provides a range of evaluative tools to measure attitudes and adoption levels among target stakeholder groups. Key dimensions include (1) Stages of Concern, which relate to the personal/affective aspects of implementation; (2) Innovation Configuration, which relates to the level of fidelity/adaptation in implementation; and (3) Levels of Use, which relates to the degree of implementation by stakeholders.	Education sector, high-income countries
Consolidated Framework for Implementation Research (CFIR) Damschroder et al. (2009)	A conceptual framework with 39 constructs that are postulated to improve implementation/outcomes. These constructs sit across five domains: (1) Intervention Characteristics, including intervention complexity and stakeholder characteristics; (2) Inner Setting, including organizational variables such as implementation climate and leadership engagement; (3) Outer Settings, including external policy and incentives to implement); (4) Individual Characteristics, including beliefs and knowledge about the interventions; and (5) Implementation Processes, including selection and evaluation protocols.	Health care explanatory model
CostOut Levin et al. (2018)	Program adoption decision tools that support the estimation of financial costs of implementation and maintenance of different interventions and the comparison of cost vs. probability and depth of impact.	Education financial modeling, U.S.
Deliverology M. Barber et al. (2011)	Designed for scaling agreed on interventions and includes processes related to (1) agreeing on success criteria, (2) establishing accountability structures and metrics, (3) creating local implementation targets, (4) performance tracking, (5) robust accountability dialogue, and (6) rewards and consequences.	Public policy implementation in high- and middle-income countries
Design Thinking Liedtka et al. (2013)	Employs a range of processes, including (1) context analysis to identify wicked issues, (2) ideation and solutions generating, (3) modeling and prototyping, and (4) testing and evaluating.	Range of commercial and public sector deployments globally

IMPLEMENTATION MODEL	DESCRIPTION	DEPLOYMENT CONTEXTS
Diffusion of Innovations Rogers (2003)	A theory of adoption model that seeks to explain how innovations spread through systems and achieve critical mass. Posits a five-stage decision process: (1) knowledge, (2) persuasion, (3) decision, (4) implementation, and (5) confirmation.	Theory of spread
Double Diamond Design Council (2021) and Nessler (2018)	A design thinking–oriented approach that traverses these stages: (1) Discover, (2) Define, (3) Develop, and (4) Deliver. Also provides a methods bank of tools and approaches.	Various
Dynamic Adaption Process Aarons et al. (2012)	Medical implementation model with a core focus on adapting the evidence-based protocols to local contexts. Posits four stages of implementation: (1) Exploration Phase, (2) Preparation Phase, (3) Implementation Phase, and (4) Sustainment. Many features overlap with the EPIS model, with an adaptation/localization lens.	Health care sector
Dynamic Sustainability Framework Chambers et al. (2013)	Focuses on maintaining and sustaining evidence-based protocols in health care settings. Key dimensions relate to maximizing the fit between the intervention, implementation setting, and wider ecological system (e.g., policy, regulation, and market forces) over time.	Health care sector
Eight-Step Process for Leading Change Kotter (2012)	Generic framework for the successful activation of change programs: (1) Create a Sense of Urgency, (2) Build a Guiding Coalition, (3) Form a Strategic Vision and Initiatives, (4) Enlist a Volunteer Army, (5) Enable Action by Removing Barriers, (6) Generate Short-Term Wins, (7) Sustain Acceleration, and (8) Institute Change.	Range of commercial and public sector deployments globally
Exploration, Preparation, Implementation, Sustainment (EPIS) Moullin et al. (2019)	Medical implementation model with four key stages: (1) Exploration (i.e., evaluating local need and appropriate evidence-based programs), (2) Preparation (i.e., developing implementation plans), (3) Implementation, and (4) Sustainment.	Health care sector
Getting to Outcomes (GTO) Wandersman (2014)	A 10-stage results-based approach for getting to agreed upon outcomes: (1) Focus, (2) Target, (3) Adopt, (4) Adapt, (5) Resources, (6) Plan, (7) Monitor, (8) Evaluate, (9) Improve, and (10) Sustain. A key focus is on organizational readiness for the identified/agreed program.	Wide ranging, including health care, community improvement, and military
Hexagon Tool Blase et al. (2013)	A six-part planning/exploration tool for schools to identify local needs and then evaluate prebuilt programs and their suitability for the local context. Focus areas are (1) Need, (2) Fit, (3) Resources, (4) Evidence, (5) Readiness, and (6) Capacity.	Education sector, high-income countries

(Continued)

(Continued)

IMPLEMENTATION MODEL	DESCRIPTION	DEPLOYMENT CONTEXTS
Human-Centred Design (HCD) IDEO (2015)	Participatory action-research approach that involves (1) immersion, (2) community brainstorming, (3) modeling/prototyping, and (4) implementing.	Range of commercial and public sector deployments globally
IOWA Model C. G. Brown (2014)	Eight-step model of evidence-based improvement: (1) identify context where improvement is required; (2) determine whether the improvement is a priority; (3) form a team to develop, implement, and evaluate the improvement; (4) review literature on the change area; (5) critique and synthesize the research; (6) stop and decide whether to proceed; (7) implement change in a pilot program; and (8) evaluate results.	Nurse practitioners in health care settings
Kaizen Graban and Swartz (2012)	Japanese quality improvement philosophy that is strongly aligned to Lean. Focused on improvement to existing processes rather than the development or implementation of new activities or "product lines." Key principles include the following: (1) every process can be improved, (2) continuous improvement is essential, (3) errors are usually the result of flawed processes, not people, (4) everyone in an organization must implement improvements, and (5) incremental changes can result in significant impact.	Global, multisector
Knowledge-to-Action Framework (KTA) Graham et al. (2006)	Focused on contextualizing health care research prior to implementing, to adapt protocols to better fit local context. Key steps include the following: (1) identify the problem; (2) adapt knowledge to local context; (3) assess barriers/enablers to implementation; (4) select, tailor, and implement interventions; (5) monitor; (6) evaluate; and (7) sustain.	Health care implementation
Lean Improvement Womack and Jones (2013)	A continuous improvement process focused on increased efficiency. Involves (1) defining customer/stakeholder value, (2) mapping the existing value stream, (3) identifying process efficiencies, (4) implementing, (5) evaluating, and (6) beginning again.	Commercial manufacturing and service sectors
Leaning to G.O.L.D. Hamilton and Hattie (2021)	Framework for education improvement in developing countries. Combines Lean processes to identify activities and programs to de-implement and then testing and scaling, with design thinking–oriented approaches for implementation: (1) Goal Hunting, (2) Opportunity Seeking, (3) Liftoff, (4) Double-Back, and (5) Double-Up.	Education systems in developing countries
Learning to Improve (LTI) Bryk et al. (2017)	LTI offers a framework for (1) the identification of areas for improvement, (2) improvement hypothesis development, and (3) Agile-oriented improvement cycles.	Education sector, high-income contexts

IMPLEMENTATION MODEL	DESCRIPTION	DEPLOYMENT CONTEXTS
Logical Framework Approach (LFA) World Bank (2000)	Used to support program design prior to implementation and for the monitoring and evaluation of live initiatives. Enables the development of theories of change and action by outlining the inputs, activities, and outcomes and how these are expected to translate into short-, medium-, and longer-term impact	International development projects in low-income countries
Perpetual Beta	Software development paradigm that involves the release of minimal viable product, reviewing user data, and adding new features in light of user experience data. Aligns with Agile methodology.	Software development
Plan, Do, Study, Act (PDSA) Deming (1986)	An action-research protocol to undertake local iterative improvement activity by (1) Planning (i.e., agreeing on what to implement), (2) Doing (i.e., putting it into practice), (3) Studying (i.e., evaluating the Impact), and (4) Acting on the evidence to decide next steps.	Global, multisector
Positive Deviance LeMahieu et al. (2017) and Pascale et al. (2010)	A framework for grassroots exploration and fact finding, to detect positive outliers or "deviants" that buck whatever issue stakeholders seek to resolve. The idea is to catalog positive outlier behaviors that can be replicated and scaled.	Community-led initiatives
Practical, Robust Implementation and Sustainability Model (PRISM) Feldstein and Glasgow (2008)	Extension of the RE-AIM model and inclusion of Six Sigma processes. Key areas of focus include (1) creating infrastructure to encourage spread, (2) sharing best practices, (3) observing impact and adjusting protocols, and (4) adapting protocols to fit new environments.	Health care sector
PRECEDE-PROCEED Freire and Runyan (2006)	Health care implementation framework with two key baskets of protocols: (1) PRECEDE, which centers on contextual diagnosis prior to implementation to ensure fit; and (2) PROCEED, which focuses on implementation and process, impact, and outcome evaluation.	Health care sector
PRINCE2 Axelos (2017)	A structured project management process with seven key themes: (1) Business Case, (2) Organization, (3) Quality Management, (4) Product-Based Planning, (5) Risk Management, (6) Change Control, and (7) Progress Tracking.	Range of commercial and public sector deployments globally
Problem-Driven Iterative Adaptation (PDIA) Andrews et al. (2017) and Pritchett et al. (2013)	Design thinking–oriented approach that provides explicit protocols for (1) identification of "problems," (2) root cause analysis, (3) searching for "solutions" in design space, (4) implementing high-probability interventions, (5) evaluating, and (6) iterating.	International development projects in low-income countries

(Continued)

(Continued)

IMPLEMENTATION MODEL	DESCRIPTION	DEPLOYMENT CONTEXTS
Project Management Body of Knowledge (PMBOK) Project Management Institute (2021)	Catalogs a range of generic project management process for: (1) initiating, (2) planning, (3) executing, (4) monitoring and controlling, and (5) closing.	Range of commercial and public sector deployments globally
Promoting Action on Research Implementation in Health Services (PARIHS) Harvey and Kitson (2016)	Posits that successful implementation (I) is a function of Evidence (E), Context (C), and Facilitation (F).	Health care
Putting Evidence to Work Sharples et al. (2019)	Developed specifically for the education sector, this outlines a four-stage process: (1) Explore, (2) Prepare, (3) Deliver, and (4) Sustain.	Education improvement, UK
Quality Enhancement Research Initiative (QUERI) Braganza and Kilbourne (2021)	Framework for the implementation of effective programs to support U.S. military veterans. Stages include (1) Pre-implementation, agreeing on goal, stakeholders, and searching for best practices; (2) Implementation, including adaptation strategy; and (3) Sustainment.	Army veterans, U.S.
Quality Implementation Framework (QIF) Meyers et al. (2012)	Proposes 14 key actions across four phases: (1) Initial Considerations Regarding the Host Setting, (2) Creating a Structure for Implementation, (3) Ongoing Structure Once Implementation Begins, and (4) Evaluation.	Health care implementation
RE-AIM (Reach, Effectiveness, Adoption, Implementation, Maintenance) Glasgow et al. (2019)	Medical sector framework from translating statistical significance into real-world clinical significance. Key areas of focus: (1) Reach (i.e., how the target population is engaged and onboarded), (2) Effectiveness (i.e., confirming that the intervention will generate positive impact for target group), (3) Adoption (i.e., processes for implementing and adapting the protocols), (4) Implementation (i.e., ensuring fidelity within the permitted adaptation parameters), and (5) Maintenance (i.e., institutionalizing as part of routine practice).	Health care rollout of new innovations at scale
Reduce Change to Increase Improvement V. M. J. Robinson (2018)	Four-phase approach to implementation: (1) Agree on the Problem to be Solved, (2) Inquire into Relevant Theories of Action, (3) Evaluate the Relative Merit of Current and Alternative Theories of Action, and (4) Implement and Monitor a New, Sufficiently Shared Theory of Action.	Education sector, high-income countries

IMPLEMENTATION MODEL	DESCRIPTION	DEPLOYMENT CONTEXTS
Replicating Effective Programs (REP) Kilbourne et al. (2007)	An initiative by the U.S. Centers for Disease Control and Prevention to codify and productize the essential features of a range of health care programs, so that new providers can adopt them out of the box/on a turn-key basis. Each protocol was field tested in a range of contexts and then translated into everyday language to facilitate adoption in next settings.	Scaling productized health care programs
Scaling Up Education Reform Bishop et al. (2010)	Proposes the GPILSEO framework of: (1) Goals, (2) Pedagogies, (3) Institutions, (4) Leadership, (5) Spreading, (6) Evidence, and (7) Ownership.	Education improvement, New Zealand
Six Sigma Pyzdek and Keller (2009)	A methodology for process improvement. Key processes include the following: (1) Define goals, (2) Measure and identify critical quality characteristics, (3) Analyze to identify alternatives, (4) Design alternative, and (5) Verify the Design.	Range of commercial and public sector deployments globally
Spiral of Inquiry Timperley et al. (2014)	Provides educators with six processes to enhance student learning outcomes: (1) Scanning, (2) Focusing, (3) Developing a Hunch, (4) Learning, (5) Taking Action, and (6) Checking. Designed for short and local cycles of inquiry and implementation.	Education sector, high-income contexts
Stetler Model Stetler (2001)	Designed for use by individuals, teams, or organizations to identify and implement appropriate evidence-based practices for the local context. The five phases are: (1) Preparation, with focus on purpose and context; (2) Validation, with focus on reviewing interventions and their evidence base; (3) Decision-making, with focus on deciding which intervention to progress; (4) Translation/Application, with focus on developing an implementation plan, including any required adaptations; and (5) Evaluation.	Nurse practitioners in health care settings
Strategic Consulting Chevallier (2016) and Rasiel (2001)	A set of tools used by management consultants on business/public service improvement initiatives. The kit set includes processes for (1) Problem Framing, (2) Root Cause Identification, (3) Determining Actual Causes, (4) Identifying Potential Solutions, (5) Selecting Solution, (6) Selling the Solution to Principal Stakeholders, (7) Implementing and Monitoring the Solution, and (8) Dealing with Complications.	Range of commercial and public sector deployments globally
Teaching Sprints Breakspear and Jones (2020)	Process for teaching teams to (1) Prepare (i.e., identify focus area and intervention), (2) Sprint (i.e., implement), and (3) Review (i.e., reflect on effectiveness and agree next steps).	Education improvement, Australia

(Continued)

(Continued)

IMPLEMENTATION MODEL	DESCRIPTION	DEPLOYMENT CONTEXTS
Understanding-User-Context Framework Jacobson et al. (2003)	Framework for the translation/application of knowledge/programs to new contexts. Focus areas include (1) User-Group Considerations, (2) the Research, (3) Research-User Relationship, and (4) Dissemination Strategy.	Health care implementation
Waterfall Royce (1987)	Linear project management model that traverses: (1) Requirements, (2) Design, (3) Implementation, (4) Verification, and (5) Maintenance.	Range of commercial and public sector deployments globally

Source: Extended from Hamilton et al. (2022).

Glossary

Agree (action): a thinking routine that forms part of the wider diverge-converge-agree protocol. It is undertaken after Convergent Thinking and is literally about agreeing what will be done.

AGREE Criteria: a rubric that can be used when deciding which de-implementation strategy to pursue. The key domains are (1) Acceptability, (2) Goal Fit, (3) Risk, (4) Ease, and (5) Expenditure.

aPpraise (4.1): the P-step focused on checking that you did what you intended and that there has been no harm; and decisions about whether to continue, to iterate, or to *stop*.

Backbone Organization: a temporary organization structure established at the system, district, or whole-school level to bring about deep and sustained de-implementation impact via the *Room for Impact* methodology.

Behavior Change Countermeasures Map: a typology of behavior change strategies that can be used as countermeasures or "antidotes" to decrease the probability that stakeholders fail to de-implement what they initially agreed on. Some of the key strategies relate to monitoring, social support, incentives, and reshaping the physical environment.

Building to Impact: our sister publication that provides a process manual for implementation. *Building to Impact* is about adding. *Room for Impact* is about subtracting.

Chalking up the wins: a tool you can use to publicly display metric data related to your de-implementation targets, to keep everyone motivated. We introduce it in (4.2) Propel, but you can use it during the whole of the De-Implement and Re-Decide Phases.

Chesterton's Fence: the act of inquiring into/understanding what sustains existing practices, so that you can decide whether to de-implement them; and so that you can map the potential derailers to de-implementation and develop countermeasures or "antidotes." The term is derived from Chesterton's (1929) book *The Thing*, where he argues that reforms should not be undertaken before the reasoning behind the existing state of affairs is understood. Chesterton gives the example of a group of people deciding to take down a fence or barrier to illustrate this, hence "Chesterton's Fence."

Convergent Thinking: a thinking routine that is deployed after *Divergent Thinking* has been undertaken. It involves narrowing in or converging on the most suitable/high-probability strategies or actions from the wider options basket.

Cost analysis: reviewing the financial cost (e.g., per student) for targeted activities/programs vs. the student outcome gains. This enables you to undertake a "cost-benefit" calculation to decide whether the outcomes are "worth" the costs.

Decide Stage: the stage of *Room for Impact* that focuses on developing high probability de-implementation strategies and plans.

De-Implement Stage: the stage of *Room for Impact* that focuses on executing your de-implementation strategy.

De-Implementation (definition): the act of removing, reducing, re-engineering, or replacing a current practice. Other terms for this include de-adoption, de-commissioning, deletion, subtraction, and cessation. The primary motivations for de-implementation include (a) reducing harms from "poor" existing practice; (b) increasing gains from a more effective alternative practice; (c) to save time/resources through efficiencies. *Room for Impact* tilts toward a focus on efficiency to reduce teacher workload but can also be used to expunge harmful practices/pivot to more effective actions.

Discover Stage: the stage of *Room for Impact* that focuses on identifying suitable de-implementation target areas—that is, the high probability "Jenga Blocks."

Divergent Thinking: a thinking routine focused on exploring a problem or opportunity as widely as possible and from as many perspectives so that all the potential options can be uncovered.

Evaluating: the act of checking whether your de-implementation actions have saved you (sufficient) time/resources and without harming student outcomes.

Fishbone Tool: a tool for mapping the variables that sustain existing practices. This links to the *Six Buckets Framework*, *Chesterton's Fence*, and the *Sub-Bone Tool*.

HEAT Criteria: a rubric that helps you to decide your de-implementation focus areas – by asking questions about **H**arm, **E**ase, **A**cceptability, and **T**ime *saved* through action.

Kill Parameters: an explicit declaration that if X, Y, or Z happens or A, B, and C do not happen, then the de-implementation initiative will be immediately killed off. Having kill parameters can help to ensure you do not continue with "zombie" initiatives that generate no impact, just because of deep emotional investment/attachment.

Monitoring: the act of systematically checking that you have completed the (de-implementation) actions you set out to.

Optimal Stopping: the decision about how long to spend searching, analyzing, and deciding before you simply get on and de-implement (i.e., your desired speed of travel). The likelihood

is that you will search longer and deeper if you are working at district or system level and/or if you are proposing a de-implementation strategy that will be very difficult to reverse from and that has a higher probability of causing harm to student outcomes.

Pareto Analysis: a decision-making protocol that focuses on identifying the activities that have the highest level of payoff vs. those that do not. The ones that do not are (potentially) good targets for de-implementation.

Permit (1.1): the P-step focused on receiving a permit/license to operate, to mitigate the guilt and shame-based drivers that often result in people doubling down on efficient practices and establishing a backbone team to undertake the *Room for Impact* inquiry cycle.

Picture (2.3): the P-step focused on the establishment of success criteria and an evaluative plan, to ensure you do no harm along the way.

P-Marathon: the act of leveraging the P-steps at a slower pace, potentially undertaking several weeks or months of inquiry before getting to de-implementation. Links to *Optimal Stopping* considerations.

Policy to Practice Mapping: the activity of mapping official policies to current practices and comparing what is being done vs. what the regulations tell us needs to be done. This enables you to compare the "policies in your head" with the policies on paper, which often do not match up!

Postulate (1.3): the P-step focused on explaining what sustains existing practices in the target de-implementation areas (a.k.a. *Chesterton's Fence*) – because in order to make change for the future we need to have a good understanding of what causes and sustains the present.

Pre-Mortem: a stress-testing strategy that involves imagining that an initiative has failed and mapping out all the reasons this could have happened, so that the de-implementation activity design can then be buttressed to mitigate these identified risks.

Prepare (2.2): the P-step focused on fleshing out a high-level de-implementation proposal into a more detailed plan of attack (i.e., what, why, when, where, who, and how).

Proceed (3.1): the P-step where you bring your de-implementation plans to life!

Professional Learning Community: a type of within-school improvement model, often employing a communities-of-practice approach that facilitates inquiry within a grade level/year group or subject department. This involves the convening of meetings to agree on priority focus areas, the undertaking of improvement-oriented (de-implementation) inquiry, and the evaluation of impact.

Propel (4.2): a basket of considerations about what you should do after you have successfully completed a *Room for Impact* inquiry cycle, including challenges related to sustainability and scale.

Propose (2.1): the P-step that centers on development of a high-level de-implementation strategy, using one or more of the 4Rs (i.e., *Remove, Reduce, Re-engineer*, and/or *Replace*).

Prospect (1.2): the P-step focused on identifying and selecting target areas that are ripe for de-implementation—that is, searching for suitable Jenga blocks.

P-Sprinting: leveraging the P-steps at a faster pace, by holding a three-to-four day "hackathon" that takes you from Permit (1.1) to Picture and then beginning your de-implementation (3.1) on day four or five! This links to both Optimal Stopping considerations and *P-marathon*, which is about operating at a slower and more considered pace.

Re-decide Stage: the stage of *Room for Impact* that focuses on appraising your de-implementation impact and on deciding what to do next; this can include embarking on another de-implementation cycle to disbanding your Backbone Organization.

Reduce: a type of de-implementation strategy that centers on a reduction in the targeted activity area—for example, reducing homework or reducing parental reporting and so forth. Reductions can be uniformly applied to all

stakeholders *or* they can be applied to selected stakeholders—for example, restricting who receives 1:1 tutoring, so that only students that meet certain criteria are eligible. You can reduce the amount (i.e., the dosage), the frequency, and/or the eligible target group.

Re-Engineer: a type of de-implementation strategy focused on reducing the complexity of how an existing process is undertaken to save time and/or budget. Re-engineering can be undertaken using Lean methodology tools and thinking to map out the existing process in full and then to test which "links in the chain" can be removed or simplified without causing harm.

Remove: a type of de-implementation strategy that centers on the complete stopping (i.e., removing) of the targeted activity area—for example, stopping all homework.

Replace: a type of de-implementation strategy focused on substituting one activity with another that takes less time/budget but that achieves similar or better outcomes—for example, replacing teacher developed materials with a third-party curriculum package.

Responsibilities and Accountabilities Framework: a tool for mapping out all the actions that need to be undertaken and assigning responsibilities and accountabilities to key individuals. This is used to ensure that everyone knows what his or her role is and no tasks slip between the cracks.

Rube Goldberg (or Heath Robinson) machine: a type of cartoon drawing named after American cartoonist Rube Goldberg (and also associated with British cartoonist William Heath Robinson). Usually, these cartoon machines consist of a series of unrelated but connected devices that generate a chain reaction, eventually culminating in an intended goal (i.e., A pushes B onto C, resulting in D). We suggest Rube Goldberg cartoons as an alternative way of presenting (and thinking through) your de-implementation plan. It can also be used for Stress Testing.

School District–Level De-Implementation: here, we refer to use of the *Room for Impact* methodology by a Backbone Organization that has responsibility for the management and improvement of multiple schools, usually within the same local geography. In the United States, Canada, and parts of Australia, this type of support is often undertaken by a school district. In England, it is often provided by a multi-academy trust (MAT); in Scotland, by the local authority; and in New Zealand, by a community of learning (Kāhui Ako).

School System–Level De-Implementation: here, we refer to use of the *Room for Impact* methodology by a Backbone Organization that operates at a regional, state, or even national level. System-level stakeholders are normally responsible for hundreds to tens of thousands of schools and often work in organizations called the department of education, ministry of education, or education services area/district.

Schoolwide De-Implementation: here, we refer to the use of the *Room for Impact* methodology by a Backbone Organization that operates at whole-school level. This would involve progressing de-implementation initiatives to across the whole school and would involve steering and support from the school leadership team.

Six Buckets Framework: a tool to help you identify what sustains existing practices. The buckets in question are (1) Regulations, (2) History, (3) Beliefs, (4) Structures, (5) Consequences, and (6) Incentives. This links to *Chesterton's Fence* consideration.

Stress Testing: the act of pretesting your de-implementation plan before activation. Some of the strategies you can use include bodystorming, pre-mortem, delivery chain mapping/Rube Goldberg Analysis, Side Effects Analysis, and variant analysis.

Sub-Bone Tool: a tool for vectoring in on specific "bones" on your fishbone map and reviewing these on more detail. This is derived from the 5-Whys tool that is commonly used in management consulting for root cause analysis.

Success Criteria: in the context of *Room for Impact*, this refers to the criteria that indicate whether your de-implementation has been successful—these are likely to relate to whether the activities were actually de-implemented, whether this saved time/resources, and whether there was any harm to students and/or staff.

Time Studies: the act of recording all the things you and your team do in a given day/week/month and time tracking the exact number of minutes spent on each of these tasks. This can be used to identify amenable areas for de-implementation during the (1.2) *Prospect*-step.

Variant Analysis: a twin-axis mapping tool that enables you to identify all the ways that a proposed activity/intervention could be varied during de-implementation. The *design features* axis refers to the things that could be varied, including dosage, duration, target group, and fidelity. The *setting levels* axis describes each of the possible variation increments for each respective design feature.

References

Aarons, G. A., Green, A. E., Palinkas, L. A., Self-Brown, S., Whitaker, D. J., Lutzker, J. R., Silovsky, J. F., Hecht, D. B., & Chaffin, M. J. (2012). Dynamic adaptation process to implement an evidence-based child maltreatment intervention. *Implementation Science*, *7*, 32. https://doi.org/10.1186/1748-5908-7-32

ABS. (2021). *Schools, Australian, 1980–2020 (Cat. no 4221.0)*. Australian Bureau of Statistics. https://www.abs.gov.au/statistics/people/education/schools/latest-release

Adam, C., Bauer, M. W., Knill, C., & Studinger, P. (2007). The termination of public organizations: Theoretical perspectives to revitalize a promising research area. *Public Organization Review*, *7*, 221–236.

Adams, G. S., Converse, B. A., Hales, A. H., & Klotz, L. E. (2021). People systematically overlook subtractive changes. *Nature*, *592*, 258–261. https://doi.org/10.1038/s41586-021-03380-y

Ahmed, S., & Nath, S. R. (2003). Public service delivery in education: The BRAC experience. Research Reports (2003). *Social Studies*, *XXXII*, 217–231. http://hdl.handle.net/10361/13456

AITSL. (2020). *School workload reduction toolkit*. Australian Institute for Teaching and School Leadership. https://www.aitsl.edu.au/reducing-red-tape

Allaire-Duquette, G., Brault Foisy, L.-M., Potvin, P., Riopel, M., Larose, M., & Masson, S. (2021). An fMRI study of scientists with a Ph.D. in physics confronted with naive ideas in science. *NPJ Science of Learning*, *6*(1), 11. https://doi.org/10.1038/s41539-021-00091-x

Altinok, N., Angrist, N., & Patrinos, H. A. (2018). *Global data set on education quality (1965–2015)* (World Bank Policy Research Paper No. 8414). World Bank.

Anderson, J. W., Konz, E. C., Frederich, R. C., & Wood, C. L. (2001). Long-term weight-loss maintenance: A meta-analysis of US studies. *The American Journal of Clinical Nutrition*, *74*(5), 579–584.

Andrews, M., Pritchett, L., & Woolcock, M. (2017). *Building state capability evidence, analysis, action*. Oxford University Press.

Arkes, H. R., & Blumer, C. (1985). The psychology of sunk cost. *Organizational Behavior and Human Decision Process*, *35*(1), 124–140. https://doi.org/10.1016/0749-5978(85)90049-4

Ashman, J., & Stobart, G. (2018) *Reducing teacher workload* (Research report). Report from Lighthouse School Partnership. DfE.

Ashmore, S., & Runyan, K. (2014). *Introduction to agile methods*. Addison-Wesley Professional.

Asimov, I. (1969). *Nightfall and other stories*. Doubleday.

Atkins, L., Francis, J., Islam, R., O'Connor, D., Patey, A., Ivers, N., Foy, R., Duncan, E. M., Colquhoun, H., Grimshaw, J. M., Lawton, R., & Michie, S. (2017). A guide to using the theoretical domains framework of behaviour change to investigate implementation problems. *Implementation Science*, *12*(1), 1–18. https://doi.org/10.1186/s13012-017-0605-9#citeas

Augustsson, H., Casales Morici, B., Hasson, H., von Thiele Schwarz, U., Schalling, S. K., Ingvarsson, S., Wijk, H., Roczniewska, M., & Nilsen, P. (2022). National governance of de-implementation of low-value care: A qualitative study in Sweden. *Health Research Policy and Systems, 20*(1), 1–13.

Augustsson, H., Ingvarsson, S., Nilsen, P., von Thiele Schwarz, U., Muli, I., Dervish, J., & Hasson, H. (2021). Determinants for the use and de-implementation of low-value care in health care: A scoping review. *Implementation Science Communications, 2*(1), 13. https://doi.org/10.1186/s43058-021-00110-3

Axelos. (2017). *Managing successful projects with PRINCE2* (6th ed). The Stationary Office.

Barber, C. (2014). How to write a speech in only 15 minutes – What's your message? *Vivid method*. vividmethod.com

Barber, M., Moffit, A., & Kihn, P. (2011). *Deliverology 101: A field guide for educational leaders*. Corwin.

Bauer, M. S., Damschroder, L., Hagedorn, H., Smith, J., & Kilbourne, A. M. (2015). An introduction to implementation science for the non-specialist. *BMC Psychology, 3*, 32. https://doi.org/10.1186/s40359-015-0089-9

Bishop, R., O'Sullivan, D., & Berryman, M. (2010). *Scaling up education reform: Addressing the politics of disparity*. NZCER Press.

Blase, K., Kiser, L., & Van Dyke, M. (2013). *The hexagon tool: Exploring context*. National Implementation Research Network, Frank Porter Graham Child Development Institute, University of North Carolina at Chapel Hill.

Braganza, M. Z., & Kilbourne, A. M. (2021). The quality enhancement research initiative (QUERI) impact framework: Measuring the real-world impact of implementation science. *Journal of General Internal Medicine, 36*(2), 396–403. https://doi.org/10.1007/s11606-020-06143-z

Breakspear, S., & Jones, B. R. (2020). *Teaching sprints: How overloaded educators can keep getting better*. Corwin.

Brown, B. R. (2019). *The Apollo chronicles: Engineering America's first moon missions*. Oxford University Press.

Brown, C. G. (2014). The Iowa model of evidence-based practice to promote quality care: An illustrated example in oncology nursing. *Clinical Journal of Oncology Nursing, 18*(2), 157–159. https://doi.org/10.1188/14.CJON.157-159

Bryk, A. S., Gomez, L. M., Grunow, A., & LeMahieu, P. G. (2017). *Learning to improve: How America's schools can get better at getting better*. Harvard Education Press.

Burkeman, O. (2021). *Four thousand weeks: Time management for mortals*. Farrar, Straus and Giroux.

Burton, C., Williams, L., Bucknall, T., Edwards, S., Fisher, D., Hall, B., Harris, G., Jones, P., Makin, M., McBride, A., Meacock, R., Parkinson, J., Rycroft-Malone, J., & Waring, J. (2019). Understanding how and why de-implementation works in health and care: Research protocol for a realist synthesis of evidence. *Systematic Reviews, 8*, 194. https://doi.org/10.1186/s13643-019-1111-8

Burton, C. R., Williams, L., Bucknall, T., Fisher, D., Hall, B., Harris, G., Jones, P., Makin, M., Mcbride, A., Meacock, R., Parkinson, J., Rycroft-Malone, J., & Waring, J. (2021). Theory and practical guidance for effective de-implementation of practices across health and care services: A realist synthesis. *Health Services and Delivery Research, 9*(2), 1–102.

Carrell, S. E., & West, J. E. (2010). Does professor quality matter? Evidence from random assignment of students to professors. *Journal of Political Economy, 118*(3), 409–432. http://www.econ.ucdavis.edu/faculty/scarrell/profqual2.pdf

Cartwright, N., & Hardie, J. (2012). *Evidence-based policy: A practical guide to doing it better*. Oxford University Press.

Carver-Thomas, D., & Darling-Hammond, L. (2017). *Teacher turnover: Why it matters and what we can do about it*. Learning Policy Institute.

Chambers, D. A., Glasgow, R. E., & Stange, K. C. (2013). The dynamic sustainability framework: Addressing the paradox of sustainment amid ongoing change. *Implementation Science, 8*, 117. https://doi.org/10.1186/1748-5908-8-117

Chesterton, G. K. (1929). *The thing*. Aeterna Press.

Chevallier, A. (2016). *Strategic thinking in complex problem solving*. Oxford University Press.

Christian, B., & Griffiths, T. (2016). *Algorithms to live by: The computer science of human decisions*. Macmillan.

Churches, R. (2020). *Supporting teachers through the school workload reduction toolkit*. Department for Education.

Cognitive Bias Codex. (2016). *Cognitive bias codex - The big picture*. ritholtz.com

Cooper, H. (1989). Synthesis of research on homework. *Educational Leadership, 47*(3), 85–91.

Cooperrider, D. L., & Whitney, D. (2000). A positive revolution in change: Appreciative inquiry. In R. T. Golembiewski (Ed.), *Handbook of organizational behavior, revised and expanded* (pp. 633–652). Routledge.

Covey, S. R. (1989). *The seven habits of highly effective people*. Simon & Schuster.

Cowan, N. (2014). Working memory underpins cognitive development, learning, and education. *Educational Psychology Review, 26*(2), 197–223. https://doi.org/10.1007/s10648-013-9246-y

Damschroder, L. J., Aron, D. C., Keith, R. E., Kirsh, S. R., Alexander, J. A., & Lowery, J. C. (2009). Fostering implementation of health services research findings into practice: A consolidated framework for advancing implementation science. *Implementation Science, 4*, 50. https://doi.org/10.1186/1748-5908-4-50

Daniels, K., Fida, R., Stepanek, M., & Gendronneau, C. (2021). Do multicomponent workplace health and wellbeing programs predict changes in health and wellbeing? *International Journal of Environmental Research and Public Health, 18*, 8964. https://doi.org/10.3390/ijerph18178964

Davidoff, F. (2015). On the undiffusion of established practices. *JAMA Internal Medicine, 175*(5), 809–811. https://doi.org/10.1001/jamainternmed.2015.0167

Davidson, K. W., Ye, S., & Mensah, G. A. (2017). Commentary: De-implementation Science: A virtuous cycle of ceasing and desisting low-value care before implementing new high value care. *Ethnicity & Disease, 27*(4), 463–468. https://doi.org/10.18865/ed.27.4.463

Dehaene, S. (2020). *How we learn: The new science of education and the brain*. Penguin Publishing Group.

Deming, E. D. (1986). *Out of the crisis*. Massachusetts Institute of Technology Center for Advanced Engineering Study.

Denvall, V., Bejerholm, U., Stylianides, K. C., Johanson, S., & Knutagård, M. (2022). De-implementation: Lessons to be learned when abandoning inappropriate homelessness interventions. *International Journal on Homelessness, 2*(2), 1–17. https://doi.org/10.5206/ijoh.2022.2.13709

Department of Education (UK). (2018). *School workload reduction toolkit*. GOV.UK. www.gov.uk

Department for Education (DfE). (2019). *School workload reduction toolkit*. GOV.UK. www.gov.uk

Design Council. (2021). Eleven lessons. A study of the design processes. *Design Council*. https://www.designcouncil.org.uk/our-work/skills-learning/resources/11-lessons-managing-design-global-brands/

DeWitt, P. (2022). *De-implementation: Creating the space to focus on what works*. Corwin.

DfE. (2016a). *Eliminating unnecessary workload associated with data management: Report of the Independent Teacher Workload Review Group*. DfE.

DfE. (2016b). *Eliminating unnecessary workload around planning and teaching resources: Report of the Independent Teacher Workload Review Group*. DfE.

DfE. (2016c). *Eliminating unnecessary workload around marking: Report of the Independent Teacher Workload Review Group*. DfE.

DuBois, D. L., Holloway, B. E., Valentine, J. C., & Cooper, H. (2002). Effectiveness of mentoring programs for youth: A meta-analytic review. *American Journal of Community Psychology, 30*, 157–197. https://doi.org/10.1023/A:1014628810714

Dupré, J. (2013). *Skyscrapers: A history of the world's most extraordinary buildings-revised and updated*. Hachette/Black Dog & Leventhal.

Durst, S., Heinze, I., Henschel, T., & Nawaz, N. (2020). Unlearning: A systematic literature review. *International Journal of Business and Globalisation, 24*(4), 472–495.

Education Week. (2022). *1st Annual Merrimack College teacher survey: 2022 results.* Ed Week Research Center. Today's Teachers Are Deeply Disillusioned, Survey Data Confirms. edweek.org

Elison, J. (2005). Shame and guilt: A hundred years of apples and oranges. *New Ideas in Psychology, 23*(1), 5–32.

Ellis, G., Bell, P., Buckle, L. A., & Shenton, A. (2017). *Reducing teacher workload: Research report into shared planning.* Report from Whitley Bay High School. DfE.

Elshaug, A. G., Moss, J. R., Littlejohns, P., Karnon, J., Merlin, T. L., & Hiller, J. E. (2009). Identifying existing health care services that do not provide value for money. *Medical Journal of Australia, 190*(5), 269–273.

Engber, D. (2019). Unexpected clues emerge about why diets fail. *Nature Medicine, 25*(11), 1632–1639.

Evidence for Learning. (2022). *Insights into de-implementation: Support for implementation. Insights into de-implementation.* E4L . evidenceforlearning.org.au

Farmer, R. L., Zaheer, I., Duhon, G. J., & Ghazal, S. (2021). Reducing low-value practices a functional-contextual consideration to aid in de-implementation efforts. *Canadian Journal of School Psychology, 36*(2), 153–165.

Featherstone, G., & Seleznyov, S. (2017). *Reducing teacher workload: Research report into marking.* Report from the Southwark Teaching School Alliance. DfE.

Feldstein, A. C., & Glasgow, R. E. (2008). A practical, robust implementation and sustainability model (PRISM) for integrating research findings into practice. *The Joint Commission Journal on Quality and Patient Safety, 34*(4), 228–243. https://doi.org/10.1016/s1553-7250(08)34030-6

Fernet, C., Guay, F., Senécal, C., & Austin, S. (2012). Predicting intraindividual changes in teacher burnout: The role of perceived school environment and motivational factors. *Teaching and Teacher Education, 28*(4), 514–525.

Figlio, D., Holden, K. L., & Ozek, U. (2018). Do students benefit from longer school days? Regression discontinuity evidence from Florida's additional hour of literacy instruction. *Economics of Education Review, 67,* 171–183. https://doi.org/10.1016/j.econedurev.2018.06.003

Finn, J. D., & Achilles, C. M. (1990). Answers and questions about class size: A statewide experiment. *American Educational Research Journal, 27*(3), 557.

Flink, C., & Odde, D. J. (2012). Science+dance=bodystorming. *Trends in Cell Biology, 22*(12), 613–616.

Freire, K., & Runyan, C. W. (2006). Planning models: PRECEDE–PROCEED and Haddon Matrix. In A. C. Gielen, D. A. Sleet, & R. J. DiClemente (Eds.), *Injury and violence prevention: Behavioral science theories, methods, and applications* (1st ed., pp. 127–158). Jossey-Bass.

García-Rodríguez, O., Secades-Villa, R., Flórez-Salamanca, L., Okuda, M., Liu, S. M., & Blanco, C. (2013). Probability and predictors of relapse to smoking: Results of the National Epidemiologic Survey on Alcohol and Related Conditions (NESARC). *Drug and Alcohol Dependence, 132*(3), 479–485.

Gardner, B., & Rebar, A. L. (2019). Habit formation and behavior change. In *Psychology.* Psychology Oxford Research Encyclopaedias. https://doi.org/10.1093/obo/9780199828340-0232

Gavin, M., McGrath-Champ, S., Wilson, R., Fitzgerald, S., & Stacey, M. (2021). Teacher workload in Australia: National reports of intensification and its threats to democracy. In A. Heffernan, D. Bright, & S. Riddle (Eds.), *New perspectives on education for democracy* (pp. 110–123). Routledge.

Gershoff, E. T. (2008). *Report on physical punishment in the United States: What research tells us about its effects on children.* Columbus, OH: Center for Effective Discipline.

Glasgow, R. E., Harden, S. M., Gaglio, B., Rabin, B., Smith, M. L., Porter, G. C., Ory, M. G., & Estabrooks, P. A. (2019). RE-AIM planning and evaluation framework: Adapting to new science and practice with a 20-year review. *Frontiers in Public Health, 7,* 1–9. https://doi.org/0.3389/fpubh.2019.00064

Global Teacher Status Index. (2018). The Varkey Foundation gts-index-13-11-2018 .pdf (varkeyfoundation.org)

Gnjidic, D., & Elshaug, A. G. (2015). De-adoption and its 43 related terms: Harmonizing low-value care terminology. *BMC Medicine, 13,* 273.

Government of Northwest Territories. (2017). *NWT teacher time and worload study.* gnwt-ece-teacher_workload_study-2015-final.pdf; gov.nt.ca

Graban, M., & Swartz, J. E. (2012). *Healthcare Kaizen: Engaging front-line staff in sustainable continuous improvements.* Productivity Press.

Graham, I. D., Logan, J., Harrison, M. B., Straus, S. E., Tetroe, J., Caswell, W., & Robinson, N. (2006). Lost in knowledge translation: Time for a map? *Journal of Continuing Education in the Health Professions, 26*(1), 13–24.

Grimshaw, J. M., Patey, A. M., Kirkham, K. R., Hall, A., Dowling, S. K., Rodondi, N., Ellen, M., Kool, T., van Dulmen, S. A., Kerr, E. A., Linklater, S., Levinson, W., & Bhatia, R. S. (2020). De-implementing wisely: Developing the evidence base to reduce low-value care. *BMJ Quality & Safety, 29*(5), 409–417.

Grisold, T., Kaiser, A., & Hafner, J. (2017). Unlearning before creating new knowledge: A cognitive process. In R. H. Sprague (Ed.), *Proceedings of the Fiftieth Annual Hawaii International Conference on System Sciences (HICSS-50), Hawaii* (pp. 4614–4623). IEEE Computer Society Press.

Gu, Q., Heesom, S., Williamson, R., & Crowther, K. (2018). *Reducing teachers' unnecessary workload: The promise of collaborative planning.* Department for Education, UK.

Gundlach, H. A. D. (2022). *Factors related to teacher turnover from schools and the profession: A systematic review, meta-analysis, and survey* [PhD dissertation, University of Melbourne]. unimelb.edu.au

Gupta, D. M., Boland, R. J., & Aron, D. C. (2017). The physician's experience of changing clinical practice: A struggle to unlearn. *Implementation Science, 12,* 28. https:// doi.org/10.1186/s13012-017-0555-2

Hakanen, J. J., Bakker, A. B., & Schaufeli, W. B. (2006). Burnout and work engagement among teachers. *Journal of School Psychology, 43*(6), 495–513.

Hall, G., & Hord, S. (2011). *Implementing change: Patterns, principles, and potholes* (3rd ed.). Allyn and Bacon.

Hall, K. D., & Kahan, S. (2018). Maintenance of lost weight and long-term management of obesity. *Medical Clinics, 102*(1), 183–197.

Hamilton, A., & Hattie, J. (2021). *Getting to G.O.L.D: The visible learning approach to education improvement.* Corwin.

Hamilton, A., & Hattie, J. (2022). *The Lean education manifesto: A synthesis of 900+ systematic reviews for visible learning in developing countries.* Routlege.

Hamilton, A., Reeves, D., Clinton, J., & Hattie, J. (2022). *Building to impact: The 5D implementation playbook for educators.* Corwin.

Handscomb, G., Palmer, L., Cousens, S., & Cunningham, R. (2017). *Reducing teacher workload* (Research report). Report from the Meads Teaching School Alliance. DfE.

Hansson, S. O. (2017). Science denial as a form of pseudoscience. *Studies in History and Philosophy of Science Part A, 63,* 39–47.

Harry, M., Mann, P. S., De Hodgins, O. C., Hulbert, R. L., & Lacke, C. J. (2011). *Practitioner's guide to statistics and Lean Six Sigma for process improvements* (1st ed.). Wiley.

Harvey, G., & Kitson, A. (2016). PARIHS revisited: From heuristic to integrated framework for the successful implementation of knowledge into practice. *Implementation Science, 11,* 33. https://doi.org/10.1186/ s13012-016-0398-2

Haselton, M. G., Bryant, G. A., Wilke, A., Frederick, D. A., Galperin, A., Frankenhuis, W. E., & Moore, T. (2009). Adaptive rationality: An evolutionary perspective on cognitive bias. *Social Cognition, 27*(5), 733–763.

Hattie, J., & Hamilton, A. (2020). *Real gold vs. fool's gold: The visible learning methodology for finding what work's best in education.* Corwin.

Hawkins, J. D., & Weis, J. G. (1985). The social development model: An integrated approach to delinquency prevention. *Journal of Prevention, 6*, 73–97. https://doi.org/10.1007/BF01325432

Hedberg, B. (1981). How organizations learn and unlearn. In P. Nystrom & W. Starbuck (Eds.), *Handbook of organizational design* (Vol. 1, pp. 3–27). Oxford University Press.

Herbert, G., Oates, T., Sherriff, T., & Walker, M. (2017). *Reducing teacher workload: The WOWs research project.* Independent research report from the Working with Others We Succeed consortium of schools. DfE.

Hogarth, R. M., Lejarraga, T., & Soyer, E. (2015). The two settings of kind and wicked learning environments. *Current Directions in Psychological Science, 24*(5), 379–385.

House of Commons (UK). (2021). *Teacher recruitment and retention in England.* House of Commons Library Briefing Paper: Number 07222, 14 April 2021. Digital Education Resource Archive (DERA). ioe.ac.uk

Huebener, M., Kuger, S., & Marcus, J. (2017). Increased instruction hours and the widening gap in student performance. *Labour Economics, 47*, 15–34. http://doi.org/10.1016/j.labeco.2017.04.007

Hunter, J., Sonnemann, J., & Haywood, A. (2022). *Making time for great teaching: A guide for principals.* Grattan Institute.

IBISWorld. (n.d.). *The 10 global biggest industries by revenue in 2021.* Retrieved January 1, 2021, from https://www.ibisworld.com/global/industry-trends/biggest-industries-by-revenue/

IDEO. (2015). *The field guide to human centred design.* IDEO.

Ingvarsson, S., Hasson, H., von Thiele Schwarz, U., Nilsen, P., Powell, B. J., Lindberg, C., & Augustsson, H. (2022). Strategies for de-implementation of low-value care—A scoping review. *Implementation Science, 17*(1), 1–15.

Ivers, N. M., & Desveaux, L. (2019). De-implementation of low-value care: Use audit and feedback wisely. *Healthcare Papers, 18*(1), 41–47.

Jackson, C. K., & Makarin, A. (2018). Simplifying teaching: A field experiment with online "off-the-shelf" lessons. *American Economic Journal: Economic Policy, 10*(3), 226–254.

Jackson, D. (2021). *Work less teach more.* Frankie Jack Publishing.

Jacobson, N., Butterill, D., & Goering, P. (2003). Development of a framework for knowledge translation: Understanding user context. *Journal of Health Services Research & Policy, 8*(2), 94–99. http://doi.org/10.1258/135581903321466067

Jansen, P. (2008). *IT-service-management volgens ITIL.* Derde Editie.

Jerrim, J., & Sims, S. (2021). When is high workload bad for teacher wellbeing? Accounting for the non-linear contribution of specific teaching tasks. *Teaching and Teacher Education, 105*, 103395.

Kahneman, D. (2011). *Thinking, fast and slow.* Macmillan.

Kania, J., & Kramer, M. (2011). Collective impact. *Stanford Social Innovation Review, 9*(1), 36–41. http://ssir.org/articles/entry/collective_impact

Karlsson, N., Loewenstein, G., & Seppi, D. (2009). The ostrich effect: Selective attention to information. *Journal of Risk and Uncertainty, 38*(2), 95–115.

Kenny, G. (2016, June 21). Strategic plans are less important than strategic planning. *Harvard Business Review.* https://hbr.org/2016/06/strategic-plans-are-less-important-than-strategic-planning

Kilbourne, A. M., Neumann, M. S., Pincus, H. A., Bauer, M. S., & Stall, R. (2007). Implementing evidence-based interventions in health care: Application of the replicating effective programs framework. *Implementation Science, 2*, 42. https://doi.org/10.1186/1748-5908-2-42

Kime, S. (2018). Reducing teacher workload: The "re-balancing feedback" trial research report. Report from Tarporley, Helsby and Queen's Park High Schools. Department for Education, UK.

King, M., Agboola, K., Perry, T., & Bradbury, M. (2018). *Workload challenge: KS5 data research report.* Report from Hatcham College. DfE.

Klein, G. (2007). Performing a project premortem. *Harvard Business Review, 85*(9), 18–19.

Klotz, L. (2021). *Subtract: The untapped science of less*. Flatiron Books.

Kokkinos, C. M. (2007). Job stressors, personality and burnout in primary school teachers. *British Journal of Educational Psychology, 77*(1), 229–243.

Kotter, J. P. (2012). *Leading change: Why transformation efforts fail*. Harvard Business Review Press.

Lawrie, G., & Cobbold, I. (2004). Third-generation balanced scorecard: Evolution of an effective strategic control tool. *International Journal of Productivity and Performance Management, 53*(7), 611–623.

Lazarus, R. S., & Folkman, S. (1984). *Stress, appraisal, and coping*. Springer.

Leach, C. W. (2017). Understanding shame and guilt. In L. Woodyatt, E. L. Worthington Jr., M. Wenzel, & B. J. Griffin (Eds.), *Handbook of the psychology of self-forgiveness* (pp. 17–28). Springer.

Leigh, J., Niven, D. J., Boyd, J. M., & Stelfox, H. T. (2017). Developing a framework to guide the de-adoption of low-value clinical practices in acute care medicine: A study protocol. *BMC health services research, 17*(1), 1-9. https://doi.org/10.1186/s12913-022-07827-4

Leigh, J. P., Sypes, E. E., Straus, S. E., Demiantschuk, D., Ma, H., Brundin-Mather, R., de Grood, C., FitzGerald, E. A., Mizen, S., Stelfox, H. T., & Niven, D. J. (2022). Determinants of the de-implementation of low-value care: A multi-method study. *BMC Health Services Research, 22*(1), 1–11.

LeMahieu, P., Nordstrum, L., & Gale, D. (2017). Positive deviance: Learning from positive anomalies. *Quality Assurance in Education, 25*(1), 109–124. https://doi.org/10.1108/QAE-12-2016-0083

Levin, H. M., Bowden, A. B., Shand, R., McEwan, P. J., & Belfield, C. R. (2018). *Economic evaluation in education: Cost-effectiveness and benefit-cost analysis*. SAGE.

Liedtka, J., King, A., & Bennett, K. (2013). *Solving problems with design thinking: 10 stories of what works*. Columbia Business School Publishing.

Loveman, E., Frampton, G. K., Shepherd, J., Picot, J., Cooper, K., Bryant, J., Welch, K., & Clegg, A. (2011). The clinical effectiveness and cost-effectiveness of long-term weight management schemes for adults: A systematic review. *Health Technology Assessment, 15*(2), 1-182.

Lovett, B. J., & Harrison, A. G. (2021). De-implementing inappropriate accommodations practices. *Canadian Journal of School Psychology, 36*(2), 115–126.

McGraw, A. P., Larsen, J. T., Kahneman, D., & Schkade, D. (2010). Comparing gains and losses. *Psychological Science, 21*(10), 1438–1445. https://doi.org/10.1177/0956797610381504

McKay, V. R., Morshed, A. B., Brownson, R. C., Proctor, E. K., & Prusaczyk, B. (2018). Letting go: Conceptualizing intervention de-implementation in public health and social service settings. *American Journal of Community Psychology, 62*(1–2), 189–202.

McPherson, M., Smith-Lovin, L., & Cook, J. M. (2001). Birds of a feather: Homophily in social networks. *Annual Review of Sociology, 27*(1), 415–444.

Meyer, E., & van Klaveren, C. (2013). The effectiveness of extended day programs: Evidence from a randomized field experiment in the Netherlands. *Economics of Education Review, 36*, 1–11. http://doi.org/10.1016/j.econedurev.2013.04.002

Meyers, D. C., Durlak, J. A., & Wandersman A. (2012). The quality implementation framework: A synthesis of critical steps in the implementation process. *American Journal of Community Psychology, 50*(3–4), 462–480.

Mencken, H. L. (1917/1949). The divine afflatus. In H. L. Mencken (Ed.), *A Mencken chrestomathy* (pp. 442–449). Alfred A. Knopf.

Michie, S., Atkins, L., & West, R. (2014). *The behaviour change wheel: A guide to designing Interventions*. Silverback Publishing.

Michie, S., Van Stralen, M. M., & West, R. (2011). The behaviour change wheel: A new method for characterising and designing behaviour change interventions. *Implementation Science, 6*(1), 1–12.

Montini, T., & Graham, I. D. (2015). "Entrenched practices and other biases": Unpacking the historical, economic, professional, and social resistance to de-implementation. *Implementation Science*, *10*(1), 1–8.

Mosteller, F. (1995). The Tennessee study of class size in the early school grades. *The Future of Children*, *5*(2), 113–127.

Moullin, J. C., Dickson, K. S., Stadnick, N. A., Rabin, B., & Aarons, G. A. (2019). Systematic review of the exploration, preparation, implementation, sustainment (EPIS) framework. *Implementation Science*, *14*, 1. http://doi.org/10.1186/s13012-018-0842-6

Nath, S. R. (2005). Reaching primary education at the doorstep of the poor: The BRAC experience. Research Reports (2005). *Social Studies*, *XXXVIII*, 415–428. http://hdl.handle.net/10361/13235

Nessler, D. (2018). How to apply a design thinking, HCD, UX or any creative process from scratch. *Medium*. Retrieved November 1, 2021, from https://medium.com/digital-experience-design/how-to-apply-a-design-thinking-hcd-ux-or-any-creative-process-from-scratch-b8786efbf812

Neuman, S. (2019). Meet John Houbolt: He figured out how to go to the moon, but few were listening. The idea that got us to the moon, and the man who pushed it. *NPR*.

New Zealand Ministry of Education. (2022). Teacher turnover – Statistics (2002–2020). Education Counts.

Newport, C. (2016). *Deep work: Rules for focused success in a distracted world*. Grand Central Publishing.

Newport, C. (2021). *A world without email: Find focus and transform the way you work forever*. Penguin Publishing Group.

Nickerson, R. S. (1998). Confirmation bias: A ubiquitous phenomenon in many guises. *Review of General Psychology*, *2*(2), 175–220.

Nielson, G. W., & Burks, B. (2022). *Stop fake work in education: Creating real work cultures that drive student success*. Corwin.

Nilsen, P., Ingvarsson, S., Hasson, H., von Thiele Schwarz, U., & Augustsson, H. (2020). Theories, models, and frameworks for de-implementation of low-value care: A scoping review of the literature. *Implementation Research and Practice*, *1*, 2633489520953762.

Niven, D. J., Mrklas, K. J., Holodinsky, J. K., Straus, S. E., Hemmelgarn, B. R., Jeffs, L. P., & Stelfox, H. T. (2015). Towards understanding the de-adoption of low-value clinical practices: A scoping review. *BMC Medicine*, *13*(1), 1–21.

Northern Territory Government (Australia). (2020). *De-implementation guide*. Prepared for the Northern Territory Department of Education.

Norton, W. E., & Chambers, D. A. (2020). Unpacking the complexities of de-implementing inappropriate health interventions. *Implementation Science*, *15*(1), 1–7.

Norton, W. E., Kennedy, A. E., & Chambers, D. A. (2017). Studying de-implementation in health: An analysis of funded research grants. *Implementation Science*, *12*(1), 1–13.

Numan, A. Q., & Islam, M. S. (2021). An assessment of the teaching and learning process of public and BRAC primary schools in Bangladesh. *Education 3–13*, *49*(7), 845–859.

OECD (2019). PISA 2018 Database. Organisation for Economic Co-operation and Development. 2018 Database - PISA (oecd.org)

OECD. (2021a). *Education at a glance 2021: OECD indicators*. OECD Publishing. https://doi.org/10.1787/b35a14e5-en

OECD. (2021b). *Not enough hours in the day: Policies that shape teachers' use of time*. Organisation for Economic Co-operation and Development. 15990b42-en.pdf; oecd-ilibrary.org

OECD. (2022). *Education at a glance 2022: OECD indicators*. OECD Publishing. https://doi.org/10.1787/3197152b-en

OECD TALIS. (2020). *TALIS 2018 results (Volume II): Teachers and school leaders as valued professionals*. TALIS, OECD Publishing. https://doi.org/10.1787/19cf08df-en

Oulasvirta, A., Kurvinen, E., & Kankainen, T. (2003). Understanding contexts by being there: Case studies in bodystorming. *Personal and Ubiquitous Computing*, *7*, 125–134. https://doi.org/10.1007/s00779-003-0238-7

Our World in Data. (2022). *Share who smoke. Smoking.* Our World in Data.

Pannett, A., Sequeira, S., Dines, A., & Day, A. (2013). *Key skills for professionals: How to succeed in professional services.* Kogan Page Publishers.

Paolucci, E. O., & Violato, C. (2004). A meta-analysis of the published research on the affective, cognitive, and behavioral effects of corporal punishment. *The Journal of Psychology, 138*(3), 197-222.

Parker, G., Kastner, M., Born, K., Shahid, N., & Berta, W. (2022). Understanding low-value care and associated de-implementation processes: A qualitative study of choosing wisely interventions across Canadian hospitals. *BMC Health Services Research, 22*(1), 1–12.

Parkinson, C. N. (1955, November 19). Parkinson's law. *The Economist.*

Pascale, R. T., Sternin, J., & Sternin, M. (2010). *The power of positive deviance: How unlikely innovators solve the world's toughest problems.* Harvard Business Press.

Patall, E. A., Cooper, H., & Allen, A. B. (2010). Extending the school day or school year: A systematic review of research (1985–2009). *Review of Educational Research, 80*(3), 401–436. https://doi.org/10.3102/0034654310377086

Patey, A. M., Grimshaw, J. M., & Francis, J. J. (2021). Changing behaviour, "more or less": Do implementation and de-implementation interventions include different behaviour change techniques? *Implementation Science, 16*(1), 1–17.

Pinker, S. (2018). *Enlightenment now: The case for reason, science, humanism, and progress.* Penguin Publishing Group.

Pinto, R. M., & Park, S. (2019). De-implementation of evidence-based interventions: Implications for organizational and managerial research. *Human Service Organizations: Management, Leadership & Governance, 43*(4), 336–343.

Pinto, R. M., & Witte, S. S. (2019). No easy answers: Avoiding potential pitfalls of de-implementation. *American Journal of Community Psychology, 63*(1–2), 239–242.

Planche, B., Sharratt, L., & Belchez, D. (2008). *Sustaining students' increased achievement through second-order change: Do collaboration and leadership count?* ICSEI.

Poulton, R., & Menzies, R. G. (2002). Non-associative fear acquisition: A review of the evidence from retrospective and longitudinal research. *Behaviour Research and Therapy, 40*(2), 127–149.

Prasad, V., & Ioannidis, J. (2014). Evidence-based de-implementation for contradicted, unproven, and aspiring healthcare practices. *Implementation Science, 9*(1), 1–5.

Pritchett, L., Samji, S., & Hammer, J. (2013). *It's all about MeE: Using structured experiential learning ("e") to crawl the design space* (CGD Working Paper 322). Center for Global Development. https://www.cgdev.org/publication/its-all-about-mee

Project Management Institute. (2021). *A guide to the project management body of knowledge (PMBOK® guide)—Seventh edition and the standard for project management.* Project Management Institute.

Protsiv, R., Pipola, P., & Welch, G. (2018). *Reducing teacher workload: Research report into planning and marking.* Report from Aquinas Teaching and Learning Trust. Department for Education, UK

Prusaczyk, B., Swindle, T., & Curran, G. (2020). Defining and conceptualizing outcomes for de-implementation: Key distinctions from implementation outcomes. *Implementation Science Communications, 1*(1), 1–10. https://doi.org/10.1186/s43058-020-00035-3

Pryor, K. (2019). *Don't shoot the dog: The art of teaching and training.* Simon & Schuster.

Pyzdek, T., & Keller, P. A. (2009). *The six sigma handbook* (3rd ed.). McGraw-Hill.

Rasiel, E. M. (2001). *The McKinsey mind.* McGraw-Hill.

Raudasoja, A. J., Falkenbach, P., Vernooij, R. W., Mustonen, J. M., Agarwal, A., Aoki, Y., Blanker, M. H., Cartwright, R., Garcia-Perdomo, H.A., Kilpeläinen, T.P., Lainiala, O., Lamberg, T., Nevalainen, O. P. O., Raittio, E., Richard, P. O., Violette, P. D., Komulainen, J., Sipilä, R., & Tikkinen, K. A. (2022). Randomized controlled trials in de-implementation research: A systematic scoping review. *Implementation Science, 17*(1), 1–13.

Richardson, R., Goodman, P., Flight, S., & Richards, G. (2017). *Reducing teacher workload* (Research report). Report from Candleby Lane Teaching School Alliance. DfE.

Rietbergen, T., Spoon, D., Brunsveld-Reinders, A. H., Schoones, J. W., Huis, A., Heinen, M., Persoon, A., van Dijk, M., Vermeulen, H., Ista, E., & van Bodegom-Vos, L. (2020). Effects of de-implementation strategies aimed at reducing low-value nursing procedures: A systematic review and meta-analysis. *Implementation Science, 15*(1), 1–18.

Riley, P., Rahimi, M., & Arnold, B. (2021). *The New Zealand primary teacher occupational health, safety and wellbeing survey 2020 data.* Research for Educational Impact (REDI). Deakin University.

Robert, G., Harlock, J., & Williams, I. (2014). Disentangling rhetoric and reality: An international Delphi study of factors and processes that facilitate the successful implementation of decisions to decommission healthcare services. *Implementation Science, 9,* 123. https://doi.org/10.1186/s13012-014-0123-y

Robinson, C., & Pedder, D. (2018). *Workload challenge research projects: Overall summary.* Department for Education.

Robinson, V. M. J. (2018). *Reduce change to increase improvement.* Corwin.

Rogers, E. (2003). *Diffusion of innovations* (5th ed.). Simon and Schuster.

Royce, W. W. (1987, March). Managing the development of large software systems: Concepts and techniques. In *Proceedings of the 9th International Conference on Software Engineering* (pp. 328–338).

Saloviita, T., & Pakarinen, E. (2021). Teacher burnout explained: Teacher-, student-, and organisation-level variables. *Teaching and Teacher Education, 97,* 103221.

Santos, I., Vieira, P. N., Silva, M. N., Sardinha, L. B., & Teixeira, P. J. (2017). Weight control behaviors of highly successful weight loss maintainers: The Portuguese weight control registry. *Journal of Behavioral Medicine, 40*(2), 366–371.

School Workforce Census. (2021). *Reporting Year 2021: School workforce in England.* Department for Education. Explore education statistics. GOV.UK. explore-education-statistics.service.gov.uk

Selby, K., & Barnes, G. D. (2018). Learning to de-adopt ineffective healthcare practices. *The American Journal of Medicine, 131*(7), 721–722.

Sharples, J., Albers, B., & Fraser, S. (2019). *Putting evidence to work: A school's guide to implementation* (Guidance report). Education Endowment Foundation.

Sharratt, L. (2019). *CLARITY: What matters MOST in learning, teaching, and leading.* Corwin.

Sharratt, L., & Fullan, M. (2006). Accomplishing district-wide reform. *Journal of School Leadership, 16,* 583–595.

Sharratt, L., & Fullan, M. (2012, 2022). *Putting faces on the data: What great leaders and teachers do!* Corwin.

Shaw, S. R. (2021). Implementing evidence-based practices in school psychology: Excavation by de-implementing the disproved. *Canadian Journal of School Psychology, 36*(2), 91–97.

Shen, L. (2018). The evolution of shame and guilt. *PLoS One, 13*(7), e0199448.

Simms, A., & Nichols, T. (2014). Social loafing: A review of the literature. *Journal of Management, 15*(1), 58-67.

Singer, P. (1981). *The expanding circle.* Clarendon Press.

Smith, J. D., Schneider, B. H., Smith, P. K., & Ananiadou, K. (2004). The effectiveness of whole-school antibullying programs: A synthesis of evaluation research. *School Psychology Review, 33*(4), 547–560.

Stecher, B. M., McCaffrey, D. F., & Bugliari, D. (2003). Relationship between exposure to class size reduction and student achievement in California. *Education Policy Analysis Archives, 11,* 40.

Stetler, C. B. (2001). Updating the Stetler model of research utilization to facilitate evidence-based practice. *Nursing Outlook, 49*(6), 272–279. https://doi.org/10.1067/mno.2001.120517

Strathern, M. (1997). "Improving ratings": Audit in the British University system. *European*

Review, 5(3), 305–321. https://doi.org/10 .1002/(SICI)1234-981X(199707)5:3<305:: AID-EURO184>3.0.CO;2-4

Stroud, G. (2017). Why do teachers leave? *ABC News*.

Tangney, J. P. (1998). How does guilt differ from shame? In J. Bybee (Ed.), *Guilt and children* (pp. 1–17). Academic Press.

Tennant, G. (2001). *Six Sigma: SPC and TQM in manufacturing and services*. Gower Publishing, Ltd.

Timperley, H., Kaser, L., & Halbert, J. (2014). *A framework for transforming learning in schools: Innovation and the spiral of inquiry*. Centre for Strategic Education.

Tobler, N. S. (1986). Meta-analysis of 143 adolescent drug prevention programs: Quantitative outcome results of program participants compared to a control or comparison group. *Journal of Drug Issues, 16*(4), 537–567. https://doi .org/10.1177/002204268601600405

van Bodegom-Vos, L., Davidoff, F., & Marang-van de Mheen, P. (2017). Implementation and de-implementation: Two sides of the same coin? *BMJ Quality & Safety, 26*, 495–501. https://doi.org/10.1136/ bmjqs-2016-005473

Varkey Foundation. (2018). *Global teacher status index*. gts-index-13-11-2018.pdf; varkeyfoundation.org\

Verkerk, E. W., Tanke, M. A. C., Kool, R. B., Van Dulmen, S. A., & Westert, G. P. (2018). Limit, lean or listen? A typology of low-value care that gives direction in de-implementation. *International Journal for Quality in Health Care, 30*, 736–739.

Visser, M. (2017). Learning and unlearning: A conceptual note. *The Learning Organization, 24*(1), 49–57.

Walker, M., Sharp, C., & Sims, D. (2020). *Job satisfaction and workload of teachers and senior leaders: Schools' responses to Covid-19*. National Foundation for Educational Research.

Walker, M., Worth, J., & Van den Brande, J. (2019). *Teacher workload survey 2019* (Research report). Department for Education. ed.gov

Walsh-Bailey, C., Tsai, E., Tabak, R. G., Morshed, A. B., Norton, W. E., McKay, V. R., Brownson, R. C., & Gifford, S. (2021). A scoping review of de-implementation frameworks and models. *Implementation Science, 16*(1), 1–18.

Wandersman, A. (2014). Getting to outcomes: An evaluation capacity building example of rationale, science, and practice. *American Journal of Evaluation, 35*(1), 100–106. https://doi.org/10.1177/ 1098214013500705

Wang, T., Baskin, A., Miller, J., Metz, A., Matusko, N., Hughes, T., Sabel, M., Jeruss, J. S., & Dossett, L. A. (2021). Trends in breast cancer treatment de-implementation in older patients with hormone receptor-positive breast cancer: A mixed methods study. *Annals of Surgical Oncology, 28*(2), 902–913.

Wang, V., Maciejewski, M. L., Helfrich, C. D., & Weiner, B. J. (2018). Working smarter not harder: Coupling implementation to de-implementation. *Healthcare, 6*(2), 104–107.

Webb, L. (2017). *Reducing teacher workload* (Research report). Report from Jurassic Coast Teaching School Alliance. DfE.

Weldon, P. R., & Ingvarson, L. (2016). *School staff workload study: Final Report to the Australian Education Union – Victorian Branch*. Australian Education Union, Victoria Branch. https://research.acer.edu .au/tll_misc/27

White, B., Barwick, T., Cook, E., Donald, L., Forde, S., King, S., Dann, R., & Sims, S. (2018). *Reducing teacher workload*. Department for Education, UK.

Wiliam, D. (2007). Changing classroom practice. *Educational Leadership, 65*(4), 36–42.

Wiliam, D. (2011). *Embedded formative assessment*. Solution Tree Press.

Wiliam, D. (2018). *Creating the schools our children need: Why what we're doing right now won't help much, and what we can do instead*. Learning Sciences International.

Wiliam, D., & Bartholomew, H. (2004). It's not which school but which set you're in that matters: The influence of ability grouping practices on student progress in mathematics. *British Educational Research Journal, 30*(2), 279–293.

Wiliam, D., & Leahy, S. (2016). *Embedding formative assessment.* Hawker Brownlow Education.

Willson, A. (2015). The problem with eliminating "low-value care." *BMJ Quality & Safety, 24,* 611–614. https://doi.org/10.1136/bmjqs-2015-004518

Wilson, S. J., Lipsey, M. W., & Derzon, J. H. (2003). The effects of school-based intervention programs on aggressive behavior: A meta-analysis. *Journal of Consulting and Clinical Psychology, 71,* 136–149.

Winter, S. R., Rice, S., Capps, J., Trombley, J., Milner, M. N., Anania, E. C., Walters, N. W., & Baugh, B. S. (2020). An analysis of a pilot's adherence to their personal weather minimums. *Safety Science, 123,* 104576.

Womack, J. P., & Jones, D. T. (1997). Lean thinking—Banish waste and create wealth in your corporation. *Journal of the Operational Research Society, 48*(11), 1148.

Womack, J. P., & Jones, D. T. (2003). *Lean thinking: Banish waste and create wealth in your corporation.* Free Press.

Womack, J. P., & Jones, D. T. (2013). *Lean thinking: Banish waste and create wealth in your corporation (Revised and updated).* Simon & Schuster.

World Bank EdStats. (2022). https://datatopics.worldbank.org/education/

World Bank. (2000). *The logframe handbook.* World Bank Group.

Wu, T., Gao, X., Chen, M., & Van Dam, R. M. (2009). Long-term effectiveness of diet-plus-exercise interventions vs. diet-only interventions for weight loss: A meta-analysis. *Obesity Reviews, 10*(3), 313–323.

Zhao, Y. (2018). *What works may hurt—Side effects in education.* Teachers College Press.

Index

Build your Visible Learning® library!

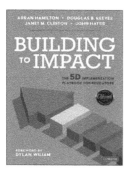

BUILDING TO IMPACT

VISIBLE LEARNING: THE SEQUEL

10 STEPS TO DEVELOP GREAT LEARNERS

GREAT TEACHING BY DESIGN

VISIBLE LEARNING FEEDBACK

COLLECTIVE STUDENT EFFICACY

10 MINDFRAMES FOR VISIBLE LEARNING

10 MINDFRAMES FOR LEADERS

DEVELOPING TEACHING EXPERTISE

Visit corwin.com/vlbooks

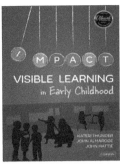

VISIBLE LEARNING IN EARLY CHILDHOOD

REBOUND

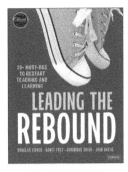

LEADING THE REBOUND

DEVELOPING ASSESSMENT-CAPABLE VISIBLE LEARNERS, Grades K–12

VISIBLE LEARNING FOR LITERACY, Grades K–12

VISIBLE LEARNING FOR MATHEMATICS, Grades K–12

VISIBLE LEARNING FOR SCIENCE, Grades K–12

VISIBLE LEARNING FOR SOCIAL STUDIES, Grades K–12

CORWIN
A SAGE Publishing Company

Helping educators make the greatest impact

CORWIN HAS ONE MISSION: to enhance education through intentional professional learning.

We build long-term relationships with our authors, educators, clients, and associations who partner with us to develop and continuously improve the best evidence-based practices that establish and support lifelong learning.